Trust

HOW WE LOST IT
AND HOW TO GET IT BACK

PRAISE FOR OTHER BOOKS BY ANTHONY SELDON

Blair (2004, revised 2005)
'This book will become an automatic point of reference for studies of a political period that promised so much.'   John Kampfner, *The Observer*

'An impressively complete and up-to-date account of the personalities and events that have formed Labour's longest-serving Prime Minister.'
The Economist

The best account so far of the high politics of the Blair era.'
Nick Cohen, *New Statesman*

'Superbly well-informed and exhaustively researched.'
Peter Oborne, *The Tablet*

Blair Unbound (2007)
'As fair a judgment on a Prime Minister as you are going to get . . . frank and fascinating.'   Mary Riddell, *The Observer*

'Modern government cannot work if its leadership is perpetually at odds with itself. In telling that tale, Seldon could not be bettered.'
Simon Jenkins, *Sunday Times*

'This is an important and good book.'   Phil Collins, *Daily Telegraph*

'This account of the Blair era, so soon after its end, is likely to be the fullest for many years.'   *The Observer*

Blair's Britain (2007)
'A compelling compendium of the Blair years from some of Britain's most authoritative figures.'   John Kampfner, *New Statesman*

'The authoritative verdict on the Blair years.'
Steve Richards, *The Independent*

'A first class resume.'   Simon Jenkins, *Sunday Times*

'Provides an intelligent, expert overview of the decade as a whole, on some 30 topics.'   *The Guardian*

'Does justice to all aspects of the Blair era.' *Irish Times*

Trust

HOW WE LOST IT
AND HOW TO GET IT BACK

Anthony Seldon

with Kunal Khatri

First published in Great Britain in 2009 by
Biteback Publishing Ltd
Heal House
375 Kennington Lane
London
SE11 5QY

Reprinted with a revised introduction 2010

ISBN 978-1-84954-001-8

A CIP catalogue record for this book is available from the British Library.

Set in Bembo and Trade Gothic by SoapBox
Printed and bound in Great Britain by CPI Mackays, Chatham, Kent

CONTENTS

I dedicate this book to the exceptionally able young men and women who helped write it, in the hope that they enjoy trust-filled lives. In particular, I would like to thank members of the 'inner team':

Kunal Khatri (co-author)
Matthew Fright
Alice Mosby
Rachel Patton
Zenobe Reade
Jess Seldon
Andrew Stevenson
Conor Turley

PREFACE

This book contains the following ten core arguments:

▶ Trusting and being trustworthy are the sovereign human virtues we need today
▶ Trust is not just about today's relationships: 'trusteeship' extends it into the future and past
▶ Trust is natural: we were born trusting and the state of nature is to be trusting
▶ A 'presumption of trust' rather than a 'presumption of mistrust' helps individuals and organisations flourish
▶ 'Blind trust' is lazy and damaging: we need 'active trust', which is informed
▶ We must distinguish trust in honesty and trust in competence
▶ We cannot *force* people to be trusting: it develops intrinsically, not by being overseen
▶ Government in Britain will gain trust if it promises less and devolves/trusts more
▶ To create a trusting world we must start with ourselves: we cannot look to others
▶ The duty to be trusting and the responsibility for being trustworthy are incumbent on all: no one can opt out

The emphasis in this book is on practical proposals: there have been many books on trust, and the arguments on either side are mostly quite well established. What we lack, however, is a working trust model demonstrating how trust can be applied in practice. The introduction sets the crisis of trust in context. Chapter 1 examines the meanings of trust and proposes our own trust model, Chapters 2 and 3 examine the factors that lead to the loss and to the building of trust, while the remaining seven chapters examine specific areas, looking at the following questions: has trust been lost, why might that be, and how can trust be rebuilt or built further? The conclusion discusses how we can rebuild trust in the most important constituent of all, ourselves.

The cumulative impact of the recommendations in this book may seem at best overly optimistic, and at worst naïve or foolish. We call for nothing less than a revolution in thinking: a shake, not a nudge. We do not imagine all these trust-based proposals would be executed within a single government's life: but we are serious about governments in the future putting the 'quality of life' agenda much higher than the 'quantity' agenda, as we explain in the introduction. The former is about being optimistic and making the best happen, as in positive health, positive policing, positive education and positive employment policy: the latter is reactive, and supportive of the *status quo*. The 21st-century battleground in British politics will not be socialism against free-market capitalism, nor progressivism against conservatism, but between exponents of the quantity and the quality of life agendas.

Anthony Seldon
August 2009

INTRODUCTION
ARE WE AT A TURNING POINT FOR TRUST?

2010: Worst crisis of trust?

The last year has filled the pages of books and newspapers with stories of greed, corruption, incompetence and misconduct. A succession of failings have involved almost everyone from politicians to policemen, from bankers to the BBC, from social workers to sportsmen, leaving the population in a state of anger, confusion and disillusion. The public feel mistrusted by government and in turn find government to be unworthy of their own trust. The professions similarly feel no longer fully trusted by a public which questions its every decision, and which is unsettled by the media and lawyers which probe trust in every corner, sometimes justifiably, sometimes not. If one was to highlight a single moment to encapsulate the 'year of mistrust', it would be in July 2009, when widely loved writers Michael Morpurgo and Philip Pullman refused to undergo 'insulting' checks that they were not paedophiles and said they will not be speaking any more in schools.[1]

Many commentators concluded that trust in British politics especially had never been so low. Philip Webster, political editor of *The Times*, talked about 'the worst year for Parliament that anyone can remember',[2] a comment mirrored by Michael White of the *Guardian*, who thought it was 'one of the worst years in living memory for British politics as a whole'.[3] The former editor of *The Times* William Rees–Mogg described it as a 'tarnished age', and said that 'the contrast between the House of Commons in 1954 and the House of 2009 is a painful one'.[4] Vernon Bogdanor, the leading authority on the British constitution, said that Britain 'was at a defining moment'.[5]

Britain is nevertheless a more trusting country than many. It has a judiciary and a civil service almost totally free of corruption, and even our much-berated politicians are rarely guilty of no more than greed, rather than the buying of influence. But it would be complacent not to recognise that trust has taken a severe knock in Britain, that it is damaging the quality of our public life, and that much needs to be done to rebuild trust. Onora O'Neill highlighted the importance of trust in her seminal 2002 BBC Reith Lectures,[6] and in the decade (almost) since she wrote her plea for trust to be taken more seriously, it has eroded in almost every sphere of British life.

The country still reels at the irresponsibility and self-indulgence of those who wrought the greatest economic crisis in nearly a hundred years. Sir Fred Goodwin, the former chief executive of the Royal Bank of Scotland (RBS) and still adorned with his knighthood for services to banking, rightly or wrongly became a particular object of hate after he walked away with a large annual pension, despite his bank recording corporate losses of £24 billion.[7] RBS is not alone. Bumper bonuses continued to be paid to bankers throughout 2009 and 2010. Whilst Lloyd Blankfein, chief executive of Goldman Sachs, congratulated himself for 'doing God's work',[8] *Rolling Stone* magazine lambasted his company as the 'vampire squid wrapped around the face of humanity'.[9]

In contrast to the swift response to the financial crisis shown by the government, politicians found themselves wanting in moral leadership in clearing up their own patch. Week after week through the spring and summer of 2009, the *Daily Telegraph* regaled us with tales of MPs claiming for anything from a bathplug to a duckhouse. All politicians, not just those from the governing party, as had been the case in most previous scandals, were the subject of public ire. The money mattered less than the principle. As the accused scurried behind the defence of parliamentary privilege, the public felt that the guilty had evaded justice. Anger had been simmering for a long time; the expenses scandal was a lightning rod for years of growing voter disenchantment and distrust in politicians.

It was also in 2009 that the spotlight, thanks to the Iraq War inquiry presided over by Sir John Chilcot, was shone on the issue which more than any other in the last ten years eroded public trust in government. Regardless of the rights and wrongs of the issue, and we will probably never know the exact truth, the public believed that Tony Blair had lied to them over the war in Iraq. They yearned for the Chilcot inquiry to skewer Blair and his cronies in Number 10. I do not believe that Blair did deliberately lie, but I do think that under intense pressure of events, and with his single-minded determination that Saddam had to be taken on, he made gross errors of judgement in the prosecution of the war and in the reasons he gave for fighting it. He damaged himself as well as the cause of public trust by not being more candid before Chilcot in January 2010.

Against such a febrile background, public servants fell under a distrustful gaze. With the fear of crime growing, and potentially explosive climate change and G20 demonstrations, the public yearned for reliable and proficient law enforcers. But the police showed themselves to be neither as proficient nor trustworthy as the public expected: a series of cover-ups and examples of incompetence culminated in excessive force on the part of the police at the G20 summit in London in early April 2009 and the death of an innocent bystander, Ian Tomlinson. Within itself, the police force was damaged by accusations of racism, corruption and incompetence by its senior officers. Further confusion was caused in February 2010 when Ali Dizaei, who had been a champion of minorities in the police force, was jailed for false arrest and fabricating claims of assault. Dizaei himself was revealed as little more than a 'criminal in uniform'.[10]

Social workers came under attack when in Haringey they overlooked the abuse of a young boy, 'Baby Peter', who eventually died at the hands of his mother and her boyfriend. The same London council had been responsible for the failure to protect Victoria Climbié from a similar fate several years before. While these council workers neglected their role, others teamed up with the police to spy on people through Britain's vast network of security cameras, abusing their powers to catch people for minor offences such as littering and dog-fouling.

In 2009 and 2010 we saw the trustworthiness of sportsmen increasingly called into question. The charismatic Dean Richards, coach of Harlequins rugby club, resigned in August 2009 and was subsequently banned from coaching in Europe for three years after his player used a blood capsule to fake an injury in a key quarter-final. At the end of the year, the world's most famous sportsman, Tiger Woods, was stung for his litany of infidelities. His widely admired moral rectitude came to be seen as little more than a diligently crafted façade. The adoration and trust of his millions of fans was not restored by his mawkish attempt to apologise in February 2010. Closer to home, Chelsea and England captain John Terry's infidelities seemed to confirm the perception of modern footballers as overpaid philanderers. At least the much-admired England manager, Fabio Capello, saw beyond technical ability to the virtue of good behaviour off, as well as on, the pitch, and removed from Terry the honour of the England captaincy.

Science, often amongst the most trusted of professions, faced a crisis of confidence with revelations of malpractice on the part of climate change scientists at the University of East Anglia. Hacked emails revealed the extraordinary deceit of a handful of scientists who selectively buried evidence contrary to their whim. Even the esteemed Intergovernmental Panel on Climate Change fell foul of scientific rigour as its claims that the ice caps would disappear by 2035 were unmasked as conjecture. Despite the overwhelming evidence from other reputable scientific studies supporting the arguments of anthropogenic climate change, public scepticism is on the rise. A Populus poll in February 2010 found that 25 per cent of respondents did not think that global warming was happening, a 10 per cent increase on a similar poll in November the year before.[11] Science, so often a bedrock certainty based in the honesty of its methodology, no longer looks as trustworthy as it once did.

Just as trust is essential within nations, so too is it vital for international understanding. Bitter division and recriminations have followed the failure of the Copenhagen Summit in December 2009 to tackle climate change. Vested national interests, from East to West and South to North, militated against the formation of trust, with the Chinese delegation obstructing negotiations and representatives from the African nations storming out. Copenhagen was a display of paralysing distrust among nations in the face of a universal and common threat with the trusteeship of the world for future generations at stake. Trust is as vital for tackling nuclear disarmament as it is for climate change. With the lurking threat of new nuclear states, the success of the Nuclear Non-Proliferation Treaty depends on the trust between its signatories as much as on the threat of sanctions.[12]

Pouring fuel on these fires in Britain was the 'feral beast' of the media. Invariably the least trusted profession in Britain, journalism thrives on scandal and recrimination and is the chief progenitor of a distrustful nation. The media itself displays no higher ethical or proficiency standards than those it derides. The *News of the World* hit the headlines in 2009 after allegations that it had tapped the phone lines of large numbers of people in the public eye. Conservative leader David Cameron's press chief, Andy Coulson, came under fire, as he had edited the *News of the World* at the time. Questions were asked as to why Cameron had gone so downmarket for his press aide, especially after Coulson was believed responsible for the Conservatives unleashing a brutal negative campaign in February 2010. But Gordon Brown was in no position to sling mud. One of his press advisors, the belligerent Damian McBride, resigned in April 2009 after it emerged that he was involved in a plan to disseminate scurrilous material about other politicians. After the departure of Alastair Campbell in 2003, who had taken media manipulation and spinning to new heights, the public had hoped that their top politicians would employ higher-minded media managers.

This widespread mistrust inevitably fed its way into opinion polls. The influential 2010 Edelman Trust Barometer revealed a continued collapse in trust in banks, with only 21 per cent of respondents considering them trustworthy, 20 points lower than in 2007.[13] Likewise, trust in politicians had also plummeted. According to the 2009 Ipsos MORI Trust in the Professions poll, trust in politicians and government ministers collapsed 8 per cent over the previous year.[14] Some 82 per cent of respondents now do not trust politicians to tell the truth, the highest negative proportion for politicians in the twenty-six years the poll has been running. Journalists, presumably buoyed by the expenses fillip, had a minor surge in trust, but still weigh as an anchor in the trust league table, with only 22 per cent of respondents considering them trustworthy.

Table 0.1: Levels of trust in various professions 1983–2009

Occupation	1983	1993	1997	1999	2000	2001	2002	2003	2004	2005	2006	2007	2008	2009
	%	%	%	%	%	%	%	%	%	%	%	%	%	%
Doctors	82	84	86	91	87	89	91	91	92	91	92	90	92	92
Teachers	79	84	83	89	85	86	85	87	89	88	88	86	87	88
Professors	-	70	70	79	76	78	77	74	80	77	80	78	79	80
Judges	77	68	72	77	77	78	77	72	75	76	75	78	78	80
Clergymen/Priests	85	80	71	80	78	78	80	71	75	73	75	73	74	71
Scientists	-	-	63	63	63	65	64	65	69	70	72	65	72	70
TV newsreaders	63	72	74	74	73	75	71	66	70	63	66	61	66	63
The police	61	63	61	61	60	63	59	64	63	58	61	59	65	60
Ordinary person in the street	57	64	56	60	52	52	54	53	55	56	56	52	60	54
Pollsters	-	52	55	49	46	46	47	46	49	50	51	45	48	45
Civil servants	25	37	36	47	47	43	45	46	51	44	48	44	48	44
Trade union officials	18	32	27	39	38	39	37	33	39	37	41	38	45	38
Business leaders	25	32	29	28	28	27	25	28	30	24	31	26	30	25
Journalists	19	10	15	15	15	18	13	18	20	16	19	18	19	22
Government ministers	16	11	12	23	21	20	20	20	23	20	22	22	24	16
Politicians generally	18	14	15	23	20	17	19	18	22	20	20	18	21	13

Ipsos MORI, 'Trust in the Professions: Veracity Index' (2009)

Question: '...would you tell me if you generally trust them to tell the truth or not?'

These polls confirm our contention that beyond politics, and elements of media and corporate life, talk of a crisis of trust across the board is less justified. Despite showing dips in ratings over the last six months, opinion polls do not reveal any longer-term institutional decline. Table 0.1 shows remarkably consistent levels of trust in different professions over twenty-five years, with doctors, teachers and judges at the top, and politicians and journalists at the bottom.

We lack the quality and consistency of opinion polls to tell us about long-term trends, and we have no polls at all before 1937, so we cannot talk with certainty about this being the 'worst' crisis of trust. Nor can we say that Britain is a broken society: at the end of the millennium's first decade, the lives of many people in Britain are positive, and are better in many ways than they were in 1990 or 2000. What we can say is that there is a short-term crisis of trust in politics, the media and finance in particular in 2010, but a much deeper and more widespread *trust malaise*, which has been building up for several years.

Everybody is talking... about trust

The growing literature on the subject of trust over the last fifteen years has analysed what trust is and why it is important, but has had less to say in practical terms about how we are to re-build it in Britain today. The most important single contribution has been Onora O'Neill's Reith Lectures, subsequently published as *A Question of Trust* (2002).[15] Some of O'Neill's principal concerns are to examine what trust means in practice, how organisations are held accountable, how far transparency boosts trust, and trustworthiness in the press. Francis Fukuyama, better known for *The End of History and the Last Man* (1992),[16] has written the other principal contribution, *Trust: The Social Virtues and the Creation of Prosperity* (1995),[17] which analyses how levels of trust have affected economic performance. He concludes that strong economic growth is intimately connected with high trust. Barbara Misztal broadens our horizons in *Trust in Modern Societies* (1996) to demonstrate how trust makes social life more predictable, creates a sense of community and makes it easier for people to work together.[18] In seeking to explain the emergence and decay of trust cultures, Piotr Sztompka in *Trust: A Sociological Theory* (1999) focuses particularly on the collapse of communism and the post-communist world order, notably in Poland.[19] Robert C. Solomon and Fernando Flores argue, in *Building Trust in Business, Politics, Relationships and Life* (2003),[20] that trust is a skill, not something innate, which must be constantly built up by integrity, with good communication imperative to building trust. Russell Hardin in *Trust* (2006)[21] builds on his earlier work, *Trust and Trustworthiness* (2004).[22] He offers a theoretical assessment of the rising distrust of politicians and argues that we can only trust others when we feel that their interests 'encapsulate our own'. We refer to many other authors who have written on the subject, notably two prominent academics, the sociologist Anthony Giddens and the historian Geoffrey Hosking.[23,24] The latter argues that trust is now based much less on family, friends and neighbourhood, and has become much more legalised, underpinned by accountants, lawyers and state bureaucrats.[25]

The 4564799710 sequence and a new paradigm

This sequence refers to the core dates of British governmental performance since 1945. All governments try to make a difference and change the agenda of British politics. Since the Second World War, only two have succeeded (and earlier in the century, just two also: the Liberal government of 1908–14 and the National Government of 1931–5). After 1945, Clement Attlee and the Labour government introduced the modern welfare state and full employment, and, for better or worse, nationalised significant swathes of the British economy. Attlee himself, as Labour MP Frank Field has said, 'personified the decency to which everybody signed up'.[26]

In 1964, the Labour government of Harold Wilson tried to make a similar impact and to kick-start the modernisation of Britain by using science, technology and centralised planning. It failed, for the same reason as did the Conservative government of Ted Heath after 1970: because the top-down, centrally imposed policies ran against the then prevailing grain of British institutions and culture. In contrast, the government of Margaret Thatcher from 1979 did manage a decisive change, ending the Keynesian social democratic consensus which had been prevalent throughout the post-war period and replacing it with a more free-market economy, though the state still retained strong central control.

Tony Blair came to power in 1997 with a determination to head 'one of the great agenda-changing governments of British history', and was blessed with advantages few incoming Prime Ministers have enjoyed: a strong economy, a united party, a landslide victory and a divided opposition. He promised a new Britain and bequeathed ten years of economic growth but only incremental change to the structure of the economy, social policy and even the constitution. Had he worked out more clearly before 1997 what he wanted to do with power, and how to use it, he would have achieved much more. Blair's failure to deliver such sweeping change fed a bitter sense of disappointment and distrust for his successor, and for politics more broadly. In the international realm, Blair offered a vision with the Good Friday Agreement in Northern Ireland of the 'road less travelled', of politicians using trust to build relations in a divided community. But instead of seeking to build on the success of this approach, he chose in the Middle East the more travelled American road, not of building trust, but trying to bomb elements of the Muslim world into submission. Force may on occasion be needed against evil, but it was misapplied by Blair, and as a result his premiership saw mistrust and suspicion grow of Britain, of the West and of Blair personally.

In 2010 there is another opportunity for whichever party wins the election to be one of the genuinely agenda-changing governments, which come every thirty or thirty-five years in British history. The inheritance will not be rosy, but neither, tellingly, was it in 1945 or in 1979. Nor was it for Franklin D. Roosevelt when he came to power in the US in March 1933, nor Barack Obama in January 2009. A year into his presidency, Obama's 'State of the Union' address did not shy away from the task he and the rest of Capitol Hill still faced in uniting a polarised nation and overcoming, as he put it, a crippling 'deficit of trust'.[27]

Whichever party wins power in the 2010 general election, rebuilding trust in the democratic process, in Britain's institutions and in our communities must be paramount. The task will be eased by the widespread recognition that change is needed, that the constitutional innovations under Labour after 1997 did not go far enough, and that the blossoming of new communications technology allows for levels of participation unknown to all previous ages in history.

The first ever televised leaders' debate could be a watershed moment for politics in the modern era. It provides an opportunity for all three leaders to display a level of honesty and openness that has been spun out of existence over the last decade. But will voters be treated to an open debate with unscripted audience participation, or will they once more be patronised with an engineered piece of political theatre?

But governments can only do so much; the shift that is required is from the politics of 'them' to the politics of 'we' and even the politics of 'I'. The current crisis of trust owes much to the almost impossible demands and expectations made by the public of 'others'. But the public must also themselves show that they are trustworthy, rather than pointing the finger of blame at others and expecting them to conform to standards that they do not observe in their own lives. The pages that follow discuss a plethora of ways of enhancing the trustworthiness of political and other institutions in Britain. At the end of the day, however, nothing will change until the public realises that trust is a two-sided coin; on one side is the trust we should legitimately expect from others, and on the other is our own trustworthiness.

Whoever wins the election should also take heed that the old paradigms – large state versus small, liberal versus authoritarian and progressive versus conservative – are redundant. The new debate is between those who see the prime objective of life as maximising quantity – gross domestic product, corporate profits, exam results, throughput of patients and solved crime – and those who highlight quality of life issues – sustainable growth, corporate responsibility, rounded human beings, a healthy nation and safe and *trusting communities*. The public want the latter, but politicians are mistakenly trapped in a logic that sees the targets and materialism of the former as the only route to it.

Parties that are sincere about quality of life as a good in and of itself, and an end distinct from quantity, and that can establish this as the country's common goal, will win the general elections over the next twenty years. Our own proposals cut across the twentieth-century political polarities: we favour big government (e.g. driving through volunteering and national service) and small government (e.g. massive devolution down to localities and institutions, and schools becoming independent); we are libertarian (e.g. huge reduction in target-setting and surveillance by government) but are socially authoritarian (e.g. on families and child-rearing). We do not believe that a 'nudge',[28] but rather a *shove*, is appropriate in many areas. Where the quantity maximisers have often trodden on trust, the quality of life agenda nurtures it in all sections of British society. How to achieve this necessary vision is what this book sets out to describe.

Anthony Seldon
February 2010

'I noticed a man building an increasingly high wall around his suburban house . . . Why the vulnerability, the need to erect ever higher defences?'
(Image Source)

CHAPTER 1
A NEW MODEL OF TRUST

The glory of friendship is not the outstretched hand, nor the kindly smile nor the joy of companionship; it is the spiritual inspiration that comes to one when he discovers that someone else believes in him and is willing to trust him.

Ralph Waldo Emerson (1803–82), American essayist, poet and philosopher

It is impossible to go through life without trust: That is to be imprisoned in the worst cell of all, oneself.

Graham Greene (1904–91), English novelist and playwright

In the mid-1990s, when driving to work at a school in south London, I noticed a man building an increasingly high wall around his suburban house, which bordered the street. The height alone never seemed to satisfy him. One morning I saw him up a ladder cementing broken pieces of wine bottles onto his wall, presumably to ward off burglars yet more fiercely. I know not whether this endeavour resulted in the safety of his home and garden, or lacerated hands – his own or the thieves'. What I do remember thinking is that any enhancement to his security would surely only have been transitory. I moved schools shortly after, and over the years would muse periodically on whether he had installed barbed wire, cemented in spiked knives, or purchased a pack of Rottweilers. Was this, I wondered, what living in urban society had become at the end of the twentieth century? Was this the same psychology that explained why nations built up nuclear armaments? Why the risk, the vulnerability, the need to erect ever higher defences? The unknown man and his fearsome wall began a quest which led eventually, more than a decade later, to this book.

What is trust?

What exactly, I asked myself, is trust? The *Oxford English Dictionary* defines it as 'confidence in or reliance on some quality or attribute of a person or thing, or the truth of a statement'. So, it is a relationship between two or more people, or between a person and 'a thing', where the person or thing has something to offer. It can also be a reliance on something factually accurate. But who should one trust, and why? What about animals, who are not mentioned in the dictionary's description? I did not find this definition wholly satisfying, and began reading about and reflecting further on trust, and what it meant in practice. I learnt that a new trust relationship usually requires an initial conscious act of will, but then becomes a habit; only when challenged or violated does trust become a visible issue again.[1] Without trust that one will not be attacked, or in the competence of a dentist, for example, life becomes difficult if not impossible. Trust is a present condition, and, as Piotr Sztompka says, 'is intimately linked to the uncontrollability of the future . . . Trust is a bet about the future contingent on the actions of others'.[2] But is trust mainly about the present, or also about a relationship with the past and future?

We learn that we give trust, and surrender something of ourselves, in the expectation that we will receive something that will enhance ourselves, others or the world at large. We lower our defences, thereby increasing our vulnerability, because greater good is expected to follow. We trust a friend because of the enhanced happiness that the friendship will generate; we trust our teachers because we believe that by giving up our leisure to work for them we will become wiser; and we suspend our caution and trust of a professional because we believe they will improve our health or material well-being. We trust politicians by giving them our vote, our taxes, or tacit compliance, in the expectation that they will improve the country and our lives. Mutual benefit lies at the heart of trust.

Trust is also a two-way process. We give trust to others, and we are thus said to be *trusting* (or not), and we ourselves are the recipients of the trust of others, and are said to be *trustworthy* (or not). They are connected. As Henry Stimson (1867–1950), the US statesman, said, 'the only way to make a man trustworthy is to trust him'.[3] It is rare for a trusting person not to be trustworthy, and it is common for a suspicious person not to be much trusted by others. We trust others and organisations to behave in predictable and appropriate ways, and in ways which accord with norms of behaviour that initially resulted in us awarding them our trust. Others trust us equally to act in predictable and appropriate ways, and in line with us meriting their own initial trust. If predictability falters, we become disconcerted and question our initial judgement. Is 'distrust' different to 'mistrust'? Some writers have defined them differently; but colloquial speech and even some dictionaries do not discriminate between them, and neither will we in this book. But is trust learnt, or is it natural – do we have our trust knocked out of us by school and by life? My questions about trust are only really beginning.

It is June 2009. A long summer term is drawing to an end, and my long-rumbling interest in trust has been taken to a new level by the apparent loss of trust in our financial sector and in our politicians. I commit myself to writing a book on trust and assemble a bright crew of 18–25 year olds (the 'we' of this book) to help me write it over the summer vacation. Their minds are much more fertile than mine, their eyes clearer, their expressions fresher. Why are they helping? There is no money to pay them unless the uncontrollable future sees to it that the book makes money. Questions are forming in my mind. What is the source of trust? Who do we trust, and why is it important?

Where does trust come from?
Trust is both innate and nurtured. Human beings are hard-wired to be trusting of others.[4] Whether this be a trait of human nature or a

consequence of immediate necessity and survival, human babies are born in trust of and trusting their mothers. Trust is then embellished by good nurturing. The baby who discovers that their parents provide for their basic needs, above all food, clothing, warmth and love, has their trust confirmed at a deep level from the very earliest days. Such children will develop more readily into trusting adults. The nurturing does not have to be excellent, but merely, in Bruno Bettelheim's words, 'good enough for trust to develop'.[5] As the baby grows, it encounters other family relationships, above all with siblings. If the young child is treated well by them, their trust will be further enhanced. Early experiences of carers and grandparents help broaden the child's sense of trust. Experiences of other children at school and in the neighbourhood become of vital importance in helping the child decide whether non-family members are fundamentally caring of their welfare, or not. The longer the child experiences trusting, loving and supportive relationships, the more deeply will their model of trust be embedded.

Where the child does not enjoy such circumstances, the patterns imprinted on their psyche will be less conducive to their trusting others. Violence or neglect of the child will severely impair their happiness, and their subsequent ability to trust others. The damage will go deeper, dependent upon the length and severity of the abuse, and upon the child's resilience, born of its nature and of its earliest experiences. It is possible to escape this vicious cycle, and there are many examples of individuals who have overcome intense adversity and who go on to live rewarding lives. Many who have been brought up in ghettos and refugee camps, who have lost both parents in natural disasters, or who have survived the most brutal foster homes, exhibit high degrees of resilience. Encounters with loving adults can transform lives. Janusz Korczak was a famous doctor and child psychologist who founded two children's orphanages in Warsaw in the 1930s, built on the ideals of 'trusting them and giving them responsibility'. He inspired the children to found Poland's first children's newspaper, and turned the schools into self-governing communities. 'Children have a right to be taken seriously,' he said.[6]

Our 'formation of trust' model can thus be shown in the simple diagram of concentric circles in Figure 1.1.

Figure 1.1: Stages in childhood trust formation

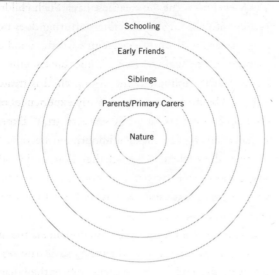

Who should and do we trust?

The summer term has now ended, and my wife and I sat at the graduation ball dinner with a group of leaving girls and their parents. I asked them whether they had a boy they trusted most in their year group. Without hesitation, all the girls came up with 'Colin'. Now, Colin was not by any means the best-looking boy in the year; he is quite small and generously proportioned. What Colin has is an extraordinary ability to make people feel good and happy. A smile hardly ever leaves his face, and for whoever he is with, old friends or those he has never met before, he has his arms out wide. It is no surprise that Colin's parents are both exceptionally warm and trusting people.

Having a trusting nature, and trusting formative relationships, is clearly a great boon, but does that mean we should trust everyone and everything we encounter in life? We have seen that people will often treat us in the way we treat them. Should I trust a stranger at a coach station to watch over my bags while I find a cup of coffee? Should I trust a dentist in rural France when I have an agonising tooth, without knowing anything about the dentist or their qualifications? Should I trust a policeman in Indonesia to point me in the right direction when I have heard, perhaps maliciously, that the police on this island are corrupt? Should I trust a child carer who I have never met?

It is not always good or wise to trust. It can lead to nepotism or cronyism, and to the trusting of the incompetent or malevolent. One can be *naïvely trusting*, without any consideration or weighing up of risks, like a child, and one can continue to trust despite evidence that one should not. We call the latter *blind trust*. It is extraordinary how ubiquitous blind trust is. It can be a lazy, an ingratiating or a fearful decision, but it is never a considered one. Husbands and wives may trust each other blindly; we may trust businessmen, doctors or friends unwisely. The pretence and the hypocrisy that lie behind blind trust are a poison that corrodes personal and organisational relationships.[7] Instead, we need to have *active trust*, where our critical faculties are engaged when deciding who to trust or not to trust. The world is full of companies using sophisticated techniques to attract our custom, 'spinning' politicians, and still less savoury people, who want us to trust them. Some, like the soldiers in the First World War, had no choice; it mattered not whether they trusted and respected their officers – they would have been shot for cowardice if they did not fight. But most of us do have a choice.

It is clear that we must make reasoned calculations on the trustworthiness of other individuals and institutions. To do so, we must rely on an array of signals. With an unknown stranger we meet on the street, we might assess their gender, age, attire and appearance before making a judgement. When appraising a restaurant, a school or a car, we may rely much on 'peer approval'. We listen closely to the advice of friends, and prefer the impartial evaluation of independent authorities when making our choices. With a doctor, for example, we are willing to give trust if we know that they have been to a selective and reputable university, that they have been approved and licensed to practise by a reliable and trustworthy authority such as the General Medical Council, and that they have been working for a number of years at an acceptable level of performance.

Trust takes time to build, and we tend more immediately to trust when a long-term reputation has been established, like Marks and Spencer among retailers, or a family lawyer who has looked after us for many years, or a GP who has spent their professional life in the community. The great value of reputation, as Russell Hardin argues, is the incentive that it gives to those who have built 'a good reputation to behave in ways that sustain that reputation'.[8] At an individual level, we have a predisposition to trust those who share our early experiences, social class, ethnicity and systems of belief. A Christian is more likely to trust a fellow Christian, a university lecturer a fellow lecturer and someone who grew up in Cardiff a stranger who was raised in the same city. People meeting for the first time commonly look for shared experiences as points of safety and common identity on which to build further trust. Our childhood and school friends can often be those who remain with us for the rest of our lives. One might not see the friend for ten years but such are the bonds of trust that have grown up that one is likely to feel 'as though we last met yesterday'. Whereas friendship can take years to develop, lovers can – albeit rarely – experience 'love at first sight'. With marriage, two individuals willingly join together in a contract of trust to sacrifice some of their personal liberties for the sake of a greater union. In the US state of Louisiana, couples can go further, and take part in a 'Covenant Marriage' whereby they forfeit their right to 'no-fault' divorce, which makes the contract still more binding.[9] Trust in marriage or long-term partnerships, and within families, are core building blocks for trust in society.

Figure 1.2 conveys a sense of increasing trust the closer one gets into the centre. Everyone will have a personal model dependent upon life experience, and drawing one's own diagram is instructive. Omitted from our diagram is trust in nature, that the sun will rise, tides will not keep rising, and that the warming earth will cool. The *Oxford English Dictionary* says trust applies to things, but there is no mutuality with nature, so we exclude it from our discussion. Omitted also is our trust in animals, and the trust they have in humans and in each other, which is based on mutuality. Animals make only one appearance in this book, which is odd considering man's work and companionship with them throughout history.

Figure 1.2: Who do we trust?

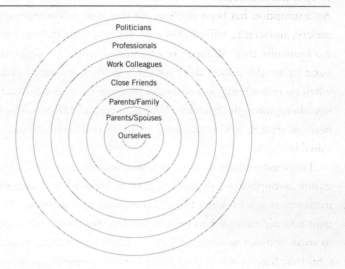

Groups that operate in secret often have high trust within the sect, but may not contribute to overall trust within society, nor merit being trusted by others. The Freemasons raise money for charity, do good works and have high levels of trust within the network, but the secrecy with which they surround themselves alienates others and detracts from their contribution. Terrorist groups require very high levels of secrecy and trust within themselves to function, as too did members of the Resistance operating in France during the Second World War. Criminal groups such as the Chinese triads or the Mafia are powerfully destructive of trust in society, as are the growing numbers of serious criminal groups in Britain, currently numbering some 4,000.[10] Youth gangs have always been part of British culture, but concerns heightened in 2009, with a high number of gang-related deaths in the first half of the year. On a social level, we are drawn to open people, and repelled by the overtly cliquey. Those living in 'gated communities' might, or might not, trust each other, but do not inspire trust in those on the outside. Secrecy and exclusivity in any form thus detract from aggregate trust.

Why is trust valuable?

An assumption has been made so far that trust is a worthy objective in society, and so it is, but why? We always gain from those we trust. There is a mutuality to it. We trust our friends to keep our confidences and to stand by us: the notion that 'you only know who your true friends are when there is a crisis', is a common sentiment experienced by those who have been through difficulty. The mutual gain which is inherent at the heart of trust is one reason why it is so extraordinarily important and valuable.

First and foremost, trust is a *fundamental survival mechanism*, and stands in opposition to those forces in life which divide us and run us down; it is a building force and it is always nurturing. We want to trust and are upset when trust is broken, because we have to be able to trust in order to survive. Trust is intimately linked to truthfulness. Children hate it when they believe their parents have lied to them. Adults express a similar outrage when they believe that politicians have lied to them, as did President Nixon over Watergate, Clinton over Monica Lewinsky, or, as some believe, Tony Blair over Iraq.[11] In her book *Lying* (1978), Sissela Bok puts forward the case for a 'principle of veracity'. We all gain greatly from living in a world where the practice of truth-telling exists, and without that strong moral presumption against lying, we would not be able to trust anyone, and would all lose out significantly.

Trust boosts *economic efficiency*. Francis Fukuyama argues in his book *Trust* that high trust within society is vital if economies are to flourish:

'One of the most important lessons we can learn from an examination of economic life is that a nation's well-being, as well as its ability to compete, is conditioned by a single, persuasive cultural characteristic; the level of trust inherent in a society.'[12] Fukuyama argues that those countries that have enjoyed the strongest economies, such as Japan or Germany, are also those that have exhibited strong elements of trust. Stephen Knack, a senior economist at the World Bank, suggests that trust is worth 99.5 per cent of the economy of the United States.[13] Economists had long been obsessed with the hard mechanisms of prices, exchange rates and contracts, and the field has only recently woken up fully to the importance of trust as a key ingredient in successful economies and companies.

Trust is necessary for *good government*. A government which is trusted has higher levels of legitimacy, and there is a greater willingness by citizens to comply with its rulings. A society that lacks trust can lead to excessive faith being placed in a radical and possibly destructive leader, in an extreme ideology or in religious fanatics. Lack of confidence in the government to ensure law and order for minorities can lead to ghettoisation, with small communities becoming ever more tightly knit, enhancing their familiarity with each other, whilst simultaneously cultivating an identity which is inevitably distant from its outside environment. A government that does not trust the public hems it in with mechanisms of accountability and surveillance.

Trust builds *better communities*. Trust is associated with 'social capital', which is described as the accumulation of mutual purpose and action. It facilitates people working together for common purposes, rests upon bonds rooted down at local level – in schools, clubs and professional organisations – and can only be built up over time. Societies with high social capital are based around trusting relationships, the willingness to accept the good intent of others, and the willingness of others to make generous judgements about one's own goodwill.

Trust makes us *happier and healthier*. People who are trusting and who live in high-trust environments lead more fulfilling and productive lives than those who are less trusting and who live in more fearful societies. They are more relaxed and open, both physically and mentally: 'We behave in a more natural way, are more ourselves, and are less inclined to adopt false personas,' says author Tony Buzan.[14] The Americans John Helliwell and Bob Putnam have conducted extensive research into the causes of life satisfaction, finding high correlations between trust and well-being.[15] Richard Layard, known as the British 'Happiness Tsar', discusses how strongly happiness correlates to trust in *Happiness: Lessons from a New Science* (2005). He notes the declining numbers of people who say they trust their neighbours, and the damage this does to the quality of life.[16] 'A person incapable of trust is a person who is something less than fully human, less than fully socialised, less than fully a member of society', say Flores and Solomon.[17] The lesson is clear: an untrusting life is a diminished one.

Finally, trust is a vital ingredient to a *good and meaningful life*. It is possible to lead a life with very low levels of trust, but it will be neither a good life nor a happy one. Trust implies vulnerability, which is precisely why some are wary of it. To trust a child means one will run the risk of being disappointed, which will almost certainly happen; to trust a friend risks betrayal and disappointment, which can happen even without one's friend willing it; to trust a lover risks damage at the deepest emotional and psychological level. But without trust, true love will never be experienced, friendship never formed, nor business operated without a huge apparatus of laws and regulations.

Should we trust the data on trust?

Politicians, professionals, the media, our neighbours and possibly even we ourselves are widely believed to be trusted less than they were a generation ago. But is that correct? Data showing apparent loss of trust are not ubiquitous, and we have drawn heavily in the pages below on polls from the best organisations: Ipsos MORI, Edelman, YouGov, Gallup and the Futures Company. We should be cautious about the data, and fully engage our critical faculties. There is a natural reason that respondents of surveys say that they 'do not trust', rather than making a positive statement that they do. Such respondents, as we know, are inclined to give the answer that they think is expected of them. Much depends on the way questions are framed. 'Do you trust X?', 'Do you trust X to tell the truth?', or 'Do you trust X to do the right thing?' will all elicit a different response from the same individual. We have no means of knowing what people at large thought about trust before Gallup produced the first opinion poll survey in 1937, so the state of trust earlier in the twentieth century, still less in the seventeenth century, when loss of trust in Charles I reached a dramatic conclusion, is a matter of complete conjecture. The survey data that are available, as seen in the chapters below, are often not directly comparable with surveys from some years ago. Robert Worcester, founder of MORI, stands by the data, but not the media's interpretation of them: 'It is a media myth that people are losing trust generally.'[18] Despite all these reservations, trust is a problem in Britain, and that trust levels could be much higher.

Government under pressure: the need for a new model

Loss of trust is endemic, but one actor is central to the whole trust question: the government. In the mid-1970s, in the midst of prolonged crises, political scientists asked whether the overload of expectations placed upon the government meant it could not cope with the pressure. The then head of the civil service, Burke Trend, would muse how the complexity and technical difficulty of government had changed beyond all recognition over his 35-year career, and asked whether the British state was equipped for the challenge.[19] By the end of the first decade of the twenty-first century, government is in a worse position. Conservatives look back nostalgically to Thatcher, who came to power a full thirty years ago, as their last strong leader, while Labour look back sixty years to Clement Attlee. Successive governments since 1945 have collapsed under the weight of scandal or from failure to meet the expectations placed upon them. What else is required before we accept that our current model of government and its relationship with citizens is flawed, and that we need a new model?

Making the case even stronger for a new constitutional settlement are the fresh challenges facing governments in the twenty-first century. The Astronomer Royal and president of the Royal Society, Martin Rees, is far from an alarmist, yet, at the beginning of this century, he wrote a book which has still failed to make the impact that it merits, *Our Final Century? Will the Human Race Survive the Twenty-first Century?* (2003). Rees estimates that the probability of human extinction before the year 2100 is around 50 per cent. He has two principal concerns. First, what the human species is doing collectively to this planet with climate change and population increases. Second, problems stemming from the empowerment of individuals with new technology. 'In the past, the individual maverick could only do limited damage, but now the risk is the global village will have its global idiot.'[20] Such threats could come from nanotechnology, uncontrolled scientific research, terrorist or fundamentalist violence and deliberately planted computer viruses. He cites the Japanese 'religious movement' Aum Shinrikyo, who released the fatal sarin gas on the Tokyo underground, using ingredients and instructions obtained from the internet as a case in point. In order to reduce the possibility of extinction of the race in the coming decades, he advocates the illiberal suggestion, as some would see it, of control of scientific research worldwide, including policing of the internet. Nuclear warfare, he believes, is less of a serious cause of extinction than major bioterrorist attacks; he fears the latter may occur within the next twenty years.

The population of Europe was three times that of Africa in 1950: by 2050, Africa will have three times the population of Europe. Within twenty-five years the UN projects that there will be more than nine billion people on the planet, the increase coming almost exclusively in the developing regions, with a projected rise from 5.4 billion in 2007 to 7.9 billion by mid-century. Pulitzer Prize-winning author Thomas Friedman in *Hot, Flat and Crowded* (2008) talks about the dangers from the growing demand for ever scarcer energy supplies and natural resources, the continued transfer of wealth to oil-rich countries and their 'petro-dictators', accelerating biodiversity loss and the division of the world into 'energy-haves' and 'energy-have-nots'. If not managed well, these could lead to irreversible destructions, and in response he calls for a global strategy of 'trusteeship'.[21] 'We need to redefine our relationship with the natural world,' he writes. In August 2009, Hilary Benn caused dismay when he raised questions about Britain's future food production: some predict significant problems feeding ourselves.

British governments certainly faced challenges at the beginning of the last two centuries. After 1800, they had to contend with Napoleon in Europe, industrialisation at home and the pressure to broaden political participation. After 1900, governments faced a militant Germany, organised labour, and widening political and social rights. And for 2000? Factoring in the seemingly intractable problems of serious organised crime, social mobility, terrorism, the pressure of a 24-hour news cycle and pandemics, and considering the apparent inability of governments around the world to cope with such demands in the late twentieth century, then the argument that major change is needed is beyond doubt. The traditional response, clawing more power into the centre and trusting less, is breaking down. A new model is required.

How does society develop trust?

Trust cannot be enforced by *extrinsic* ways, from forces coming from outside the individual. Rigid laws and harsh punishments will at best produce compliance, but not trust. A harsh government, an intransigent boss, teacher or father who runs a regime of rules and punishments, will inspire fear but not trust. Religions and sects that stress divine punishment, equally, do not generate trust, but rather submission through fear. Trust is not a commodity that can be forced into anyone. Autocratic teachers and parents cannot comprehend why their classes or children are not trusting of them. But to inspire trust in others requires one to give trust, to be trusting. Harsh and strict regimes do not give trust, so do not receive it. As Plato said: 'Good people do not need laws to tell them to act responsibly, while bad people will always find a way around the laws.'

Society has fallen back on a whole panoply of *middle ground* trust developers. We refer here to contractual understandings, financial incentives and bonuses, regular inspections and measurable targets, all designed to boost accountability. None of these are wholly satisfactory as a way of generating trustworthy behaviour as they deny trust in the first instance. Contracts, like all formalisation of relationships, are only created because of a lack of initial trust. A contract depersonalises a relationship between two people or organisations and can be as likely to detract from trust as to add to it. Initially under Thatcher in the 1980s, and still more under Blair after 1997, modern business practices spread into the professions and across the civil service in a bid to increase efficiency and accountability. The philosophy was guided by public choice theory, which saw public servants as acting like businessmen, wanting to maximise the size of their domains. It denigrated the established public service ethos, which assumed that civil servants and even professions would behave in a public-spirited fashion. There is a presupposition that the individual is not able or willing to perform at their best professionally without targets or accountability. They are motivated by suspicion, and do not have a belief in human nature at its best.

Targets often bring out the worst in human nature: even good people will sail as close to the wind as they dare without missing them, while the authorities will feel compelled to punish a conscientious person who just breaks a target while letting off those who just meet it but whose work is shoddy. Organisations bend and twist their resources to meet the targets, sacrificing other worthy but unmeasured ends. The quality and richness of schools have been twisted by the requirement to meet targets, and they feel further devalued by the oppressive inspection regime which grew up in the 1980s. Health workers feel excessively monitored, and can fall into assessing each other in terms of performance ratings rather than on the basis of trust and altruistic cooperation. Incentive pay can demoralise people. The assumption is that the only motive for someone in a vocation such as teaching or nursing is the earning of money, rather than a desire to do something worthwhile with pay a secondary factor. I remember a bizarre conversation with an official in Number 10 soon after Blair came to power, about what I thought of introducing incentives to improve teaching. 'It would be a big mistake as it will belittle the motivation of those who try hard, cut across collegiality, demotivate and divide,' I said. They went ahead with their incentive pay.

Much faith has been placed on increasingly sophisticated technologies of surveillance as the solution to the problems of trust, by aiming to minimise the available opportunities people have to break the law or perform poorly. Visibility and transparency certainly can enhance law-abiding behaviour in the professions, business and private lives. If it is the case that transgressions are likely to be seen and noticed, people will be more likely to behave in ways that avoid them being seen to break the law. But they are not ideal ways of building trust, because the motivation is fear of being found out rather than being trustworthy for its own sake. Parents who spy on their young do not produce trustworthy children. Prying into our lives by government, the police and by journalists carries its own risks, and can readily infringe on individual rights. With modern communication and information technology, as with the arms race, a serious opponent can develop equally sophisticated technologies to combat the enhanced surveillance.

We believe a presumption of trust is better than a presumption of distrust. Trust in the professions has not risen in the twenty years since targets and enhanced accountability measures have become more widespread. Accountability measures failed to prevent the financial crisis and MPs' expenses. There is a better way to conduct society.

None of these middle ground methods will be 'de-invented'. But the only enduring way to ensure that trust becomes the dominant value is for trust to be *intrinsic*. It must come from within us, something that the young grow up with and want to live by themselves and expect others to live by. This book calls powerfully for intrinsic trust to be developed across British society, and is based upon our belief in the natural goodness of human beings, and accordingly in a presumption of trust. Methods include the rewarding and celebrating of ethical and altruistic behaviour, giving all individuals opportunities to learn to give and receive trust, and encouraging families and schools to let children grow up in trusting surroundings so their inherently trusting natures can blossom rather than be stunted. The motivation to stimulate trust can be represented diagrammatically, as in Table 1.1.

Table 1.1: Intrinsic / middle ground / extrinsic motivations

Intrinsic	Pure altruism/service
	Educate ethics and duties / responsibilities
	Sense of personal development and fulfilment
	Role models who display high trust
	Intangible recognition from peers – gratitude/stigma
	Accountability within the organisation itself
Middle ground	Public recognition and status
	Inspection, oversight and surveillance
	Accountability to external parties
	Monitoring, regulation and targets
	Financial inducement and incentives
Extrinsic	Approval of the powerful
	Arbitrary laws and indiscriminate rules
	Threat of divine punishment
	Threat of dismissal
	Threat of imprisonment

Can we learn from political philosophy?

Political philosophers have been writing about the ideal way to order government and society for 2,500 years. They have much to say about trust and in producing our model of trust we draw heavily on their inspiration.

Plato (429–347 BC) offers a vision of an imaginary state ruled over by 'philosopher kings', and says that government is best left to those properly trained in the art of philosophy, who he defines as the enlightened men of society. These 'philosopher kings' would epitomise the four virtues of temperance, prudence, fortitude and justice. But Aristotle (384–322 BC) argues that such enlightened action is not solely the purview of an exclusive realm of philosopher kings, it is open to *all*. He says that the highest purpose of man, and the objective of his life, is to achieve *eudaimonia*, which he defines as 'a happiness or joy which pervades the good life'. He teaches that man must, and is able, to find the right balance in his own life between deficiency and excess, describing this as the 'golden mean'. A life that is lived in excess is damaging to society overall, as are lives devoid of basic needs.[22]

Confucius (551–479 BC) pre-dates Plato and Aristotle, but only in the last century did his ideas begin to filter significantly into Western thinking. He saw trust as absolutely fundamental to a good society; even in facial expressions, he said, truth must be represented, as honest communication is elemental in the building of trust. Like Plato and Aristotle, he believed in the duty of rulers to lead by example. 'The moral character of the ruler is the wind; the moral character of those beneath him is the grass. When the wind blows, the grass bends.'[23] Superior leaders, Confucius believed, possessed the moral power to lead without having to rely on force or bullying. He valued humility, politeness and decorum highly. Cicero (106–43 BC) echoes him: 'popular' politicians do and say things that will be popular among the multitudes; virtuous politicians, who lead upright lives, do what is right, and are rewarded by the approval of the virtuous.[24]

In contrast to their heady optimism, some writing in the last three centuries have proved more cynical. The Englishman Thomas Hobbes (1588–1679), as with the Italian Niccolò Machiavelli (1469–1527), adopts a much more pessimistic view on human nature and motivation. Hobbes writes in *Leviathan* that life in the 'state of nature', i.e. before the advent of government, was 'solitary, poor, nasty, brutish and short', and this justified strong authority which would use force arbitrarily to ensure that order was kept.[25] For both Hobbes and Machiavelli, trust was an irrelevant adjunct to such a society. The English novelist William

Golding was equally pessimistic: he wrote his dystopian novel *Lord of the Flies* (1954) about the breakdown of order within a group of English schoolboys forced to look after themselves on a tropical island following a plane crash. The book was influenced by his own experience of the tumultuous years that had preceded the book's publication. Our own judgement about how humans treat each other without strong authority over them is as such fundamental to our whole understanding of trust. Advocates of extrinsic ways to motivate the public are of a school cynical of human nature.

Baron de Montesquieu (1689–1755) was less pessimistic than Hobbes but similarly argued that the self-regarding pursuit of honour and distinction came more naturally to men than a commitment to the public interest. He argued that though democracy and monarchy provide citizens with greater security than the inherent corruption of despotism, both must be hemmed in through the institutional 'separation of powers'. It is only through such checks and balances that power will not be abused such that government would be worthy of trust and its citizens guaranteed the greatest possible liberty. This view owed much to Plato and Aristotle, but Montesquieu was fêted for it by the founding fathers of the US Constitution, and his influence and stature has thus been immense.

Jean-Jacques Rousseau (1712–78) writes in stark contrast to Hobbes, and has an altogether sunnier view. He sees not man but, like Montesquieu, arbitrary government as the source of danger and woe. He famously wrote: 'Man is born free, but everywhere he is in chains.'[26] For Rousseau, the fundamental requirement was to find a form of association which would articulate the common good and allow each citizen to enjoy maximum freedom. His solution was the 'general will', which he saw as the moral and collective will of the citizenship at its best. Laws should come from the people as a whole, and any law that is not thus ratified is 'null and void'. Rousseau was a 'social contract' theorist whose work built on that of John Locke (1632–1704), whose ideas of a contract between the rulers and the ruled meant that arbitrary rule was out, and rulers had to operate under the 'rule of law'. Rulers had a duty to look after the interests of the ruled, and if they sacrificed that trust could expect to be replaced. The ideas of the social contract theorists flowered in the American Declaration of Independence of 1776 and less enduringly in the French Revolution in 1789.

The dramatic overthrow of the monarchy in France that culminated in the guillotining of Louis XVI in 1793 catalysed a conservative reaction, embodied in the personality of the Irishman Edmund Burke (1729–97). Burke published the pamphlet *Reflections on the Revolution in France* in 1790, written in disapproval of the revolutionary chaos of the late eighteenth century. Burke was a strong supporter of nationality, conservatism and traditional constitutions, which he believed were God given and sanctioned by historical tradition. He cautioned against change which went against the grain of tradition, and which was not 'organic'; such change would not endure. Continuity and tradition were what he wanted; this underpins his strong support for the family. He spoke warmly about the 'little platoons', described as 'the first principle (the germ as it were) of public affections'.[27] In similar fashion, Alexis de Tocqueville (1805–59) argued in his studies on America that it was the country's network of civil associations that was critical to combating destructive individualism and sustaining a healthy and vibrant democracy.[28] For both Burke and de Tocqueville, love for the country begins with love for these smallest groupings or associations with which each individual and family can identify, and on which the nation and society are built.

The tide of liberal and revolutionary ideas could not be stymied and in 1791 the Englishman Thomas Paine (1737–1809) wrote *The Rights of Man* in response to Burke's *Reflections*. Paine went further than the earlier exponents of social contract and argued that the first of all rights of man is liberty – which governments had to be trusted to respect. But with rights came responsibilities: 'A Declaration of Rights is, by reciprocity, a declaration of duties also,' he wrote. 'Whatever is my right as a man is also the right of another man and it becomes my duty to guarantee as well as to possess.' Paine argues that revolution is justified when trust is broken and 'government fails to safeguard its people and protect their rights'.[29] Paine's arguments had a profound impact on those drafting the Declaration of Rights of Man and Citizen drawn up by the National Assembly of France in 1789. His influence further extends from the 1791 United States Bill of Rights to the 1948 UN Universal Declaration of Human Rights, but his emphasis on duties that come with rights has not spawned any influential 'Bills of Responsibilities'.

Yet responsibility to one another is critical to our trust model, and helps us identify the necessary goals and direction of our ideal society. We need something more to cover freedom of expression, goodness and justice. John Stuart Mill (1806–73) was a pupil of Jeremy Bentham (1748–1832), who developed the theory of utilitarianism, in which actions are justified according to whether or not they lead to the greatest happiness for the greatest number. Mill's seminal work, *On Liberty* (1859), was written in reaction to contemporary moralists and political reformers and what he saw as the Victorian ethos with its 'yoke of opinion'. He asserts the sovereignty of 'one very simple principle', that the only reason for which man is entitled individually or collectively to interfere with the liberty of another individual is for 'self-protection'.

John Rawls (1921–2002) has been the most prominent political philosopher of our time, and in his *A Theory of Justice* (1971) provides a definitive statement on the ordering of a just society. His concern was to ensure that social and economic inequalities in society should only exist where advantageous positions were open to all, under conditions of equality of opportunity, and where they could ensure the greatest benefit to the least advantaged. To Rawls, our innate sense of justice is cultivated through our upbringing and the trust we develop in family relationships. The guilt we feel when we breach these trusting relationships with our family is equivalent to the sense of guilt that we feel about injustice among the least well off in society. Rawls's theory nonetheless remains a hypothetical thought experiment. It is a society as ideally constructed as it is practically unrealisable. The utilitarian 'greatest happiness principle' likewise collapses in practice into a conflict between 'rules'-based and individual 'act'-based utilitarianism. Indeed it is a damning feature of philosophy in the last two centuries that it became a self-referencing and inwardly focused domain, increasingly abstracted and detached from actual experience and reality.

It is on these grounds that the British novelist and philosopher Iris Murdoch (1919–99), who wrote *The Sovereignty of Good* in 1970, dismisses all previous philosophy because of its inability to provide us with a system which 'one could live by'.[30] Her starting point is a decline of faith in God, but she argues that we should focus our attention instead on what is 'good' to help us improve morally. Goodness is related to knowledge of the 'true nature of things', which can be attained by experiencing life moment by moment: 'If I attend properly I will have no choices, and this is the ultimate condition to be aimed at.'[31] The perfect model of such attention is offered by the 'humble man', she says, 'because he sees himself as nothing [and] can see other things as they are'.[32] Murdoch emphasises the importance of art and literature as teachers of virtue and providers of truth, for they both serve to free man from his selfish consciousness, as a result of which we can discover objective reality. Her advocacy that we can only achieve virtue and attain humility by defeating the ego, and living in the present, marks her out as a highly spiritual philosopher, much in tune with mystical traditions.

Amartya Sen, the Nobel prize-winning economist, fits within this critical tradition. In his influential *The Idea of Justice* (2009), he disputes that people will ever agree – in direct contrast to Rawls – on what is a 'just society'. Instead of asking absolute questions about what a perfect just society should be like, he calls for a comparison of actual human lives and inequalities to enhance justice and remove injustice. Trust is placed in the enlightened leadership of those who are called upon to take global decisions in our interconnected world.

From this canter we can extract several lessons helpful in designing a new model of government and society for the twenty-first century built around trust.

▶ We must train leaders in virtue so they become worthy of trust (Plato, Cicero)

▶ Citizens should aim for virtue and happiness in society through their own endeavour (Aristotle, Mill, Murdoch)

▶ Leaders must act in trustworthy ways and communicate honestly (Cicero, Confucius)

▶ Trust in government will be enhanced if power is separated and if there are in-built checks and balances (Plato, Aristotle, Montesquieu)

▶ Society is made up from the bonds of trust within families and of a plethora of small associations and if change is too sudden, it will erode trust (Burke, Tocqueville)

▶ Sovereignty lies with the people, and they have a right to eject the government if it does not prove itself worthy of their trust (Locke, Paine, Rousseau)

▶ With rights come responsibilities (Paine)

▶ Family nurturing is essential to the formation of trust and to a sense of justice (Burke, Rawls)

▶ Truth can be comprehended from living in the present and from immersing oneself in great art and literature (Murdoch)

▶ Experience teaches us that inequality in and between nations is untenable, and leaders should seek to reduce it (Rawls, Sen)

Our trust model

We are now ready to put forward our trust model. We believe that trust – being trusting and being trustworthy – is the sovereign quality that is most needed to build a flourishing Britain in the twenty-first century. Our trust model rests on some clearly defined principles.

It incorporates *trusteeship*, i.e. it does not just encompass contemporary relationships but extends into the future and past. It extends into the future because we have a duty of trust to future generations to look after and husband the planet so that it will nourish and delight them, rather than bequeath them an inhospitable or uninhabitable mess. We need to care for our institutions, buildings and families, leaving them stronger than we found them. We need to assess our 'trust footprint', the balance of trusting and untrusting actions in our lives, and develop a 'trust trade' equation: where it is unavoidable to scar natural beauty, we must compensate by bequeathing beauty. The National Trust shines out as an exemplar with its commitment to protect special places in England, Wales and Northern Ireland 'for ever, for everyone'.[33] The architects of medieval cathedrals knew they would not live to see their creations completed, but have left us objects of enduring beauty. Trust extends into the past. We have insufficiently honoured our trust relationships with those who sacrificed their lives fighting for the country and even with our own family who came before us. In China, derived from Confucianism, is a paramount respect for ancestors: Chinese families regularly pay homage to their forefathers going back several generations with many overseas Chinese communities forming clan associations, *Kongsi*, for individuals with the same family name. In Britain, despite our Christian heritage and the fifth of the Ten Commandments, parents are respected less by their children, while grandparents are often sidelined, considered to be an inconvenience. As Jonathan Sacks has argued, 'home is as sacred as a house of worship',[34] not least because it is a place where all generations of the family gather together. Societies, companies and associations of all kinds need also to show that they are trustees of all that earlier generations built up. Too many think that our institutions began the day we joined them and will cease to matter the day we leave, or think life began the day we were born, and will cease the day we die. Failure to respect trusteeship is solipsism gone mad.

At the core of our thinking is the *presumption of trust*, grounded on the psychological proposition that people will behave as they sense they are expected to behave. Where people and institutions feel themselves not to be trusted, they will not behave in trustworthy ways; where they do sense themselves trusted, they will behave in a more high-minded way. The lack of a presumption of trust by government, police, media and lawyers has diminished us all as human beings. Building trust in society is difficult because of what we might term 'the one and twenty rule'. It is far easier to damage trust than to build it up. Imagine that you help an elderly lady on a train, take her suitcase off the shelf and place it on the platform for her. If you do that, she will feel an automatic surge of trust and happiness, and you too will feel a sense of goodness. But if you took her bag off the shelf and ran off with it, she would feel profoundly unhappy and her mistrust of others would deepen. Impossible to quantify, the feeling of unhappiness and mistrust might be said to be twenty times more powerful than the goodness that would be generated by the kindly act. It is hard work building trust.

We believe trust is *innate*, and that we flourish in a trusting world. Performing trusting acts makes us feel happy: there is a natural compulsion to give and receive trust, and to be honest. We do not believe, as do the rational choice theorists, and philosophers like Robert Nozick in *Anarchy, State and Utopia* (1974), that humans are essentially happy or at their best when they are out for themselves. The eighteenth-century philosopher David Hume wrote that humans think first of themselves, then of their families, and only then of others. We do not believe human nature is so self-centred, but rather that there is a balance, perfectly encapsulated by Rabbi Hillel in the second century BC: 'If I am not for myself, then who will be? If I am only for myself, then what am I? If not now, when?'[35] One can live a life in a bubble without trust, but man is not at his best, nor entirely human, nor happy if he does so. We are all inextricably interconnected. John Donne's words have been studied more closely in English lessons in schools than practised in our lives day by day: 'No man is an island, entire of itself . . . Any man's death diminishes me, because I am involved in mankind.'[36] Every single human being on the planet is involved in mankind, and every one of our actions affects not only other human beings but nature as well. If I drive dangerously, then I not only endanger others but also encourage others to emulate my behaviour. If I drive a petrol-guzzling car I use up the planet's resources quicker than they may otherwise be consumed. If I throw rubbish out of my car's window, it pollutes the road. We want to do good to others because at the very deepest level we recognise that we are all part of each other; to do good brings happiness, to do harm to others causes us to be unhappy.

As man is innately trusting, and responds best when there is a presumption of trust, the optimum motivation is *intrinsic*, generated from inside. External sanctions and motivations belittle human beings' dignity, professional pride and imagination, and should be avoided. Human beings thus have to *take responsibility themselves* for being trusting. Only if we achieve this autonomously will we move to a more trusting society.

As role models, leaders across society must meet two key criteria of trustworthiness: behave ethically and be technically proficient. The power of leaders to build or destroy trust is vast. Without honesty and competence, suspicion will grow, as will the threat of corruption. Politicians need also to speak the language of trust much more. British politicians in the late twentieth and early twenty-first centuries were reluctant to talk about morality, not because they thought the subject unimportant, but because they feared that the press would alight on alleged immoral behaviour of some of their own number and open up charges of hypocrisy. The 'M' word (morality) acquired the stigma that the 'L' word (liberal) had in the previous decade in US politics. It is not a matter of left or right, conservatism or progressivism. Our failure to talk about morals has meant that we lurch from one epidemic of moral outrage to another, as with the cash for questions scandal in 1994, cash for honours in 2006–7, the MPs' expenses scandal in 2008–9. We all need to talk more about right and wrong.

The trust we advocate is an active trust, with critical faculties consciously engaged, and where the trustworthiness of others is fully assessed. It is the opposite of blind trust. Trust has to be earned, and a teacher or leader who says 'trust me', or a politician who has to tell us he is honest or trustworthy, is asking for our blind, not active, trust.

Trust requires a balance of individual and collective needs. If an individual action is too individualistic and rides over others, then it will be a selfish and untrusting act. If the collective impulse is too strong, then individuality is swamped, as Mill foresaw in *On Liberty*; equally, if the government is too collectivist, it stifles individual and corporate enterprise. A trusting society needs a sensitive balance between the freedom of expression of the individual person or company, and the claims of the collective: that medium ground is expressed in Figure 1.3.

Figure 1.3: The individualist–collectivist continuum

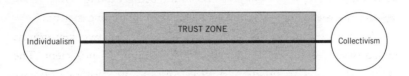

The trust approach finally does not rely on any religious authority and can be supported by the non-religious and religious alike. Belief systems such as Buddhism, which place trust highly, and enshrine the doctrine of *mudita* or happiness in another's good fortune – which is the opposite of *Schadenfreude* – can help spread trust. But closed and exclusive religions or sects which may have high trust internally but distrust externally can damage trust in society overall. Ideologies can also be damaging of trust in society if, like Marxism or extreme environmentalism, they place the achievement of their ends above human needs. Everyone in life has a guiding philosophy, be it religious, nationalist or altruistic. At the other end of the scale, one can place the modern drive for scientific managerialism in the form of regimentation and accountability. Too much of it belittles values, marginalises ethics and chokes trust. So again, we have a continuum, with the middle ground between both poles being the area where we find most trust (see Figure 1.4).

Figure 1.4: The ideology/religion–regulation continuum

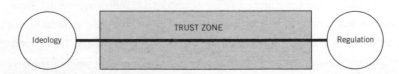

Placing both of these lines together forms a cross with a middle area, which will be the 'high trust' area. When an individual or organisation operates here, there will be a natural tendency for the actions to help build trust in society. If an individual or state is operating at the outer margins, there will be a tendency to spread mistrust, and to contribute towards a dysfunctional society. This is represented in Figure 1.5.

Figure 1.5: Complete trust diagram

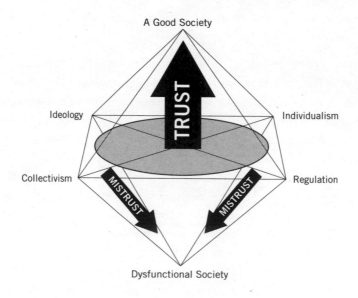

To ensure that individuals, organisations and society move most speedily towards increasing trust, we propose a 'Trust Test' (TT) as the measure by which all actions can be assessed. An action is judged to have passed the TT if it builds trust with other individuals. An action that detracts from or destroys trust is an action that fails the TT. This trust relates not only to other individuals and organisations in Britain and abroad today, but also with future generations, and with those who have gone before us. Can it really be this simple? Yes, and if the man with the wall operated with the TT in mind, he would have been wiser and happier. If indeed he had been burgled, he would have realised that nothing more valuable had been taken from him than his goods.

Jeffrey Archer would say 'I'm worth £5 million' in the 1980s.
Since that decade, material and consumer values have proliferated,
at the expense of the civic and collegiate. *(AFP/Getty Images)*

CHAPTER 2
HOW IS TRUST LOST?

The trust of the innocent is the liar's most powerful tool.

Stephen King (1947–), author

We need to comprehend why trust has been lost in Britain, to the extent it has been, if we are to work out how to rebuild it. There was never a 'golden age' of trust in the past; Classical Greek and Roman politicians and businessmen could be venal as well as virtuous, as could their sportsmen, their military and their law enforcers. The centuries that followed the fall of Rome were not remarkable for their trust either. In our own lives, we tend to look back at a time which we think, rightly or not, was more trustful than now. When I first went to university, I could go to the local Blackwell's bookshop and buy whatever books I wanted. There, the staff would make a note of the title, my name and the price, to be settled at the end of term. A year or so on, the bookshop began to demand personal ID. In my final year, they asked not only for ID, but also required that one open an account with proof of ability to pay. Everyone seemed to lose out from this formalisation. The bookshop became burdened with bureaucracy, the customers were inconvenienced and the sense of belonging to a community evaporated. I imagine that the dishonesty of a small number caused the change. Or maybe it was the arrival of a new accountancy firm with bright new business management techniques. Why is it that we sacrifice trust so readily, when it is so clearly something that we desire? There are no definitive answers, but this chapter offers ten possibilities.

1. Decline of religious and moral codes

Throughout history, the existence of religious and moral codes has acted to help bind society together around certain predictable norms of behaviour which have helped to boost trust. Humanist camps in summer 2009 taught the young about moral standards devoid of religion, but throughout history it has traditionally been religion that has bequeathed a set of moral codes. The team who worked with me on this book are mostly atheists or agnostics and they protested, as will many readers, at the idea that religion should be put forward as a source of trust. Indeed, one need only contemplate the horrors of the Crusades, the blood lust of Protestants and Catholics in the wars of religion in the sixteenth and seventeenth centuries, ethnic cleansing in the former Yugoslavia, and the clashes between Sunni and Shia Muslims in contemporary Iraq to realise how frequently organised religion has brought about war and the destruction of trust.

But for all the mistrustful and evil acts that have been perpetrated in the name of religion, the advocacy of good actions and service to others, which are common to all religions, have been powerful forces binding societies together and contributing to trust. At the core of Christianity, Judaism and Islam, the three main monotheistic religions, is the service of a single entity: God. The polytheistic religions of Hinduism, Buddhism and Sikhism emphasise this idea of service, but to multiple gods. Their existence may be disputed by many people, but in all cases, these deities demand not selfishness, nor violence, but loving acts towards others. Whatever their services to scholarship and to journalism, the writings of Richard Dawkins, most recently in *The God Delusion* (2006),[1] and Christopher Hitchens in *God Is Not Great: The Case Against Religion* (2007),[2] have been a disservice to the understanding of religion. They equate the worst actions committed by people with religious labels to religion as a whole. One would not seek to diminish science because there have been bad or even malevolent scientists. Besides, Karen Armstrong in her *Case for God* (2009) says that they attack not religion but fundamentalism, and have little to say about God, who is beyond the scope of language to comprehend. Even the non-religious must accept that religion has inspired much of what is finest in life.

Without the clear moral codes that religion provided, Geoff Mulgan writes, 'it is much harder to understand your place in society; it is much harder to picture what is going on'.[3] Marek Kohn argues similarly in his book, *Trust* (2008): in our contemporary world, where agreed social norms have diminished, he argues 'people tend to converge upon the relatively limited number of poles of attraction, sustaining a mass culture based on best selling music, images, and styles of adornment', but this has led to 'extensive social uncertainty'.[4] For trust to be built up, predictability and agreed norms of behaviour are fundamental. The non-religious, for all their strengths, have not produced codes of comparable reach and influence to the religious codes. Utilitarianism and Rawls's *A Theory of Justice* (1999) have not provided a universal moral code.[5] Codifications of rights, most notably the Universal Declaration of Human Rights of 1948, have often been so general that they have made little difference to people's lives. Onora O'Neill writes: 'Declarations of rights ostensibly offer something to everybody, without coming clear about the costs.'[6]

2. Decline in family and sense of belonging
In 1945 in Britain, it was common for families to live together, with children leaving home only once they were married, and grandparents often living in the same house.[7] By 2009, children would leave home at eighteen to go on to work or higher education (43 per cent of 18–30s enter higher education),[8] grandparents would live separately (42 per cent of grandparents lose contact with their grandchildren after a family break-up),[9] and parents would often be living apart. The decline of

the traditional family in Britain, and together with it, the change in the stability of the mother–child bond, has been significant because children first learn about trust in the home.[10] 'The most devastating effects for the impulse to trust are brought about by the decay of the family,' says Piotr Sztompka.[11] The trusting impulse, he says, has been replaced by an inherent suspicion. Where the family unit is strong, there will be higher levels of trust. However, we must beware of easy correlations between a decline of the traditional family and the breakdown of trust. Scandinavian levels of family breakdown are high too, but trust is believed to be higher as are levels of reported well-being. The Dutch are celebrated for their liberal attitudes toward drink, drugs and sex, yet are reported to have far higher levels of trust: a key factor here might well be the greater support that families receive.[12]

A wider sense of community belonging has broken down too in the last twenty-five or more years. The American author Robert Putnam, in Russell Hardin's *Trust* (2006), notes that in the US from the mid 1960s onwards, 'the resources people, neighbourhoods and large families once had to organise themselves to deal with problems have gone into steady decline'.[13] He describes how during the last forty years the activities that isolate us from one another have steadily increased. Television keeps us at home in the evenings, and often in separate rooms. Multiple ownership of cars means fewer people use public transport. The decline of local employment means many now work away from home communities. Life has become increasingly atomised. 'Relationships that can be organised by norms that are locally, spontaneously enforced are no longer part of many, if any important aspect of our lives,' says Hardin.[14] Instead we fall back on 'abstract principles and legal constraints'.[15] Regular contact with fellow human beings is essential for trust and understanding to grow: the more opportunities for fulfilling relationships, the more predictable life becomes, and the more individuals can relax into letting go of their apprehensions and giving back trust. Society might enhance individual freedom, but it has been to the detriment of trust. The balance has shifted far in the direction of solitary life, and opportunities for belonging have been significantly reduced.

3. Continued social exclusion

Continued social exclusion has damaged trust because political parties have promised to extend opportunities for all, yet British society has remained steeply stratified. William Beveridge, the founder of the modern welfare state, said that government would slay the five giants of 'Idleness, Want, Squalor, Ignorance and Disease'.[16] From 1945, governments encouraged the belief that they would be able to achieve this end. But they have been unable to eliminate poverty, sickness or the other ills, despite pumping billions of pounds into the welfare state. Disparities between the rich and poor continue and maybe are widening.[17] The Organisation for Economic Co-operation and Development declared in 2008 that Britain remains one of the most unequal countries in the developed world, with the richest 10 per cent of the population earning nine times more than the poorest 10 per cent.[18] Inequality and a chronic sense of exclusion do not make for trust.

The Panel on Fair Access to the Professions, chaired by Labour MP Alan Milburn, reported in April 2009 that 'many of Britain's professions have become more socially exclusive and, as a consequence, bright children from average income families, not just those from more disadvantaged backgrounds, are missing out on a professional career.'[19] His final report in July 2009 concluded that Britain was a 'persistently unequal society', and that the great post-war surge in social mobility ground to a halt in the 1980s. Despite twelve years of a Labour government committed to improving social inclusion, with its policies such as tax credits, Sure Start, nurseries for all, improved schooling and greater access to university and apprenticeships, the panel concluded that class had become more rigid.[20]

These findings have been challenged by many, including David Goodhart, who believes that social mobility 'still remains quite high', except at the very top and in the long tail at the bottom.[21] Nevertheless, it is hard to be trusting of a state which has promised equality of opportunity, yet seems to have not dealt equally with all citizens. Richard Wilkinson and Kate Pickett argue in *The Spirit Level* (2009) that 'the scale of inequality provides a powerful lever on the psychological well being of all of us'. Their very clear finding is that levels of trust between members of the public are lower in countries and states where income differences are larger.[22]

It is not just the less well-off and ethnic minorities who feel themselves excluded. Peter Oborne's book *The Triumph of the Political Class* (2007) argues that a self-perpetuating cadre has continued to dominate political society, reminiscent of the eighteenth century, and despises attempts to limit its power.[23] Power has become unacceptably centralised in the British state. Despite attempts by Margaret Thatcher and subsequent Prime Ministers to devolve government, decentralise management and, more recently, directly facilitate greater representation of ethnic minorities and women in Parliament, huge swathes remain excluded from the political process.[24]

4. Corporate greed and corruption

Companies which make large profits but charge high prices to customers have a negative impact on trust, still more so when they award very high bonuses. Anger at the credit crunch was exacerbated in July and August 2009 by news of high bank profits and talk that the 'big bonus' culture would return to the City in the new year.[25] The high bonuses and reckless lifestyles of bankers, which began in the 1980s, has fuelled deep mistrust, as caricatured by the 1987 film *Wall Street*, in which the lead character, Gordon Gekko, epitomises greed.[26] Surveys repeatedly show that news of very high salaries, especially when the public cannot understand why the money is justified, creates mistrust. Damage has been done to trust in Britain by a few individuals and corporations that have behaved recklessly or who have cost the British public jobs, savings, holidays and homes. Nick Leeson caused dismay in

1995 when his actions resulted in the collapse of Barings Bank, which had been trading since 1762. Leeson lost £827 million speculating, primarily on future contracts.[27] Arthur Andersen was one of the big five accounting firms until 2002, when it ceased to practise after being found guilty of criminal charges relating to its handling of the auditing of Enron, the US energy company. This resulted in the loss of 85,000 jobs worldwide.[28] Arms companies arouse less trust than consumer companies, for obvious reasons. In 2004, the Serious Fraud Office made two arrests during their investigation into secret offshore payments to the Middle East as part of the 'al-Yamamah' £40 billion arms deal with Saudi Arabia.[29] Robert Klitgaard, a leading analyst on corruption, has reached the formulation that corruption is 'more pronounced in systems characterised by the formula $C = M + D - A$', or, 'corruption equals monopoly plus discretion minus accountability'.[30]

5. Rise of consumerism and the rights culture

There is nothing wrong with consumerism *per se* but a balance between it and communal or civic values has been lost. A civic ethic educates the young to be public minded and to show trust; the consumer mentality is concerned more with personal satisfaction and corporate gain. Between the 1960s and the 1980s, a fundamental shift occurred in British society, away from hierarchy and deference, towards one based upon market values. This change happened across the world and was associated with thinkers like the Austrian Friedrich von Hayek and the American Milton Friedman. It happened at all levels of society from local communities up to the City of London. David Kynaston entitled the final volume of his history of the City *A Club No More* (2007).[31] 'Up to the 1980s', he said, 'the City of London had been a club or a series of clubs: people knew each other, shared the same values and had been to the same schools and universities. From the 1980s onwards, it became a much more market-driven and harder place.'[32] British companies like ICI and BP changed from being relatively sedate places, to tougher and more competitive ones. A job for life in one company, which helped to build trust, increasingly disappeared. Into the civil service came market testing and business techniques. The old world of the dependable Whitehall official, with a tradition of public service, effectively died. Under threat too came the notion of a 'vocation', a calling to a public-spirited job, where financial remuneration was only a part of the motivation for the individual entering that career. The conventional wisdom, developed in the 1940s and based on Maslow's 'Hierarchy of Needs', placed self-actualisation as the highest motive for work, but now money was all.[33]

Some of these changes were overdue, others were inevitable. But the message that the young absorbed were that success and financial wealth are the ultimate validations of the good life. A defining moment for me came when I invited Jeffrey Archer to a school in Croydon in the 1980s to speak to the pupils. He boasted to them that he had lost all his money and said he was 'now worth £5 million'. It was the first time that I, as well as the pupils, had heard someone equating their human existence to a lump of money. Some time after, I began to notice that the young increasingly said they wanted careers where they would earn lots of money, so they could have fast cars, big homes and lots of holidays. In *Affluenza* (2007), psychologist Oliver James analyses the compulsive drive for material affluence in modern society, and argues that it has failed to bring the enhancements to happiness and well-being that we all assumed it would.[34] In 2008, the Association of Teachers and Lecturers warned that children were coming under excessive commercial pressure to be seen buying and wearing fashionable brands.[35]

The concern with rights, rather than duties and responsibilities, has coincided with the rise of consumerism. Rights are stressed by government, in our legal system, in our hospitals and our schools, and when we are disappointed we want to know what 'they' are going to do about it. Rights are important for trust, because we need to feel that organisations are trustworthy and will respect us as citizens, consumers and individuals. But they need to be balanced by duties and responsibilities. Rights imply what you can take out; duties are what you give back. Duties build more trustworthy people; rights build trust-demanding people.

A new consensus is being built in Britain that our consumerist priorities are wrong. Nic Marks of the New Economics Foundation (NEF), Jules Peck, the former advisor on quality of life to David Cameron, and Robert Phillips of the PR company Edelman are part of this new view. They argue that the championing of consumerist values has diminished the intrinsic values of community involvement, emotional intimacy, familial ties and institutional loyalty, and that our physical and mental well-being have suffered.[36] 'The more we value materialism and hedonism,' Marks says, 'the less we value communities. This is particularly true of the younger generation, who live in a world where what you have defines you and who you are. Our surveys show them strongly endorsing material values over extrinsic ones.'[37] We have gone too far in letting consumer values and an obsession with rights predominate, and trust has been the casualty.

6. The rise of violence and fear of violence

Violence and the fear of violence, including terrorism, has detracted significantly from trust. It has made us suspicious of neighbours, wary of strangers, and angry that the police and government cannot do more to make us safer. Crime has risen steeply since 1945, and even though figures show that it may have decreased since 1995, the fear of crime has continued to rise, and with it suspicion of the police. On a daily basis our newspapers and television screens seem full of some new, horrific act of violence, often unrepresentative of the overall picture, but with great power to alarm. 9/11, 7/7 and the persistent threat from terrorism have increased levels of fear, while the response by government has led to parallel fears of an encroaching police state. We live in a climate of suspicion which predisposes us to think ill of other people's intent. Is it surprising then that we do not trust those around us?

While I was researching this chapter, the following e-mail arrived in my inbox: 'THIS IS NOT A JOKE; READ IT AND PASS IT

ON TO ALL YOUR FEMALE FRIENDS AND FAMILY . . . IT COULD JUST SAVE THEIR LIVES – An important message from the Police – This actually happened a few weeks ago on the M3 FLEET SERVICES!!! It was early evening, and a young girl stopped to get petrol. She filled her tank and walked into the store to pay. The cashier told her, "A man just got into the back of your car. I've called the police, and they're on their way". When the police arrived, they found the man in the back seat of the girl's car and questioned him. He stated he was joining a gang, and the initiation to join is to kidnap a woman and bring her back to the gang to be raped. If the woman is still alive by the time they finish with her then they let her go . . . According to the police, there is a new gang forming here. The scary part of this is, because the guy didn't have a weapon on him, the police could only charge him with trespassing . . . He's back on the street and free to try again . . . LADIES, you or one of your family or friends could be the next victim.' Was this a hoax? I have no idea. The e-mail continued about why women should not trust men, citing recent lurid attacks, and offering advice. It finished: 'As women, we are always trying to be sympathetic: STOP IT!' It matters perhaps less whether the police sent the original e-mail than that the contents are widely believed. They offer some wise counsel, but add significantly to fear and anxiety.

The spate of knife crime in Britain in 2007, and gun crime since 2008, have caused increasing levels of mistrust, while talk in summer 2009 of cuts of 10,000 local policemen because of the need to reduce expenditure have caused public concerns. Many members of the public cannot understand why individuals are let out of prison merely to reoffend, and why sentences are not longer to safeguard the public better. They cannot comprehend why the prison service is seemingly incapable of keeping drugs out of prisons and crime bosses from continuing to operate their crime empires from behind bars. They do not know why some judges continue to give lenient sentences, a concern exacerbated by the right-wing press.[38] They do not see why they have to be putting ever-greater security measures into their homes, and why they can't walk through the park or certain streets at night. What they do know is that they can no longer trust the police to tell them the truth.

7. *Disappointment in politicians: scandals and expectations*

The British electorate has long been used to disillusionment with their Prime Ministers; from Lloyd George, the first 'bad man' of the twentieth century, to Blair, who never recovered from the loss of trust for going to war with Iraq. Monarchs and princes throughout history have not behaved well, but the disillusion with the antics of the Queen's children and Princess Diana in the 1980s and 1990s contributed to loss of trust not only in the monarchy, but in authority in general. Then again, nothing prepared the country for the widespread disgust at politicians of all parties in the 2009 expenses revelations. The public becomes alarmed when it cannot trust those who they expect to be of high repute to run the country. The implicit question behind it all is *quis custodiet ipsos custodes*; who will watch over those who watch over us?

Both major political parties in Britain have contributed to a lack of trust by arousing expectations in the electorate as a means to be elected and then failing to satisfy those expectations. The belief grew, and with it disillusion, that politicians were 'only in it for themselves.' In the 1970s and the 1980s, both Labour and the Conservatives used advertising agencies extensively to rally support, the most famous emblem being the 1979 Saatchi and Saatchi billboard 'Labour isn't working'. Increasingly in the 1980s, political parties adopted sophisticated electoral techniques copied from the United States with focus groups and private polling increasingly used by all parties. With the decline of political ideology, they became like any company conducting market research into what their customers wanted and then satisfying their customers with products, which in this case were policies, albeit policies which rarely delivered on their promise. Labour and Conservative politicians were increasingly driven to make commitments which they could never possibly deliver, usually concerning public services and taxation. Blair made countless promises of the '50 per cent reduction' variety but little or nothing happened, except where, from 2000 to 2009, public spending was ramped up, despite tax being left broadly unchanged.[39] 'I think great cynicism was caused by attempts', says Polly Toynbee, 'by Thatcher first of all, and then by Blair to create the idea that they could change Britain.'[40] Gordon Brown similarly aroused expectations over many years of how he would transform Britain once he became its Prime Minister. They promised much, but did not build trust. Churchill, who promised 'blood, toil, tears and sweat' in May 1940, and promised little when he again returned to power in 1951, did earn trust.[41]

8. The ubiquitous media

Writers and artists throughout the ages have sought to attract and stimulate audiences by pushing boundaries – look at the writing of dramatists Christopher Marlowe or John Webster. The repeated cry has gone up that a latest work of art is 'the most shocking ever' and 'depraved'. The film *Antichrist* by the director Lars von Trier in summer 2009 is merely the latest to push expectations, using the protection of *auteur* cinema to put on screen images of intense violence that would never have been allowed had the film been produced by the pornographic industry.[42] Censorship is odious, but artists need to be responsible, expressing their thoughts with appropriate rigour and force while avoiding the gratuitous insult that many seek deliberately to evoke.

Not all media exposure builds trust: the diaries of Richard Crossman, Barbara Castle and Tony Benn lifted the lid on how Whitehall operated in the 1960s, but diminished respect for ministers and civil servants. The 1969 documentary *Royal Family* on BBC television was designed to show the human face of the Queen and her family, but it arguably removed some of the mystique and did little to enhance the public's trust.

Competition between media outlets has further been to the detriment of trust. The highlighting and dramatisation of stories to sell newspapers, and gain viewers for broadcasts – political stories, medical stories, criminal justice stories, education stories, financial news, history, even worries about the future – has not built trust. It has spread fear by giving a heightened impression of danger in the world at large and uncertainty about what is true. Good news does not sell. Great writers throughout history, Shakespeare in *King Lear* and *Hamlet* or George Eliot in *Adam Bede* and *Mill on the Floss*, have highlighted the dramatic, the abnormal and the violent. But the greatness of their stories and ultimate value lie in their redemptive quality. There is no redemption in much that one encounters in the media; just tales of ugliness, corruption, mean, twisted people and lurid stories that leave one demoralised.

The rise of the internet, which began as recently as the 1980s, has grown in Britain by 180.7 per cent since 2000 to 43.8 million users in March 2009.[43] In many ways the new technology has enriched life, spread participation and enhanced democracy. Robert Phillips of Edelman has spoken about 'the need to capitalise on the Information Age to bring the enlightenment home'. But as he notes, 'the information age can as easily be a force for bad as a force for good'.[44] In practice, the information age has indeed done more to erode trust than to build it up. The accumulation of information in databanks by governments and other agencies has eroded trust because of fears of it falling into the wrong hands, fears which appeared all too real with the loss of child benefit records by a courier in 2007, or when a secret terror file was left on a train in 2008. The internet has also become a vast depository of crankiness and half-truths, as David Aaronovitch describes in his book *Voodoo Histories: The Role of the Conspiracy Theory in Modern History* (2009).[45] Richard Sambrook of the BBC said that 'it is not only cynics who don't believe anything . . . because there is so much contradictory information'.[46] As Onora O'Neill has observed, 'openness and transparency has done little to build or restore public trust. On the contrary, trust seemingly has receded as transparency has advanced . . . technologies that spread information so easily are every bit as good at spreading misinformation and disinformation.'[47]

The anonymity of the internet removes the mechanisms by which we interact with each other to assess trustworthiness, Hardin argues. The widespread concern about chat rooms, and their abuse by paedophiles and others who prey on the young, is real. The young, and not only the young, may naturally assume that a seemingly friendly correspondent has good intent and should be trusted, when face-to-face contact would provide a very different story.[48] Without the internet, al-Qaeda and other terrorist groups would be unable to operate, or groom fresh targets. In July 2009, former public school boy Isa (né Andrew) Ibrahim was convicted of plotting terrorist acts; he admitted that he had been radicalised by reading material from Abu Hamza on the internet.[49] The internet has provided further opportunities for corporations to market their wares. It is fifty years since Vance Packard wrote *The Hidden Persuaders* (1957), which powerfully showed how advertisers were manipulating consumers with quasi-scientific methods which they had derived from psychology and sociology.[50] The work of the Advertising Standards Authority has ameliorated the worst aspects of manipulation by advertisers, but the gulf between the perception of the product and the reality has still been responsible for erosion of trust. Although the internet has rightly lifted the veil of mystery and secrecy across many aspects of society, it is also clear that knowing all does not mean trusting all.

9. Increase in accountability and surveillance by government
Government has extended inspections, regulations and targets into almost every facet of our lives, saddling business with bureaucracy that cuts across its creativity, and limiting the freedom of action and imaginative capability of professionals. Targets have been helpful in many ways in focusing attention on key objectives, but they have also been destructive. Gwyn Bevan has written on how regulation by targets assumes that priorities can be targeted, the part can stand for the whole, and what is admitted does not matter.[51] Antony Jay, co-writer of *Yes Minister*, the 1980s television series, unleashes a diatribe against central government in a 2009 pamphlet for having initiated 'a vast proliferation of tribunals, inspectorates, regulatory authorities, quangos, bureaux and councils,

taken on an army of consultants, advisory committees, coordinating bodies, tsars, initiatives, action groups and task forces' which, taken together, have 'spelt the death of trust and common sense and created the bureaucratic nightmare of Twenty First Century Britain'.[52] Fear has been the driver of this obsession with accountability and investigating professionals and ordinary citizens. The fear is that, without a strong controlling presence from the centre, people cannot be trusted.

It is over sixty years since George Orwell published *1984*. In it, he portrays a dystopian world in which the state is constantly watching each citizen. A television screen is in every room of every home, which observes every action that takes place. The state is even able to observe people having sex in bushes. Helicopters have prying eyes which look in through windows. The 'thought police' monitor what everyone says and what people think. In the sixty years since, computers, in their infancy when Orwell was writing, have penetrated everywhere in our lives. The state and other bodies now hold more information about us than anyone might have imagined, apart from Orwell. On an average day in London, CCTV cameras will capture one's image up to 300 times, and there is one camera for every twelve citizens in the UK, giving the country the title of the 'world's most watched society'.[53] Henry Porter has written tirelessly about the abuses to civil liberties under the Blair government. 'It was once possible to believe the government's unusual attention to law, order and behaviour', he writes, 'was benevolent yet ill-conceived. Now it looks more like the result of late-onset sociopathy, influenced by a long period in power and the degenerate entanglement between Downing Street and the seething red-top newspapers.'[54] The belittling bureaucratic intrusions into our lives, and the intrusive prying nature of the modern state, have enraged us all.

10. Dehumanising scale and pace

Trust has been eroded because modern life demands a level and intensity of interaction with human beings and institutions which means that the friendly and the familiar are often not possible. A hundred years ago, people would rarely meet others beyond their local community. Relationships were predictable and the norms of behaviour widely understood. Now we encounter as many people in a day as our forefathers did in a year. Trust is closely related to familiarity. In the twenty-first century, we constantly have to assess people we do not know, and judge their likely trustworthiness in situations of day-to-day discourse; in a bar, on a crowded train or in a business meeting. We also have to continuously assess the array of organisations, associations and institutions which increasingly impact upon our lives. In both instances, where we are unfamiliar with our new encounters, there is a degree of risk and vulnerability. In this society, we need to have far higher guarantees of trustworthiness. The decline in the stability of families, in relationships and in work, call for a new understanding of trust. Anthony Giddens writes about how we have moved from 'facework commitments', where we have regular person-to-person encounters, to 'faceless' commitments', where we develop faith in expert or abstract systems.[55] It is clear we can never go back to our villages of old, and will continue to live in a village which is increasingly global; a village where we have to find better ways of learning how to assess each other, and how to give and receive trust.

The pace of life has additionally been corrosive of trust. We no longer have the same time to spend with our families, our partners, our children or friends. Time for solitude and quiet reflection is squeezed. The result is that we lose touch not only with others, which is the essential prerequisite for trust, but with ourselves. This is a significant loss, as Flores and Solomon tell us; 'the heart of both the practice and the strategy of building trust is first building self-confidence and self-trust: trust in one's own abilities, skills, knowledge, preparation, and know-how, as well as trust in one's own body and body language, impulses, emotions, self control, moods, thinking, intelligence, and sensitivity to others'.[56] One can see other reasons for the loss of trust, such as the current lack of a common enemy to unite us, as seen in the Second World War. But in a century which will bring unprecedented global challenges, necessitating global solutions, the distinction between a 'them' and 'us' is at best unhelpful, and at worst, destructive.

As such, these ten factors, seen as the most significant, are the building blocks for the more pressing question on how trust can be rebuilt.

Desmond Tutu, chair of the Truth and Reconciliation Commission, which helped rebuild trust in South Africa after apartheid, is pictured handing over copies of the final report to Nelson Mandela. *(AFP/Getty Images)*

CHAPTER 3

HOW IS TRUST RECOVERED?

The chief lesson I have learned in a long life is that the only way to make a man trustworthy is to trust him; and the surest way to make him untrustworthy is to distrust him and show your distrust.

Henry L. Stimson (1867–1950), US statesman

How is trust built?

Are there common characteristics of successful societies, organisations and companies which have high levels of trust? In this chapter, we look at some possible examples and see what can be learnt from them, before proposing ten factors which build up trust, each of which correspond to the trust eroding characteristics.

Trust has manifested itself in different ways in history at different times. Geoffrey Hosking identifies seven phases of society with evolving structures of trust. Initially, in tribal society, trust was centred in kinship, and was placed in the leader and in God. When city states emerged, trust came to be placed more in the citizen body as a whole. The age of empire secured trust, in part, by generating myths about the empire, as well as in religion, to establish a hierarchy and consensus in the wake of military conquest. Medieval feudalism saw trust rooted in patronage and in the local lord, and was cemented by the church. Post-medieval monarchy saw honour moving from chivalry to 'courtesy', with science creating new systems of knowledge. With the development of nation states, trust came to be placed in democratic structures with institutional guarantees being placed in a stable currency and statute law. Finally, with the advent of the global economy, and doctrines of individual self-fulfilment and economic liberty, trust was underpinned by the establishment of universal human rights. Trust is difficult to secure in this final era because the strong affluent nations expect developing ones to follow free market policies, while at the same time they want to protect their own vulnerable sectors. Trust only operates successfully where there are not blatant inequalities either between or within nations.[1]

Anthony Giddens sees a different form of trust in pre-modern and modern society. In the former, trust focused on kinship structures, on tradition, on religious cosmology, and on communities, which were essentially local. The modern world, having been shaped by the printing press from the fifteenth century, the industrial revolution from the eighteenth century, the increased movement of people from the nineteenth century, world wars and the technological revolution of the twentieth century, and the information age of the twenty-first century, is very different. Trust in this modern world is much more diffused, and it is placed as we have seen amongst far higher numbers of people, in business partners, many of whom never meet face to face, and in impersonal systems such as the law, financial processes and medicine, whose expertise one has to trust.[2]

Turning to some specific examples, Athens in the late sixth century BC can be said to provide a model of a successful society.[3] During that century, Athens's diverse trade network had produced considerable wealth, but also a high degree of polarisation between rich and poor. Those who found themselves in debt became slaves to their creditors, resulting in serious social unrest. The reforms of Solon included the forgiving of debt, the freeing of indebted slaves, the redeeming of their land and the forbidding of future debt bondage. The reform of Cleisthenes subsequently reconstituted the basis of the tribal society on which Athens had been based, creating a new kind of entity, the *polis* or city-state, governed by its own citizens, rather than by tribal leaders or tyrants.

The reforms overall saw trust shift from being rooted in tribal loyalty to those of a stakeholding city-state, which laid the foundations for Athens' prosperity and extraordinary culture for the next couple of centuries.

When Augustus seized power in Rome in the first century BC, he outbid the warlords by converting the army from a militia to a professional one, using the Roman treasury as well as his own wealth to pay for it, and endowing needy veterans with their own land. Public entertainment, municipal works and relief for poverty were directed towards Rome's poorest inhabitants, including Augustus's popular *panem et circenses* (bread and circuses) scheme. Consequently, both the military and civilian elements of Rome gave their trust to him, and this enabled Rome to make the transition from a city-state to a vast overseas empire, the basis for Roman rule for the next two centuries.

Hosking provides historical comparison with the various European communities that saw significant trust levels develop, such as late medieval Venice and Genoa and the Netherlands from the fifteenth to the seventeenth centuries. But we now shoot forward to the nineteenth century in Britain, which saw the development of a variety of associations which excelled in trust. Robert Owen (1771–1858) is considered the father of the 'cooperative' movement. He proposed forming 'villages of cooperation' where workers would raise themselves out of poverty through their own efforts and mutual support. He believed firmly in workers being placed in a pleasant environment with access to education not only for themselves, but also for their children. A core plank in the cooperative thinking was a rejection of the principles of charity that underpinned the welfare reforms being introduced by the government. 1844 saw the formation of the Rochdale Society of Equitable Pioneers, with tradesmen banding together to open their own stores selling food at affordable prices. 'Friendly Societies' spread throughout the British empire, based on the principle of mutuality, committed to self-help and to the welfare of all workers. A common thread in mutual organisations is the principle that an enterprise or association should be owned and controlled by the people it serves, and should share surpluses on the basis of each member's contribution rather than on their ability to invest capital, which is based upon the possession of wealth.

The nineteenth century saw examples of high-trust *commercial* companies. Cadbury, based at Bournville, Lever Brothers (later Unilever), based at Port Sunlight and Rowntree, based at York, all stand out for the quality not only of their products but of the way they looked after their employees. Interestingly, all three had Quaker influences. Cadbury was the first firm to introduce a Saturday half-day holiday and to set up democratically elected 'works councils'. Young employees were encouraged to go to night school, and allowed to leave early twice a week. Rowntree produced one of the first pension schemes and widows' benefit funds; it had a company gym and pool and introduced one week's holiday with full pay. Lever Brothers provided a hospital, school and concert hall; 'profit sharing' involved profits being directly invested in the community. It is easy to be dismissive of all these high-minded Victorians, and the reality on the ground often fell far short of the ideals, but they are still shining examples of how high-trust organisations could flourish even in the highly competitive nineteenth century when exploitation of workers, including children, was commonplace.

The National Trust was created in 1895 as an independent charity by three Victorian philanthropists, Miss Octavia Hill, Sir Robert Hunter and Canon Hardwicke Rawnsley, to 'preserve and protect the coastline, countryside and buildings of England, Wales and Northern Ireland'. As Octavia Hill put it, 'The need of quiet, the need of air, the need of exercise, and . . . the sight of sky and of things growing seem human needs, common to all men.'[4] It is important to the theme of this book because it enshrines the notion of preserving the best of the natural environment for the benefit and enjoyment of future generations, beyond the time span that characterises the mental world of politicians. This sense of 'trusteeship' implies that we are only the tenants, not the possessors, of the world we inhabit. We have a duty to leave behind us not a depleted, but a richer and more vital, world for future generations, to last, as the National Trust motto says, 'For ever, for everyone'.

The Second World War and its ending stand out as a time when enlightened individuals planned how to make the post war world more peaceful and trusting between nations.[5] In place of the interwar League of Nations, which failed to establish legitimacy or authority, came the United Nations. The Bretton Woods currency agreement, the International Monetary Fund, the World Bank, and the General Agreement on Tariffs and Trade were all multinational bodies founded in the wake of the war. The European Union (or Common Market as then known) was set up in 1957 to boost trade and reduce the prospect of further European wars, that had so blighted the first half of the century. None of these bodies has been perfect, but their intent has been laudable. All have tried to build trust through international cooperation, and they have sought to spread the benefits of prosperity, enlightened government, and scientific knowledge.

Germany was broken by the Second World War, and had to rapidly recover a sense of direction. Trust had to be built not only between the new government elected in 1949 and its demoralised population, but also with the occupying powers. The country had to cope with division and the stigma of defeat. Yet under Konrad Adenauer, it established a stable democracy, made lasting reconciliations with its former enemies, and underwent *Wirtschaftswunder* ('economic miracle'). Outstanding leadership, a high sense of collective moral purpose and international cooperation were the keys.

More recent, but no less daunting, was the restoration of trust in post-apartheid South Africa, a nation deeply divided even before apartheid was introduced in 1948. Nelson Mandela was released in 1990 after twenty-seven years of imprisonment, and in South Africa's first multiracial elections in 1994, the African National Congress won the election by an overwhelming majority, Mandela becoming the first black South African president. A new constitution was agreed in 1995 and the Truth and Reconciliation Commission, chaired by Archbishop Desmond Tutu, was established. This was a court-like body, empowered to grant amnesty to all who had committed wrong-doings during the apartheid era, as long as there was a full disclosure by the person seeking amnesty. South Africa has had great difficulties since, but not emanating out of the trust–building work for the first few years after 1994.

Palo Alto is a US city located in the San Francisco Bay area of California with a population of about 60,000. It is a charter city, meaning that its governing system is defined by its own charter document which can be amended by a majority vote of its residents, which helps give those residents a sense of ownership, pride and respect. The result is a community with high levels of trust. The social psychologist Philip Zimbardo performed a famous experiment in 1968 when he parked two cars in the street, one in New York and one in Palo Alto. Before long, the Bronx car was a wreck. In Palo Alto, however, nothing happened for a few days, until a kindly man came and closed the bonnet when it began to rain.[6] Steve Hilton, David Cameron's senior aide, admired the communal spirit, the confidence to leave one's front door unlocked, and the sense of police being familiar to the residents.[7] Fraser Nelson thought similarly in *The Spectator*: 'It is where a dynamic economy meets the family-friendly workplace.' Palo Alto residents also take full responsibility for their local environment – 'environmentalism is part of the culture', he wrote.[8] Others look to Davis, also in California, named 'one of the friendliest cities in the United States',[9] as an example of high levels of trust and community fellowship. Highlights are its status as the 'most bicycle friendly town in the world' (its motto), with its proportionally high bike path mileage, and its annual Picnic Day, a bustling festival organised by students and attended by over 50,000.

Palo Alto and Davis are privileged, small and homogeneous communities. Ladakh is none of these. One of the highest and most sparsely populated communities on earth, and set at 9,800 feet, it lies deep in the Himalayas in the north Indian state of Jammu and Kashmir. Ladakh, renowned for its remote mountain beauty and its Tibetan-influenced Buddhist culture, is a strategic location at the crossroads of major trade routes; China to the north and east; India to the south; Afghanistan and Pakistan to the west. Despite its proximity to the ongoing Indo-Pakistan turbulence, Ladakh is a striking example of a multicultural society – made up of Buddhists, Muslims and Christians – functioning with high levels of trust. The Ladakhis are renowned for being a hospitable and simple people, with small communities living self-sufficiently, sharing a strong ethos of mutual cooperation. High trust communities are often spurred initially by a common enemy, human or natural. With the Dutch Republic it was the sea; with Ladakhis, the intense winter cold.

Characteristics of trusting organisations

What can be learnt from studying these selected examples of high trust societies and organisations? Ten features, exhibited by some or all of these bodies, stand out:

▶ Many are grounded on ethical values, sometimes based upon religious principles
▶ Those within the organisations exhibit pride and a sense of ownership
▶ Several have a wider responsibility than the mere maximisation of profit and personal gain
▶ Those within the organisation have responsibilities and duties, rather than just rights, and actively contribute to its success
▶ They have regimes which help guarantee a freedom from fear
▶ They are well and often wisely led: law-enforcers win our hearts and minds
▶ Communication, within and aimed at outside the community, is honest
▶ Those within the organisations are looked after and have rights guaranteed
▶ The family is respected and supported
▶ There is a human scale: individuals feel known and valued.

We can expand the thinking behind these common characteristics, and offer ten preferred ways for trust in societies, organisations and countries to be rebuilt. They all emphasise intrinsic ways of rebuilding trust and are based upon there being a presumption of good faith, rather than of mistrust.

1. Need for a universally accepted moral code

The decline of religious observance and of accepted ethical codes has contributed to the moral uncertainty in Britain. This vacuum needs to be addressed. Religious leaders argue for the need for ethical codes, but with the marginalisation of religion throughout society, their calls lack wide impact. Perhaps religion will see a renaissance in this new century, but we should not rely on that; nor, given the rise of fundamentalism, can we rely on religion to produce the benign ethical framework society needs. Politicians are wary of talking about moral questions for fear of being labelled hypocrites, or arousing ridicule. So we bumble along without an agreed moral compass to guide us, lurching like an intoxicated driver from side to side, occasionally crashing into the pavement because we lack a sense of direction.

Contemporary political philosophers have each stressed the need for one goal to be placed above all others: Justice (Rawls); Liberty (Nozick); Happiness (Layard); or Capabilities (Sen). We favour 'Trust' as the best overarching idea for reinvigorating society and bringing back purpose and legitimacy to government. Utilitarian thinking resulted in much good including an extension to social rights and improvements to education. But utilitarianism has also been used as a recipe for selfishness: still more has libertarianism. Rawls and Sen, for all their intellectual cogency, do not translate easily into a readily understandable ethical code. A new principle is necessary, above all if the twenty-first century is to be more public spirited. The moral code that we need is trust, in the form of the 'Trust Test' (TT), according to whether actions add or detract from trust and trusteeship. It is the measure by which all actions of the individual, association or government are to be judged. The chapters that follow elaborate on a wide variety of ways for making ourselves and our institutions more trusting and trustworthy.

Building trust with the future is an aspect that needs highlighting. We should not have needed the panic of the last few years over climate change to remind us of our duty to look after our planet. Politicians, chief executives and leaders of all kinds need to think beyond their own personal careers and legacy. Jim Collins in *Good to Great* (2001) says that a characteristic of a 'level 5 leader' is that they think about their succession in a selfless way; they don't just think about their own legacy.[10] Great leaders should want to see '*après moi, le succès*' rather than '*après moi, le déluge*'. Shakespeare wrote in *Julius Caesar* 'The evil that men do lives after them; the good is oft interred with their bones.'[11] We will fail, though, if we just look to leaders. What matters most is what we can most affect: our own lives, and ensuring that we have a positive trust footprint. It is indeed much easier to destroy than to build trust, yet building trust for the future is fundamental to everyone.

2. Support families and enhance opportunities for belonging

We need better education in the responsibilities of parenting. The model of parenting we adopt has been conditioned subconsciously by our own experience of being parented; a vicious circle has thus developed whereby the young, who were inadequately parented, know little about how to bring up their own children. They in turn may prove to be less trusting of their parents. If experience teaches babies and young children that they are not able to trust their own parents, they will not themselves develop trusting attitudes in later life. Marriage or stable partnerships which produce children need to become sacrosanct: vows should be respected, not because of extrinsic laws or fear of public exposure, but out of an intrinsic sense of responsibility, care and love for each other and for one's offspring. Some are lucky to have stable partnerships, which appear to take little work; most require intense devotion and care. However, the good that comes is immeasurable. The state could do more to support marriage, but the primary impetus has to come from the individuals themselves. The state and society need to do more to discourage young women from having babies until they are emotionally and economically prepared, and have the support of a stable relationship or wider family, to give the child the best prospect of being reared in a secure environment.

Atomisation in society beyond the home needs to be counteracted by enhancing the opportunities for belonging. The successful societies discussed above commonly had at their heart the spreading of ownership, rights or membership. Martin Seligman, the founder of positive psychology, tells us that belonging to something bigger than oneself is a core factor that makes for a meaningful life.[12] Belonging to a society, an institution or a club confers a sense of belonging and dignity, as well as opening up an abundance of opportunities to give trust and to be trusted. What we need to do much more is build opportunities for people to belong. For many in Britain, the cornerstones of life for much of the last century were trade unions, working men's clubs, team sport clubs, the local pub and the Church. Now, many of these opportunities for belonging have decayed.

The experience of fighting in both world wars last century was one of unspeakable horror mixed with prolonged periods of boredom. It is ironic that many veterans looked back on their experiences in the conflicts as high points in their lives, and regularly attended regimental reunions until they died. No more graphic illustrations of the power of belonging can be given than this. The comradeship, the requirement to trust others and be trusted oneself, the sense of belonging and feelings of pride in oneself and one's regiment are the essence of the sense of belonging found in the military during this time.

More team opportunities for sports need to be created, which not only afford a sense of belonging but also allow for physical exercise. Few activities are more binding than playing in a team oneself, whether football, hockey or athletics. New organisations need to be created, and existing organisations need to do far more to reach out. Schools, police stations, hospitals and fire stations can all do much more to connect with their local communities. Companies should enhance opportunities for involving employees and their families. The *Sunday Times* said: 'Many firms have dispensed with the social side of working life – such as subsidised sports clubs and Christmas parties.'[13] To the extent this has happened, companies should reverse this trend. Opportunities for volunteering could be enormously enhanced, whether with the police, the Territorial Army, local charities or conservation groups. Every eighteen year old should undertake a year's national community service (discussed later). For trust to be developed, we need to belong again, which means we need the institutions that allow for this.

3. Enhance social inclusion

Britain will always be socially and economically unequal. Debates may rage about whether inequalities are increasing, and whether it matters.[14] But the evidence is clear, from Wilkinson and Pickett in *The Spirit Level* (2009), from Rawls, Hosking and a host of other authorities we have drawn on, that blatant inequality, and the perception of failure to address it effectively, detracts from trust. Addressing this is best done at three levels: family, education and jobs. Helping ensure children have the best possible start, through secure homes, will help them develop with order and stability. Schools need to improve rapidly: they need to be smaller, free from centralised control and chosen by parents. They also need enhanced parent involvement. Academically able children will thus be much better provided for, removing the need for positive discrimination at universities. Finally, improved schools and a year of national community service will prepare people much better for the job market. Meanwhile professions need to develop much better outreach programmes – such as that of St George's Medical School in London – to encourage those from a wide range of social and ethnic backgrounds to join by training them to meet the required standards, instead of creating artificially lowered standards. A fully equal society is as impossible to achieve as it is wrong. By greater focus on quality of life, we can do far more to ensure that what is unequal in quantity need not be so in quality.

4. Enhance corporate responsibility and reducing greed and corruption

Given the ubiquity of corporations in all of our lives – they provide much of what we eat, wear, live in and move about the world in – building trust in them is essential. It should not be difficult. Because of the ubiquity of the corporate sector, it is particularly important that it is seen to operate ethically if we are to rebuild trust in society. Bonuses need to be tied to genuine long-term success, rather than the 'quick buck' mentality that caused so much offence in the credit crunch. Transparency of pay differentials from top to bottom would also help recover trust. Companies need to be deeply socially responsible to their very core. Sponsoring a school in Kenya, or holding Christmas parties, is nothing if the whole practice of the company is not ethical. Companies in the UK that rank high on the 2009 Reputation Institute study, such as Marks & Spencer, Smith & Nephew, Cadbury and William Morrison supermarkets,[15] show that businesses can behave as ethically and responsibly in the twenty-first century as did the best in the nineteenth. On corruption, Robert Klitgaard suggests that when it becomes systemic, the best approach is to attack it as one would a resilient disease: corrupt activities should be analysed for their weaknesses before being actively subverted. Through deeds more than words, a credible signal must be sent that corrupt systems are being changed. One way of doing so is to make an example of a prominent corrupt figure, to show people that the period of impunity is over.[16,17] Identifying culprits, rather than the 'cover up' culture prevalent today, is indeed necessary so that the public can see justice is being done.

5. Educate civic values, duties and responsibilities

David Puttnam, the film director, has challenged schools to develop civic values above consumer values in young people.[18] The young everywhere are told that consumer acquisitions and values make life more meaningful or bearable. Children start seeing advertisements on television before they can string a sentence together. They see their parents and siblings enjoying being consumers, and they want bigger and better toys than their friends. They come to believe that they will not be happy without them.

Families and schools have a vital part to play in educating and re-educating the young. The former must help children to understand the importance of behaving in trustworthy ways, of civility and of carrying out duties and responsibilities. Parents are often reluctant to do this, yet their example is central to how their children will behave at school and as adults. The best schools teach civility and trustworthiness as a core part of their daily provision for the young. How students are spoken to, how they hear adults addressing other adults, the messages they receive from the school, and the behaviour they see rewarded or punished are vital. Children can learn about the damage of cheating and corruption. US schools make much of their 'honour codes', drawn up by the students, to reduce plagiarism. In Hong Kong, the government developed a comprehensive anti-corruption programmes for schools, and in 1986 75 per cent of the 15–24 group, the first to experience the approach, believed corruption was a serious problem compared to only 54 per cent of the 45–64 age group.[19]

The young should also be taught well-being as a core part of the curriculum. These classes, misleadingly named 'happiness classes' by the media, help the young to learn how to live a good life and to discover how their bodies, minds and emotions work optimally. The classes cannot prevent unhappiness and misfortune in life, but they do help give the young the tools to take responsibility for their actions and to respond to misfortunes when they occur. The thinking is based upon the pioneering work of Martin Seligman. When president of the American Psychological Association in 1998, Seligman questioned why the field of psychology was so heavily weighted towards the understanding of neuroses, psychoses and abnormality. He asked why more work was not being conducted to widen understanding of the development of a meaningful, a good and a happy life. This gave birth to positive psychology and to understanding how a pessimist, whose outlook is one of 'learnt helplessness', could adopt an optimistic outlook. Key ingredients of an optimistic life are caring for others and acting in a way that builds trust. As Tal Ben-Shahar of Harvard University said, 'if you want to feel good, do good.'

It is half a century since President Kennedy spoke the famous words in his inaugural address: 'Ask not what your country can do for you; ask what you can do for your country.' Like so many pithy sayings, his words are oft repeated but little practised. Successive British governments have been like the worst kind of parent: they indulge and give handouts in the hope of gaining popularity (i.e. votes at elections), but have been far too weak in setting boundaries and saying there are responsibilities, which have to be met. Parents need to ensure that their children carry out chores; schools that students are instilled with a sense of duty and hold responsibilities; and government that with citizenship comes responsibilities. We have to tilt the balance in surveys away from asking whether we trust the government, companies, schools and so on, and towards asking whether we are trustworthy in our own actions.

6. Reduce fear in public spaces and enhance safety

How does one build trust where violence and the fear of violence, bullying and terrorism destroy it? To develop trust, children and adults need to feel safe not only in their homes but in public spaces, in streets, in stations and in parks. At present, they are insufficiently comfortable. Without an appropriate sense of safety, we will never trust each other, the government, the security services or the police.

Streets, parks and open spaces need to be reclaimed for families and those of all ages, so that they may feel free to wander with complete safety and trust that they will not be attacked, abused, threatened or shocked, nor see public spaces vandalised. How do we achieve this vital goal? Parents have become so fearful of danger to their children outside the home that many no longer feel entirely happy with them venturing outdoors unsupervised, and supervision is often difficult to achieve. Reforming the police, shifting their focus to prevention of crime, and bringing officers back on the street working with local communities is fundamental. David Willetts is one of the leading Tory thinkers on quality of life issues. He writes: 'The loss of confidence in outside spaces . . . and a growing culture of risk aversion are significantly harming the childhoods of too many children.'[20] The Palo Alto illustration shows the advantages of having policemen on the beat, who are familiar to, and trusted by, the community. Paying for more adults to supervise public spaces and enhancing and improving play areas for all children is a key part of the solution.

Ugliness breeds ugliness, and dereliction breeds vandalism, but beauty inspires good behaviour. We need to create more places of beauty, as has been achieved with the walkways along the river Thames through central London, and the beautification of the heart of Newcastle-upon-Tyne. Society needs to help children and adults realise that acts of violence against others and against property are not harming 'them', but damaging everyone. With greater affinity with the neighbourhood, and more awareness of the TT, more will realise that each of us is connected, and that we all suffer, the perpetrator as much as the victim, by anti-social acts. Having families, schools, the media and politicians far more intrinsically attuned to the TT will, in time, be of far more enduring value to the reclaiming of safe public and private spaces than relying on extrinsic responses.

7. *Enhance the integrity and quality of leadership*

Politicians and civil servants should be the most highly principled and practised members of our society, as many philosophers have observed. Societies which have been conspicuously successful have often been characterised by leaders who have exemplified virtue and nobility of purpose. The American Presidents whom polls show are the most highly respected include George Washington, Thomas Jefferson, Abraham Lincoln and F. D. Roosevelt.[21] These men combined effectiveness with moral quality.

The challenge in Britain is to bring in at central and local level politicians and civil servants who combine high moral character with considerable ability in the dispatch of business. Once elected, politicians need to show more trust in the public, which scoring cheap points against the opposition, behaving in uncivil ways, and spinning the truth fail to achieve. All who have positions of influence and power in society need to be far more aware of their actions and to measure them against the TT. Members of the Royal Family below the Queen (whose behaviour is impeccable), business leaders, and leaders in the media, sport and the arts need to recognise that with the privilege of their position comes responsibility, in recognition of their power to influence, for better or worse, the lives of others. Politicians and officials need proper training in ethics and in the art of governance; constitutional changes need to be introduced to build new mechanisms of communication between the electorate and politicians to ensure trust is entrenched. Expectations have done much to damage trust in politicians. The public need to be educated into realising that politicians, while important, do not make all the difference to their lives. It is they themselves who must be responsible for bringing about improvements in their own lives and in those of others. As Elie Wiesel said at the White House in 1999, 'indifference can be tempting – more than that, seductive. It is so much easier to look away . . . to avoid such rude interruptions to our work, our dreams, our hopes.'[22] Rather than blaming 'them', the language must change to 'me' and to 'us' being responsible for our lives and to society at large.

8. Need for honesty and responsibility in the media

The media needs to honestly and responsibly reflect politicians and leaders to the public. Those societies that have flourished have tended to have leaders with the ability to communicate clearly to the public at large. Whereas Julius Caesar and Cicero addressed audiences of thousands, as did the nineteenth-century Prime Minister William Gladstone, with the coming of broadcasting (radio in the 1920s and television in the 1930s) politicians now rarely address audiences face to face beyond Westminster and party conferences. Broadcasting has transformed the ability of politicians to communicate directly to the public. But no amount of modern technology can make an honest or excellent communicator out of a politician who is not.

The best way for media outlets to gain trust is for them to develop intrinsic means of gaining trust. The media, even in its hunger for audience, should pay far greater attention to trust and truth. Too much output panders to our lower natures, the desire for sensation, material gain, violence, sex and the enjoyment in seeing others humiliated.

Have I Got News for You and *Mock the Week* can be brilliant, but they can also cross the line between satire and cynicism, undermining confidence in good people as well as in the untrustworthy. The message audiences receive from seeing *Who Wants to Be a Millionaire?*, *The Apprentice*, *The X Factor* and celebrity chat shows is that money and fame equal happiness, that they can come easily, and that these are the desired ends of society. Media companies, large and small, could do far more to emulate the responsibility of the best commercial companies from other sectors. Does the media ask itself often enough the effect its output will be having on the thinking and attitudes of its audiences? Everyone, from executives and editors down to individual writers, needs to act in ways that consciously merit trust. The best are excellent. Many newspaper articles, television and radio programmes and internet sites do inform and civilise people. The media could become the most powerful and transformative vehicle in Britain for creating trust across society.

9. A more trusting state and a more trustworthy population

The state needs to reverse its increasing culture of suspicion and lack of trust in professionals, corporations, and individuals. Government needs to move away from extrinsic towards intrinsic methods of ensuring civilised behaviour and high levels of corporate and professional conduct. People will break the law. But if government and the police treat the public with respect, they will have them on their side in apprehending those who do wrong. Some individuals in companies and in the professions will be dishonest, incompetent or corrupt. But that does not mean that everyone has to be dragged down to their level, and be hemmed in by counter-productive regulations, as happens after crises such as the killing of Stephen Lawrence in 1993 and of Baby Peter in August 2007. Government must have a presumption of trust rather than a presumption of mistrust, as it does at present. When government or other institutions do make mistakes, as with the killing of Jean Charles de Menezes in July 2005 by the police, or child abuse by Catholic priests, the public needs to believe that the truth is being sought out and communicated, rather than being covered up. The population, equally, needs to respond to this new culture of trust by ensuring that their own conduct, in private and at work, is responsible and is in accordance with the trust principle.

10. More human scale and more reflection

All successful countries, societies, corporations and other organisations, even when very large, still have subsidiary units, to which the individuals within them can relate. Soldiers who fought in Agincourt, the school boys at Thomas Arnold's in Rugby and the employees at GlaxoSmithKline all owe their primary allegiance to smaller units led by individuals whom they know and who know them. We will never return to a land of villages and small towns, but we can do more to create a sense of identity with those people who oversee our lives. In *The Tipping Point* (2000), Malcolm Gladwell talks approvingly of the work of the British anthropologist Robin Dunbar, who argues that 150 represents 'the maximum number of individuals with whom we can have a genuinely social relationship'.[23] In place of myriad superficial encounters, we need to renew and deepen our core relationships, as outlined in Figure 1.2, 'Who do we trust', beginning with family and our oldest and closest friends. Most lives needlessly sacrifice the potential for joy and meaning that comes from time spent with those close to us. To spend more time with our friends and family is to see afresh the meaning and value of trust.

Trust requires time to build. The easy mobility of modern life and the pace of technological change have undercut the time available for trusting relationships to develop. Our leaders, whether political, business or military, need to take time out each day for reflection. So too do we all. A more rested and reflective life is a more considered and meaningful one. The battle to live in a more trusting world begins with oneself. If we want to be our best, if we want to be our most authentic, as opposed to acting out other personas, we have to find the space within us. That means taking time for ourselves. Unless we detach ourselves from the noise of modern life, we will never be able to find the time to give trust, or to be fully trustworthy.

In June 2009 Michael Martin was forced to resign as Speaker of the Commons in the wake of the parliamentary expenses row. It was the first time the Speaker had been ejected in 300 years. *(WireImage)*

CHAPTER 4
TRUST IN GOVERNMENT, POLITICS AND LOCAL DEMOCRACY

*If the people cannot trust their government to do the job for which it exists
— to protect them and to promote their common welfare — all else is lost.*

Barack Obama (1961–), 44th US President[1]

Have we lost trust?

If politicians are not trusted, then democracy cannot function properly. Governments need to be trusted to fulfil certain basic minimum responsibilities, including protecting their citizens from harm, foreign attack and violence at home, and ensuring justice and a certain level of welfare, especially for those unable to look after themselves.

To be sceptical about politicians can of course be a desirable thing and should not immediately be a cause of worry. From the 1970s until the mid- 1990s, almost all industrialised democracies recorded a decline in levels of trust in their respective governments except for the Netherlands.[2] British levels of trust in their national government are below the EU average. Whereas in 2008, 66 per cent of the Dutch, 60 per cent of the Danish, 56 per cent of the Swedish and 31 per cent of the French people questioned said that they 'trusted' their government, only 29 per cent of British did — compared with a figure of 34 per cent for the EU overall.[3] More worryingly, in polls of trust in differing professions, politicians in the UK come out low, or near bottom, compared to others.

The figures for politicians are certainly troubling and are even more worrisome when considering the Ipsos MORI poll in June 2009, which found that three quarters of those surveyed thought Britain's government needed improving. The survey showed that whereas in 2001, 45 per cent were satisfied with the Westminster system, by June 2009 this figure had fallen to only 20 per cent.[4] Back in 1973, 48 per cent of respondents thought that the British system of governance worked well or extremely well, according to another poll. By 2009, the figure had fallen to 24 per cent.[5] Parties and MPs in the House of Commons seem to be the primary focus of concern – even before the expenses scandal of the summer of 2009. A British Election Study survey from May 2009 found that nearly a quarter of those surveyed had no trust *at all* in political parties and nearly a third said that they had no trust at all in politicians in general.[6] However, the trends are not all negative: 37 per cent believed in 2009 that MPs had a 'high moral code', whereas in 1993 after the 'back to basics' furore (when John Major's attempt to raise moral questions at the 1993 conference backfired after a series of Tory scandals), the figure was only 28 per cent.[7]

We tend to trust those whom we know, and so it is no surprise that the local MP is much more trusted than MPs in general. The pie chart from the June 2009 survey reveals that 76 per cent of MPs in general were not trusted to tell the truth, as opposed to 44 per cent of the local MPs (see Figure 4.1).

With declining levels of trust has come dwindling memberships of political parties. In the 1950s, the Conservative Party boasted three million members; now they have less than 10 per cent of that figure, just a quarter of a million. Labour claimed to have 830,000 members when Harold Wilson became Prime Minister in 1964, but by the middle of 2009 this had fallen to 177,000, while the Liberal Democrats had just 60,000. In 2005 only 1.3 per cent of the electorate was a member of one of the three major political parties, compared to 4 per cent in 1983.[8] Being prepared to belong to a political party is not the only measure of the health of a democracy, and of trust in it, but it is a significant factor, especially when active participation in and membership of other activities has not been in decline and many pressure groups have seen a significant increase in membership. To put all this into perspective, however, there is not the widespread lack of trust in British parties and the system of government that there was in the 1960s and 1970s, the late 1920s and early 1930s in Britain or in the inter-war years in Germany. For all the groans and screeching of the plates of the British body politic, no one is seriously advocating junking the entire system.

Figure 4.1: Trust in MPs[9]

Q: I am going to read out some different types of people. Please tell me which you would generally trust to tell the truth and which you wouldn't

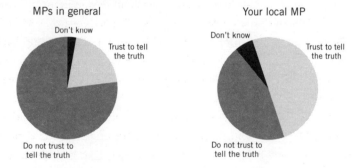

Base: 1001 British adults, 29th-31st May 2009
Source: Ipsos MORI, 'Three in four believe Britain's governance needs improving', 3 June 2009

Why have we lost trust?

People hate being lied to. Politicians are judged by exacting standards and we are revolted when our leaders behave poorly. Scandals have been a regular feature of British political life but no scandal this century has so damaged a prime minister as that over claims that Iraq had WMDs ready to be launched in forty-five minutes as the basis for going to war against Saddam Hussein in 2003. The subsequent investigations into the alleged 'sexing up' of the intelligence document overseen by Alastair Campbell, and the concern over the hounding and subsequent death of the government scientist David Kelly in July 2003, ignited the public's distrust.

Leaders always fall further when they make particular claims about themselves against which they will be judged. Tony Blair said that he would lead a 'whiter than white' government after the years of 'Tory sleaze'. His religious faith, even though he downplayed it in office, was clearly the guiding principle of his life, and it was inevitable that he would be judged by higher standards. The first cloud on his blemishless horizon, the Ecclestone affair, came within months of him taking over, after which he made the claim to John Humphrys on television that 'most people who have dealt with me think I am a pretty straight kind of guy'.[10] He nevertheless continued to enjoy high levels of trust during his early years, with 57 per cent identifying him as 'honest' in 2000.[11] His standing began to slip, however, long before Iraq, though his personal rating ran higher than that of the government. Polling in April and May 2002 showed that while 43 per cent of respondents trusted Blair less than they did the year before, over half said the same of the government.[12,13] By 2004, Blair's honesty rating had slipped to 37 per cent and he found it hard to recapture the integrity in the eyes of the public, which always mattered so much to him.[14]

The expenses scandal unleashed a pent-up fury which had been brewing for several years about the self-seeking behaviour of MPs. David Smith of the *Sunday Times* described it as 'almost mob rule against MPs'.[15] The scandal differed from earlier ones because it exhibited a disillusion with MPs in *all* major parties, not just in the governing party, as had been the case in the latter days of the Major government from 1993 to 1997, notably with the 1994 'cash for questions' scandal. This earlier episode powerfully paved the way for the perception that MPs were lining their own pockets rather than serving the public interest. At the height of the expenses row, an Ipsos MORI poll for the BBC found that 62 per cent thought that MPs put their own interests above the interests of their party, constituents and country. This was the highest score the company had ever recorded on that question, compared with 45 per cent taking this view in 2006.[16] The poll found that only one in five of the public trusted MPs to tell the truth,[17] while 52 per cent of respondents in another survey said that they would vote for a candidate not caught up in the scandal in the next election, even if it meant voting against the party they wanted to win.[18]

Furthermore, political parties were singled out as the institution perceived to be most affected by corruption in the UK in a Transparency International survey, and were rated worse than the civil service, the judiciary and other groups.[19] To put the corruption concern in perspective, Britain is still believed to have one of the least corrupt systems in the world. In the Corruption Perception Index, which measures the degree to which corruption is thought to exist among politicians and public officials, the UK was ranked sixteenth least corrupt out of 180 countries.[20] For all that, scandals have powerfully corroded trust in Britain.

The young in Britain feel particularly disillusioned with politicians. A Hansard Society survey in 2009 found that only 30 per cent of 18–24 year olds said they have discussed politics or political news with someone else in the previous two or three years compared with 47 per cent of their parents' generation.[21] Younger generations have been raised in a media environment wholly different from that of their parents, which has profoundly affected their attitude to politics, not least because they regularly absorb far higher levels of cynicism, such as from the television programme *Mock the Week*. A report in 2006 'Power: An Independent Inquiry into Britain's Democracy',[22] found that support was being lost less from those in 'the margins' than from 'the young, better educated, and upper-status citizens who have benefited most from social progress'.[23] The loss of trust and interest amongst the young is particularly worrying as a facet of the general decline of trust in politics.

The 'decline of conviction' among party leaders is another potent cause for loss of trust. Polls in the UK regularly show that most admired leaders are those such as Attlee, Churchill and Thatcher, who knew their own minds and gave a strong conviction lead.[24] To many voters, it seems that leaders have become more concerned with the opinions of swing voters, whose views they learn about from focus groups, rather than with speaking their own minds. A popular belief is that merely following the 'floating voter' has taken over from actually leading the country. Jules Peck and Robert Phillips write in *Citizen Renaissance* that the public are no longer being asked to think of themselves as active citizens, but rather as consumers who pay taxes and in return receive just what they themselves, and not others, need and want.[25] This logic was explicit in the Thatcher government's introduction of poll tax. The Power Inquiry concurred with Peck and Phillips's conclusion, finding that a major reason for this disengagement was that the main political parties were widely perceived to be lacking in principle and too similar.[26]

The perception and reality of an increasingly centralised government have played their part in the loss of trust, as the public feels that government is increasingly remote from their everyday lives. In a 2005 survey, 67 per cent of people said they wanted to have an influence on how the country was run, but only 27 per cent felt that they did have that say.[27] The 2009 Communities and Local Government Committee report argued that 'since the Second World War, the trend has been for central government to increase its powers and responsibilities at the expense of local government'.[28] The 1980s were a significant turning point in their loss. Simon Jenkins has written forcefully about the damage done by Thatcher's centralisation, extending to the running of the NHS, new police authorities, housing, the railways, schools and universities, and the justice system.[29] Her legacy meant that in 1997 'the reserve powers contained in Thatcher's statutes would give Labour more power over the state sector than any other European government'.[30]

Labour after 1997 restored some local power with devolution in Scotland and Wales. It also reinstituted a London-wide authority. But its attempts to revitalise the power of local government, for example through elected mayors, fell flat when cities like Manchester and Brighton rejected the option. A nagging fear with devolution is that it would facilitate an even greater inequality of performance to emerge between regions. Indeed surveys already show a very uneven spread across Britain of satisfaction with local councils and with opportunities for participation. As demonstrated in Figure 4.2, there is significant variation in satisfaction levels. Kensington and Chelsea residents expressed very high satisfaction with their council, with an approval rating of over 75 per cent, and nearly 40 per cent of those in Gateshead were satisfied with opportunities for participation in the council.[31]

Figure 4.2: Satisfaction with opportunities for participation

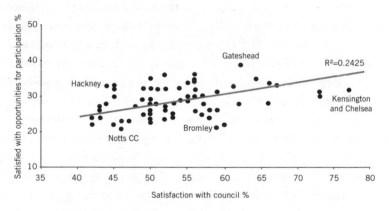

Base: BVPI 2006 (70 District, County and Unitary Authorities)
Source: Ipsos MORI/BVPI, *General User Survey for East Sussex County Council* (2006)

The increasing *professionalisation* of politics may have contributed to loss of trust. Tocqueville warned against the emergence of a political elite with 'an almost infinite distance from practice' who bring 'all habits of literature into politics'.[32] A common route for young people entering politics is to start off as party workers then move on to special advisors, before becoming MPs and then ministers This familiar path has tended to make Westminster much more inward looking. The perception of elitism in our political ranks is not necessarily anything new. David Marquand writing in his book *Britain since 1918*, comments that critics in the 1950s similarly condemned 'the very idea of a governing class with an inherited vocation from leadership [as] a symptom of ossification and decline'.[33] Yet even twenty-five years ago, MPs were drawn from a much wider field, from trade unions, businesses and the professions. The growing insularity of Westminster has spread disillusion with politicians. In the 2008 US election, John McCain and Barack Obama used public dissatisfaction with politicians as part of their platform. Indeed, Obama won in part on the back of the disillusioned youth vote. The British system of government is far less likely to throw up candidates who can capitalise on being anti-political establishment, apart from at by-elections and the flurry of anti-corruption parliamentary candidates thrown up by the MPs' expenses row, though this sentiment will probably have lost momentum by the coming general election. Indeed, apart from directly elected mayors, there are no opportunities in Britain for Obama-style candidates to jump over the party political caucuses to win power. We need to rebuild confidence that Westminster and Whitehall are places that people can be proud of, rather than places from which people want to distance themselves.

One of the most graphic illustrations of the loss of confidence in the British political system is the decline in turnout for voting at general elections. At the 1951 election, when Churchill's Conservatives beat Attlee's Labour Party, the turnout was 83.6 per cent. In 1992, it was 77.7 per cent, which fell to 59.2 per cent in 2001, rising only slightly to 61.4 per cent at the 2005 general election.[34] Many explanations have been offered for the decline in turnout, including the outcome being foregone, and party platforms being very similar. But it is a hugely worrying indicator on the barometer of trust, if in the most important election in the country, which takes place every four or five years and generates four weeks of intensive coverage in the media, politicians are still only able to entice three fifths of the electorate to the ballot box.

The restoring of trust

The expenses row 'has created an opportunity for constitutional change unseen since the Great Reform Act of 1832', said one commentator.[35]

Parliament is in a state of flux with the first resignation of a Speaker for 300 years,[36] and the prospect of potentially 140 to 150 MPs standing down at the 2010 general election provides a unique opportunity for a fundamental rethink about the relationship between the electorate and government at both central and local levels. Such a move has popular support. Research by YouGov for the Fabian Society found that over half the respondents agreed with the proposition that there is now a 'once in a generation chance for a major overhaul to improve our democracy'.[37] It would be hard to imagine a worse catastrophic loss of confidence in our elected MPs than that over expenses, and if this episode does not lead to significant change, it would be difficult to know exactly what could. Geoff Mulgan described the bedrock on which any new formulation must be built. We need in the future to start 'seeing government as a relationship, a dialogue not a monologue, and being willing to earn trust not just once, but again and again'.[38]

To earn trust again and again to the degree needed for a vibrant democracy, politicians have to show that they are *trustworthy*. Parliamentary sovereignty has been a core tenet of British democracy, and it resists any notion of parliamentarians being scrutinised by external bodies. But in the wake of the expenses row, a poll for the BBC found 85 per cent of the public supported the idea of an independent judicial body to scrutinise MPs' activities, including expenses.[39] On our model of intrinsic–extrinsic motivations, we favour internal above external monitoring, because the latter has the presumption of mistrust, and the public has a right to MPs whom they can presume to be honest and trustworthy in their day-to-day dealings. The job of an MP is rightly very demanding, with on average 68,500 constituents to represent,[40] and they do need adequate staffing and resource allowances, and competitive salaries. A better way than external regulation is to have high degrees of visibility, with all financial transactions of MPs properly accounted for and available to scrutiny by the public at large. Penalties for transgressions need to be much harsher. More on this later.

Trust is typically lost where different groups in society feel they have no voice and do not receive fair representation. Increasing the *diversity* of

MPs, with greater numbers of women, working class and ethnic minority candidates, would immediately make the House of Commons a more just, legitimate and effective legislature. The reason why so many MPs are white, male, and middle-class is largely because the caucuses, who select candidates in constituencies, predominantly choose those who are most like themselves. The solution is to institute the system of primaries, which function well in the United States. With open primaries, candidates no longer have to win the support of the wholly unrepresentative caucuses of the party faithful, but convince potentially thousands of local voters within their constituency. This reform is already gathering support from prominent figures such as David Miliband.[41] It will also spread opportunities for democratic expression, as was shown recently when an extraordinary 16,639 people turn out in Britain's first open primary to select Dr Sarah Wollaston as Conservative candidate for the seat of Totnes at a cost of £40,000.[42] But systematic change will not happen of its own accord; as was recently argued in *The Times*, the small numbers who currently choose election candidates would never voluntarily give up their privilege.[43] The change would have to be imposed from the centre and be funded from the public purse.

Trust in the legislature might well be further enhanced by the introduction of fixed term (of say four year) elections (supported by 73 per cent of respondents in May 2009)[44] and reform of the House of Lords. As a wholly elected chamber, the newly named Senate would have a particular brief not only to scrutinise the operations of the legislature better than at present, but also to implement enhanced checks and balances over the judicial and executive arms of government. The reforms of 1999 dragged the House of Lords into the twenty-first century, removing all but ninety-two hereditary peers and increasing the appointment of more women and ethnic minority peers, so that by 2009, it was able to boast the same percentage of women as the House of Commons (20 per cent), while 5.4 per cent (forty peers) belonged to an ethnic minority compared to just 2.3 per cent of members of the House of Commons.[45] But reform is incomplete and must go further, especially after the allegations in January 2009 by the *Sunday Times* which revealed that four peers had indicated a willingness to accept financial inducements from an undercover reporter to influence legislation due to be scrutinised in the Upper House. A YouGov poll for the *Daily Telegraph* revealed in May 2009 that 69 per cent of people wanted further reform including all members to be directly elected.[46]

Many have fallen back on electoral reform as the panacea to restore trust and correct all evils. The arguments have raged intensively for thirty-five years and more, since before even Samuel Finer's *Adversary Politics and Electoral Reform* (1975) made such an eloquent case for proportional representation, and we do not need to go into them in detail here. A compelling argument for reform is that in so many seats in Britain the result is a foregone conclusion and so there seems little purpose in voting, when only 10 or 15 per cent of seats might realistically change hands at any one election. Some 52 per cent of respondents in May 2009 favoured directly linking the number of seats won in a general election to a total vote for each party.[47] Peter Kellner has recently made a compelling argument for the Alternative Vote, which he argues would better reflect the votes of the public whilst maintaining stable government and also preventing extremist parties, such as the BNP, from winning seats to Parliament.[48] Some moderate electoral reform would help give voters meaningful choices in even safe constituencies, but we fall short of favouring any measure of electoral reform which damages the relationship between an MP and a geographic constituency, or which hands the power to form governments to party leaders to form coalitions, thus taking power even further away from the electorate. One should also be cautious about whether reform would enhance trust. In both New Zealand and Japan, trust decreased after the electoral system was reformed in the former, and restructured in the latter.[49]

What is essential to restoring trust is to bring into politics a far higher calibre of individual, in terms of both integrity and also effectiveness in the art of politics. A report into public standards in 2008 found that 85 per cent of those asked considered it 'extremely important' for public officeholders not to take bribes, and 73 per cent not to use power for their own gain, both significantly above the 61 per cent who said that it was 'extremely important' for them to be 'competent at their jobs'.[50] Plato in the *Republic* emphasised the need for long training for political leaders, and though this may be impractical in 21st-century Britain, the understanding that MPs have to embody the virtues that he described of justice, wisdom, temperance, and courage could not be more apposite. One can immediately see that had MPs behaved in a more just, wise, and temperate way, and been more courageous, then the expenses scandal would never have occurred. Confucius said rulers should further be self-disciplined, lead by example and treat followers with love and concern.[51] What characterised superior leadership for him was the possession of a moral virtue or power, which allows the ruler to win over followers without the recourse to force. Kautilya is a lesser-known figure in the UK. He wrote *Arthashastra*, an ancient Indian treatise on statecraft, and spoke of the extreme importance of self-discipline, which can only be acquired if the individual is capable of learning and practising what is learnt. A determination to learn and improve oneself needs to be ingrained in any elected politician.

High-minded thoughts such as these are in fact enshrined already in Parliament, in the Robing Room, to inspire the monarch in her leadership of the legislature. Around the walls are painted five frescoes, which were intended eventually to number seven, representing the seven desired virtues of a good monarch, as drawn from the knightly virtues of Camelot and Arthurian legend. The virtues of hospitality, generosity, mercy, religion, and courtesy are painted, but ironically, fidelity and courage were never completed. These virtues would all, if followed, allow individuals to become much higher-quality MPs and to become real leaders, rather than mere followers of public opinion and focus groups. Practising these virtues would develop more authentic leaders, who would be deserving of more authentic trust.[52] Cicero's distinction between popular politicians, who do what is popular, and virtuous politicians, who do what is right, is pertinent here.[53] How would one ensure that MPs were acting in line with these values? A code of ethics would be an excellent way forward and it could enshrine the principles of the Trust Test. It would provide a minimum guarantee to voters about what they could expect from their elective representatives. It would outline the role of an MP against which their behaviour and performance could be judged, and it would be intrinsic, rather than extrinsic or legally enforced. It would constitute an act of faith for MPs in which they would be saying: 'Here are the standards by which you should judge me, but I will strive to do better.'

The Committee on Standards in Public Life has been in existence for nearly fifteen years, but has had little visible effect upon trust. The very vagueness of the current Code of Conduct for MPs is part of the problem: it stresses that members 'shall at all time conduct themselves in a manner that will tend to maintain and strengthen the public's trust and confidence in the integrity of Parliament and never undertake any action which would bring the House of Commons, or its Members generally, into disrepute'.[54] The code of ethics we propose needs to be much sharper and more visible. Each MP would have to sign it at the beginning of each parliament and, if their conduct failed to live up to what was written, they would be disciplined and then ejected, with local constituents also being able to trigger a 'recall' by-election, if they felt the code had been breached, a development favoured by 79 per cent of those polled in mid-2009.[55] Ideally, such dramatic moves should not be necessary because the new kind of MP coming into Parliament would change the culture sufficiently for them to desist from breaching the code of their own volition. MPs would be imbued with a vision of their role as 'trustees', heirs to a tradition of serving in the oldest parliament in the world, and with a profound commitment to leaving British democracy in a more respected state than it was when they were first elected. Trust in the government would also be considerably enhanced if ministers and civil servants were to have a similarly bracing visible and enforceable code of ethics.

Ministers, and still more the Prime Minister himself, are placed under almost intolerable strain, and they mistake actions for effective action.

They have been caught up in a vicious circle, fuelled by the 24-hour news cycle, of having to show that they are busy and doing things. The more exaggerated the claims they have made to win elections, the harder their little feet have pattered on the treadmill. 'Government has earned public dissatisfaction . . . by promising to remedy . . . economic and social problems and then not being able to keep the promises.'[56] Under such circumstances it has been hard for ministers and the Prime Minister to give sufficient time to reflect upon whether their behaviour is ethical. What has struck me most vividly when writing about Prime Ministers is the mismatch between their own views of their behaviour and that held by others. From Wilson to Brown, they have believed that they are behaving ethically and in tune with high principles, yet they have not given themselves the space to reflect deeply upon their personal mission in this, the most important office in the country.

Openness and transparency are key factors highlighted in the Edelman Trust Barometer for building trust.[57] President Obama, a significantly younger figure than many in Washington, set the tone when on his first day in office he established the 'open government initiative'.[58] Much greater use should be made by the British Government of the new electronic mediums of communication, to listen to the public and to communicate back with them. In Britain in 2008, 65 per cent of households could access the internet,[59] a rather higher percentage than those who voted in the 2005 general election. Of the two main political leaders, Cameron has shown himself more adept at understanding the new cyberworld than the sixteen-years-older Brown, whose performance on YouTube in April 2009 was mawkish.

Our mechanisms of democracy are still determined by eighteenth- and nineteenth-century ways of thinking. On polling day we travel, sometimes long distances, to polling stations, to be secreted in a screened-off booth to mark a cross on a ballot paper which is later collected and delivered to a central location, to be counted by hand. It is hard to imagine that in 2100 this is how democracy will function. At some point between today and then, the system will change. We argue that it should change now, with increasing use made of blogs, Twitter, Facebook, MySpace, Flickr and the like to communicate with the public, and for the public to communicate with their representatives and government. Twitter was used by candidates in the 2008 US presidential election, and in February 2009 the Australian Prime Minister, Kevin Rudd, used it effectively to send out information about the bush fires. The latest technologies should be used extensively: to allow constituents to raise issues with their representatives, for representatives to sample opinion among their constituents and to communicate their rationale for voting on bills in Parliament. Using these methods more would do much to stimulate interest amongst the increasingly turned-off young.

E-communication could be used further to test support for which bills could be introduced into Parliament and with what content, to poll opinion on government policy, as the FCO did when asking about the UK's foreign priorities, and to use government websites more imaginatively to provide far better and more honest communication with the public. The Number 10 petition website has proven remarkably successful in increasing engagement, but is limited by virtue of the fact that there is often little follow-through. Consideration should therefore be given to the idea of a People's Bill, which would be voted on by the public on a yearly basis. Brazil is one of the few countries to have seen an increased trust in politicians during 2008–9.[60] Its Trust in Politics online database made its public officials accessible to voters, communicating information on political donations and expenses of elected members, and consulting on emerging thinking about the budget. E-technology itself will not, of course, itself restore trust. It also poses its own problems, including internet users not being representative of the public as a whole. But the direct and open communication that it facilitates will take us a long way away from the grotesque episode of Jo Moore, a government specialist advisor, who famously described 9/11 as a 'good day to bury bad news' and the world of Alastair Campbell, whose regime (1997–2003) did so much to epitomise everything that was wrong with the old world of spin and general control of information.

The executive needs to weaken its tight grip over the legislature to let Parliament breathe. Government must reduce the power of whips and allow more free votes, allow Parliament to select committee chairs, give select committees more genuine authority, staffing resources and power and allow Parliament to scrutinise appointments.[61] We do not favour the use of hypothecated taxes, which has been advocated by some, whereby revenue from that tax is ring-fenced for a specific purpose. Rather than giving the electorate a direct say over use of revenue, we believe that Parliament should be trusted to spend taxes appropriately.

Number 10 and the Cabinet Office have been allowed to become a crazy mess of duplicating functions since the 1980s. Power has largely accumulated at the centre because of a lack of trust of Whitehall departments, just as Whitehall departments had grabbed power to themselves because of a lack of trust in regional and local government. Number 10 and the Cabinet Office have worked best under Prime Ministers such as Churchill, Attlee and Thatcher, when they were relatively small, staffed by high grade personnel who provided what the Prime Minister needed to know only in the core functions of the job. The ineffectiveness of premiership in Britain is not unconnected with the Prime Minister forgetting what their job is, and Number 10 and the Cabinet Office becoming choked up with functions that have no place there.

Neither do we favour the direct election of a president, as in the republics of France or the United States, on the Burkean grounds that one should not tamper with time-hallowed traditions unless there is a very good reason. The monarchy and the office of the Prime Minister are positions that play an important role in the British state. Neither do we favour regular uses of referendums, with the exception being when changes to the Constitution are proposed. For all the seeming appeal of a referendum in encouraging popular interest and building trust, regular usage would bypass both Parliament and Government. In practice they are open to exploitation by powerful interest groups: Peter Kellner in his article 'Down with People Power' points out that most of the twenty-one referendum votes in California within the preceding year had been funded by billionaires or powerful lobby groups.[62] We should be looking to ensure that government and Parliament perform in a way that is worthy of our trust, not trying to emasculate or bypass them.

Trust can be restored to central government by devolving power massively to local government, reversing the centralising trend which has been in place since the end of the Second World War and given Britain the most centralised government in Europe. 'No one in Germany thinks Mrs Merkel is responsible for what goes on in hospitals in Düsseldorf,' says Tony Travers, director of the Greater London Group at the London School of Economics. 'Everyone understands her primary job is foreign policy, security and the economy. Compare the faces of John Major and Tony Blair before and after they left office, and look at Gordon Brown before and now. We should not try to carry on running the country as if it is a city and the Prime Minister is the mayor with sixty million people to look after.'[63]

We have seen how we are most likely to trust those closest to us, and the ubiquitous aspiration 'to be heard' is most likely to be answered at a *local* level. Yet trust has collapsed locally, less because of anything that local politicians and officials might have done wrong, than because of the steady leeching away of influence. The electorate has little trust in local government because local government has little power, and thus has little meaning in their lives. Rebuilding authority in local politics is therefore the essential precursor to rebuilding trust locally, and nationally. Distrust of local government from the centre drove the loss of its powers: indeed sometimes local government did behave in untrustworthy ways, such as the Liverpool City Council's illegal 'deficit budget' fiasco in 1985.[64] Local government now feels ready to be trusted again. The Audit Commission concurs, rating 42 per cent of local authorities in the highest performance categories in 2008 compared with just 15 per cent in 2002.[65] Genuine local government is known to work in other countries: in Denmark, the municipalities have wide responsibilities. 'The philosophy [is] that citizens should have – with very rare exceptions – only one entry point to dealing with the public sector, and that it should be the municipality.'[66]

Counties in Britain should be given back powers they have lost progressively since the 1940s. In the nineteenth century, the great municipalities competed against each other, and the competition resulted not only in improved standards, but also a healthy diversity of provision. One reason British politicians look endlessly to the United States is because its government permits diversity, whereas the British uniformity strangles it.[67] Counties could assume charge of commissioning the local health service and accountability for police services from the NHS and police authorities. At present, health and policing remain insufficiently accountable to local populations. Running health across England is far too big a job for the NHS. Scotland and Wales manage their own health services, and so too could English counties. Skills and further education could also be returned to counties, where local politicians have a much clearer understanding of local employment and training needs. Schools should be overseen by county halls, which would provide the funding, while schools themselves, like hospitals, should be given wide measures of individual autonomy. Counties are a much better unit in England for organising local affairs than regions. Labour's referendums on regional assemblies failed to receive the popular mandate they required, and regional government in England is probably dead for many years.[68]

The introduction of *elected mayors* has worked well in the Greater London Authority, with first Ken Livingstone and then Boris Johnson since May 2008, and in the London boroughs of Hackney, Newham and Lewisham. Turnout jumped to 45 per cent in the 2008 mayoral contest, a reassuringly healthy level for a local contest.[69] They have been less successful in Doncaster and Stoke-on-Trent, but that has had more to do with local politics than a systemic failure with elected mayors *per se*. Travers argues that they can fit in well with the desire for a recognisable face to personify a political district.[70] We would also favour having directly elected leaders at county level. Imposing mayors on metropolitan districts and governors on communities would be a breach of trust, but ensuring that each community had the opportunity to vote in a referendum on whether or not they wanted to have a mayor or governor would be democratic.

Trust would be significantly boosted by giving greater powers to the parish/urban parish/community level of local government. Matters such as planning, street-cleaning, lighting, antisocial behaviour, upkeep of public areas could all be governed at this most local of levels. The police could also be bonded into small units, and answerable to parishes through elected representatives. The sense that the community belonged to all, and was run by local people, would enhance the sense of ownership, with it being cared for by those who live within it. Pride within local communities will help restore trust.

Critical to increasing the power and respect of local government is giving back greater control over its own finances.[71] Reversing the decline of financial powers can be achieved in a number of ways, including local income taxes, allowing local authorities to determine the business rate, and allowing local government to raise council tax above capped limits. In retaining financial muscle, the local electorate will come to more directly feel the presence and influence of their local government, stirring a greater level of engagement than is currently the case.

As part of the new constitutional settlement we advocate, we call for the doctrine of 'subsidiarity' to be legally entrenched, as is currently the practice in the EU. It is a guiding principle, which states that no function should be performed at any level that could be performed equally well at a lower level. The new settlement would need to be underpinned with the same safeguards, as have been enshrined in the Scottish and Welsh devolutions. Given the chronic tendency of central government to take powers away and to intervene, local government needs this safeguard. Standards and a broad equalisation of resources would be determined centrally, as would regulations and monitoring by the Audit Commission and other bodies, but local autonomy as to ultimate use of resources would be sacrosanct.

The culture in Britain would need to change to that which exists in France and many European countries. This has been neatly encapsulated by Martine Buron, ex-mayor of a small municipality in the centre of France: 'Nobody from the national state would ever dare to intervene in the effectiveness of local services. This is unheard of. If people aren't satisfied, they don't vote for you next time.'[72] Parliament, too, needs to stop rushing into local government's jurisdictions as soon as something goes wrong, as happened with the Baby Peter case in 2008. The more Parliament and central government intervene, the more the public and the media will look to the centre to provide the answer and the more overloaded, and thus mistrusted, it will become.

The change in culture must come most fundamentally from the electorate at large. Polls show clearly the public's concern with crime, schooling and planning issues, but they do not relate their concern to the political institutions that can help remedy their anxieties. The Local Government White Paper of 2006 went some way in proposing some of what we seek, including community calls for action, the creation of parish councils and the empowerment of local people to manage their own local neighbourhoods more. The Sustainable Communities Act 2007 helped allow for some sensible devolution, subject to Whitehall agreement. But as such the proposals are overly bureaucratic and have yet to connect fully with the local public.[73] Revitalising local politics will not be easy. It will require an influx into local government of a more committed and capable grade of volunteer than we have seen to date, with the current trend towards an increasingly older councillor (the average age has risen from fifty-five to fifty-nine in the past decade).[74]

Polly Toynbee is one of the sceptics. 'All parties are supporting localism, but I worry it will just lead to postcode lotteries, inequalities, and plain bad government. I am far from convinced that local government can do a better job than the centre'.[75] It is certainly true that people are much busier and have more leisure opportunities than they had in the past, and persuading able people to give up their time to serve the community for no financial reward might be hard. But that does not mean that we should not try, and the case for shifting powers down from central government is overwhelming. Other countries manage vibrant local democracy, and so must we. More importantly, weak local government will eventually undermine – and may already have undermined – Parliament. Councillors and local activism are the bedrock of democracy in Britain.

At the heart of our proposals lies the conviction that trust will only be rebuilt if each citizen behaves in a trustworthy and responsible way. The words of Kennedy, exhorting citizens to ask what they can do for their country, could not sum up the approach more clearly. We have to think about duties and responsibilities as well as rights; many people are reaching the same conclusion that 'the contemporary democratic process requires more of its citizens'.[76] Peck and Phillips in *Citizen Renaissance* argue that the impetus for the change we seek will come from the conjunction of cataclysmic threat, a widespread demand that we take 'well-being' more seriously, and the possibilities being opened up by the information revolution.[77] What is certain is this: unless active citizenship becomes the norm in Britain, and if *trust* does not become the dominant ethos, then the bonds that have held our society and government together will weaken, eventually to a disastrous extent.

Despite leading the Royal Bank of Scotland to the biggest annual loss in UK corporate history, Sir Fred Goodwin walked away unrepentant, with an annual pension of £703,000. For many, Goodwin came to personify the abuse of trust in the banking sector. *(Jim Kuhn)*

CHAPTER 5
TRUST IN BUSINESS, BANKERS AND THE ECONOMY

How selfish soever man may be supposed, there are evidently some principles in his nature, which interest him in the fortune of others, and render their happiness necessary to him, though he derives nothing from it except the pleasure of seeing it.

Adam Smith (1723–90), *The Theory of Moral Sentiments*

The global financial crisis has shaken trust in corporations, banks, and even in the capitalist model. The crisis grew not out of a systemic failure of capitalism, but from people and institutions behaving carelessly, dishonestly and greedily; the answer to both of these lies in trusting and being trustworthy. Adam Smith, the father of modern economics, placed self-interest high. In a much quoted passage, he wrote: 'It is not from the benevolence of the butcher, the brewer, or the baker, that we expect our dinner, but from their regard for their own interest. We address ourselves, not to their humanity but their self love, and never talk to them of our own necessities but of their advantages.'[1] Many have drawn inspiration from these words, and they have fostered a greedy materialism whereby individuals maximise their personal financial gain; trust and honesty are deployed only as contingent devices to achieve it.[2] Many have overlooked Adam Smith's lesser-known text *The Theory of Moral*

Sentiments, which instead emphasises the need for shared moral behaviour as the backbone of a functioning society.

It is this softer tone which has resonated with many recent authors, including Francis Fukuyama, who in *Trust* (1995) demonstrated the positive correlation between trust and economic growth: 'There is no necessary trade-off, in other words, between community and efficiency; those who pay attention to community may indeed become the most efficient of all.'[3] Kenneth Arrow, Nobel Prize winner, argued in *The Economy of Trust* (2006) similarly, that 'people do have aims in life, and not just the grand achievement of material gains.'[4] Being trustworthy makes increasing economic sense, as 77 per cent of consumers reported in 2009 that they had refused to buy a product or service from a distrusted company,[5] and 54 per cent said they would make a personal recommendation to others of a company that had earned their trust.[6] Increasing trust in management can increase revenue by up to 30 per cent.[7] But trust, we argue, should be an end in itself, not a boost to profit maximisation. Otherwise trust becomes little more than a manipulative tool that will foster distrust and resentment over the long run.

Have we lost trust?

Edelman's 2009 Trust Barometer shows there was a massive loss of trust in business (amongst the 'informed public' between the ages of thirty-five and sixty-four) in the US in late 2008/early 2009, bringing it close to the levels for Britain, France and Germany, which have been persistently low (see Figure 5.1).

Looking at Europe exclusively, Figure 5.2 shows trust in business in Britain remaining steady between 2008 and 2009 on 45 per cent but at a level described as 'low'. Trust levels for the first half of 2009 were nevertheless above Spain (40 per cent), Germany (33 per cent), France (29 per cent) and Italy (27 per cent). Furthermore Figure 5.3 shows a significant decline from 2003 to 2008 in the perception of British businesses behaving ethically.

The most trusted sectors within Britain are entertainment and leisure

Figure 5.1: Trust in business in the US[8]

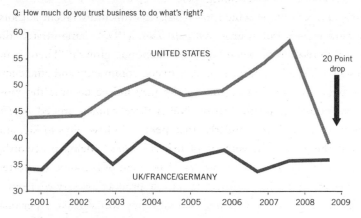

Q: How much do you trust business to do what's right?

Informed public ages 35 to 64 in the US, UK/France/Germany
Responses 6–9 only on 1–9 scale; 9=highest
Source: Edelman, 2009 Trust Barometer

(67 per cent), food companies (64 per cent), supermarkets (64 per cent), technology (64 per cent), while those that are the lowest are tobacco (15 per cent), fast food (27 per cent) and petrochemicals (28 per cent). The summer of 2009 saw trust in business internationally on an upswing

Figure 5.2: Trust in business in Europe[9]

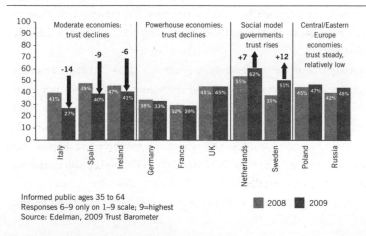

Informed public ages 35 to 64
Responses 6–9 only on 1–9 scale; 9=highest
Source: Edelman, 2009 Trust Barometer

2008 ■ 2009

according to Edelman, with the US up from 36 per cent to 48 per cent and Germany from 34 per cent to 39 per cent. Trust in British business however, continued to fall, from 46 per cent to 44 per cent.[10]

Figure 5.3: Ethical behaviour of British businesses[11]

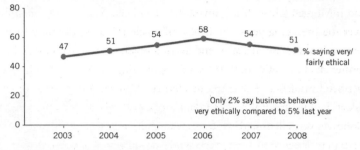

Q: How ethically do you think British business generally behaves?

% saying very/fairly ethical

Only 2% say business behaves very ethically compared to 5% last year

Base: c. 1000/2000 British adults aged 16+/15+ each year
Source: Ipsos MORI, Annual IBE/Ipsos Mori Survey of UK Adult Opinion on Business Ethics (2008)

Why have we lost trust?

The word 'credit' comes from the Latin verb *credere*, meaning 'to believe' or 'to entrust'.[12] A breakdown of trust between customers, investors, banks, government, regulators and the media lies at the very heart of the financial crisis. It is true that some banks lent money they did not have to lend and customers spent some money they did not have to spend. As Joe Garner of HSBC put it, 'the financial crisis is not a crisis of funding, liquidity and capital, but rather a crisis of character and ethics.'[13] Blind trust, rather than the active trust we advocate, lay behind the whole credit crunch and financial crisis. 'The very success of the economy led to people suspending the need to question the drivers of that success – people assumed trust because the system was working – and so trust morphed from active to assumed trust, which was not consciously challenged,' said Tony Manwaring of *Tomorrow's Company*.[14]

In those banks that became unstuck, like the Royal Bank of Scotland (RBS), Citigroup, Merrill Lynch and UBS, blind trust, or a 'suspension of distrust', on the part of shareholders, investors and regulators was at the fore. Within these organisations, caution was sacrificed in the pursuit of higher short-term profits. Internal risk departments, the monitors of prudence and guardians of trust, were utterly marginalised. In Merrill Lynch, the risk department operated in a silo separate from trading operations, while in Citigroup and UBS, risk managers were given a similarly low status. In banks that came through the crisis, such as Deutsche Bank, Goldman Sachs and JPMorgan Chase, heavy investment had been made in risk-monitoring over the preceding years; the banks still made mistakes, but their focus on a more 'holistic risk management' averted disaster.[15] Sir Fred Goodwin, the former chief executive of RBS, was the worst single example of a leader who sacrificed prudence. According to Herman Mulder, former head of group risk at the Dutch ABN AMRO Bank, acquired by RBS and others in 2007, Goodwin was still trusted by those around him, internally and externally, and wasn't challenged. Such was Goodwin's domineering aura, many were too afraid to challenge him whilst others 'believed in his Midas touch'.[16] As banks continued to indulge in repackaged loans and collateralised debt obligations, profits grew in tandem with ever growing complexity. The mathematical models the banks relied on became increasingly opaque and oblivious to the growing systemic risk. Mulder continued: 'Risk managers were struggling to keep the pace and fully appreciate the risks in our own portfolios, let alone the systemic risk that accrued. If we were unable to understand our own risk portfolio, how would we trust that of our peers?'

Greed, which we can define as seeking individual gain without consideration for others, drove the credit crunch. It was not just the bankers and investors driving the greed, nor our seemingly insatiable demand for ever more consumption, but also that of the politicians. The Financial Services Authority (FSA) came under immense pressure from Gordon Brown, Number 10 and the Treasury, who in turn yielded to the banks' demands for freedom from the FSA's bureaucracy. Since the 1980s, deregulation had fuelled intense competition in the City and brought immense pressure on institutional investors and fund managers to perform. These imperatives inevitably transferred to the business world. Greed perpetuated greed, and in this Anglo-American version of stock market capitalism, the criterion of success became shareholder value as expressed by share price.[17]

Goodwin became the scapegoat for much of what went wrong in the credit crunch. He provided an appetising target when, having led RBS to the brink of dissolution, with losses totalling £24.1 billion for 2009, the largest annual loss in UK corporate history, he still walked away with a £703,000 per annum pension, which he adamantly refused to forgo. When in June 2009, he finally agreed to reduce his pension to £342,500 a year,[18] the damage to his reputation had already been done. The image of financiers and business people receiving exceedingly high salaries, bonuses and benefits causes great resentment and loss of trust in the probity of banks and companies. The 1980s saw British banks and corporations adopt American thinking that huge salaries and bonuses were an appropriate reward for high flyers and top executives as, the argument went, they were in limited supply.[19] The residual distaste was fuelled by images of young Bollinger-swilling, cocaine-snorting and Porsche 911-driving 20-somethings making absurd amounts of money in the City of London in the 1980s, gaily flaunting their easily obtained wealth. This 'me-first attitude' was satirised by comedian Harry Enfield in his 'Loadsamoney' character on television. Polly Toynbee, author with David Walker of *Unjust Rewards* (2008), said: 'It is when the public cannot see why such high financial rewards are being given to people who do not seem to merit it that they grow suspicious, and mistrust and disillusion are spread.'[20]

Reports in mid 2009 that there is a new city buzz word, BAB, 'bonuses are back', in the City of London, with a return of the champagne parties and higher bonuses anticipated at the end of the year, has provoked fury, just when the temperature was beginning to cool among the public. The statement by John Varley, CEO of Barclays, that the banks' obligation was to ensure they paid appropriate prices, comparing city traders to footballers, was not well judged.[21] Stephen Hester, the new chief executive of the Royal Bank of Scotland, which is 70 per cent owned by the British taxpayer, has been given a £9.6 million pay package, and came under fire when RBS reported a mid-year loss of £1 billion.[22] The Centre of Economics and

Business Research has suggested bankers are in line for bonus payments worth £4 billion in 2009.[23] Politicians, including Alistair Darling, George Osborne and Vince Cable, have all condemned this 'business as usual' mindset. With Darling indicating a willingness to use legislation to curb such excesses,[24] it shows that significant measures will have to be taken if trust is to be regained in and between British companies and banks, and it is to this subject we now turn.

Restoring trust in banking and business

Consumers are very clear about the steps that business needs to take to rebuild trust after the financial crisis. They want 'increasing shareholder value' and 'protecting profit margins' placed at the very bottom of corporate priorities, and 'treating employees well', 'keeping producing quality products and services' and 'transparent and honest business practices' at the very top (see Figure 5.4).

Figure 5.4: Measures to rebuild trust[25]

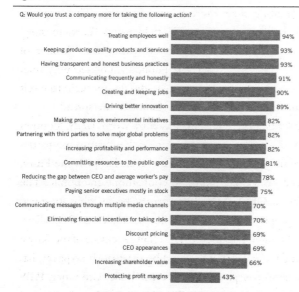

Q: Would you trust a company more for taking the following action?

Treating employees well	94%
Keeping producing quality products and services	93%
Having transparent and honest business practices	93%
Communicating frequently and honestly	91%
Creating and keeping jobs	90%
Driving better innovation	89%
Making progress on environmental initiatives	82%
Partnering with third parties to solve major global problems	82%
Increasing profitability and performance	82%
Committing resources to the public good	81%
Reducing the gap between CEO and average worker's pay	78%
Paying senior executives mostly in stock	75%
Communicating messages through multiple media channels	70%
Eliminating financial incentives for taking risks	70%
Discount pricing	69%
CEO appearances	69%
Increasing shareholder value	66%
Protecting profit margins	43%

Informed publics aged 25 to 64; responses 6–9 only on 1–9 scale; 9=highest
Source: Edelman, 2009 Trust Barometer

The first response to any crisis is to bring in the heavy guns to restore order. There is a natural preference for extrinsic means of ensuring that trustworthiness returns, but it will never succeed because it is not based on giving trust, which means responsibilities need to be taken far more seriously. The 'middle ground' range of devices – targets, inspection, oversight, monitoring and regulation – have all been popular responses to the financial crisis. The review by Adair Turner, chairman of the FSA, recommended in August 2009 an array of measures including increasing capital requirements and counter-cyclical conditions such that they rise in upswings and fall in recessions.[26] Alistair Darling produced a White Paper on regulation which proposed a Council of Financial Stability within the Bank of England. Some form of enhanced regulation is indeed inevitable until confidence recovers. But regulation alone will never be sufficient.[27] As Professor Paul Zak, a prominent figure in the field of neuroeconomics, writes: 'Legal regulations may perversely lead to an increase in immoral behaviours by crowding out our innate sense of fair play.'[28] Regulation by external bodies with legal powers only encourages trusting actions through forced compliance and through fear of exposure, rather than through an inner determination to act morally.

A better form of regulation is self-regulation, from within the organisation itself or by the professional or trade association. The financial services industry should create a forum for self-regulation articulating the very highest principles. Inspiration could be drawn from a variety of bodies, including the National House Building Council, which for decades has set an industry-led standard to protect customers from poor quality building, or even the Association of British Travel Agents, whose travel bond gives customers some protection against default by its members. Companies themselves need to set much higher standards internally. Employees take their lead from the top.

Restricting salaries and bonuses is necessary but will only happen with broad consensus internationally. A sense of proportion is required to bring pay back onto a responsible basis. In the UK, bonus payouts increased from 2006–9 from £5 billion to £15 billion.[29] Treasury

Minister Lord Myners wants the government-commissioned review to force banks to disclose the names and pay packages of their top earners, irrespective of whether they are on the board.[30] A variant is to link pay and bonuses to *long-term* success, and could be made in restricted stock, dependent upon performance, redeemable over perhaps ten years.[31] Some see such moves as unduly restrictive on freedom of action. But J. P. Morgan, one of the founders of modern banking, believed that to motivate people you did not need a ratio of more than ten between the highest and lowest paid, a commonly discussed ratio in management schools but unfamiliar, it would seem, in the boardrooms of the real world.[32]

Informing the public about top pay is one method of facilitating clearer communication, which Edelman emphasises is essential: 'In a time of utter distrust, business leaders must make the case for actions and then demonstrate their progress against those goals.'[33] Leaders need to be much more honest about mistakes when they occur, about what needs to happen to correct them and how to avoid repetitions. Chief executives need to be more visible and be able to communicate honestly and convincingly. Companies and banks need to come out from behind the shadows, work more openly with the media, and communicate directly with the public electronically. CEOs need also to communicate much better within their organisation, imbuing their companies with 'very simple, common sense standards of decency'.[34]

Looking after all stakeholders i.e. all those who have a stake in the company, is essential to the rebuilding of trust. It is now fifteen years since Will Hutton wrote *The State We're In*, which launched the modern phase of thinking about stakeholding. His aspiration was 'to create a new financial architecture in which private decisions produce a less degenerate capitalism.'[35] The economic crisis could well provide the very opportunity we need for stakeholding to be taken far more seriously: Robert Peston believes it could be more significant in its impact on the economy than the collapse of communism.[36] Wise communities learn from disasters and good comes out of them. We need to ensure the financial crisis becomes the catalyst for addressing all the long-standing problems in the financial and corporate sectors.

Employees need to be treated well, not just because it makes good business sense, but because they are human beings. The ability to distinguish between employees as instruments and employees as individuals is the mark of a moral and a mature company. Even Jack Welch, former CEO of General Electric (1981–2001), and heralded as the godfather of stock market capitalism, said in March of 2009: 'Shareholder value is the dumbest idea in the world . . . Your main constituencies are your employees, your customers and your products.'[37] Britain is still dominated too much by a Taylorite mentality, which takes its name from early twentieth-century management thinker Frederick W. Taylor.[38] He sought to maximise labour efficiency by very high degrees of specialisation, which minimised the need for workers' initiative, judgement and even skill. His thinking was based on a presumption of distrust: motivation was to be induced by better pay, directed at the more productive. But distrust breeds distrust and an assertive trade unionism was the inevitable reaction. Clear demarcation between white- and blue-collar workers was the result, an officer and a soldier class, with few opportunities for promotion from the rank and file. In stark contrast, in Germany blue-collar workers have much higher skills levels, greater responsibility and much more mobility into white-collar occupations. Compared to Britain, Germany has much flatter pay scales, and bonuses are paid far more on the basis of group rather than individual achievement.

Trust will be built with employees if companies consciously nurture their quality of life. The 2008 report *Working for a Healthier Tomorrow* found: 'A shift in attitudes is necessary to ensure that employers and employees recognise not only the importance of preventing ill-health, but also the key role the workplace can play in promoting health and well-being.'[39] The report estimated that £100 billion is lost each year because of working-age ill health. The New Economics Foundation has produced a five-point plan, adopted by Business in the Community, for companies to create a genuinely healthy work place – mentally, physically and psychologically.[40] No corporation has any reason not to be aware of the benefit and need for implementing, and practising such a policy – from top to bottom.

Stakeholding means that customers are treated in a much more trusting way. In particular, communicating with customers needs constant attention. Sixty per cent of Edelman respondents said they needed to hear information about a company three to five times before it sank in.[41] E-communication has opened up pathways for business and banks to listen to customers better. Johnson and Johnson run a particularly effective blog which serves as an online feedback website. The literature, the slogans and the CEO might be admirably clear, but the messages need to be repeated by others throughout and beyond the organisation many times over. Trust takes a long time to build, but can be easily shattered.

Shareholders need to enter a new relationship with their companies. In 1963, individuals held over half the shares in British companies: now they hold an eighth. Institutional investors such as pension funds and insurance companies held over half of UK shares in 1995, but have now slipped back to a quarter. Foreign investors over the same period have moved from less than a sixth to owning half the shares in the UK-listed corporate sector.[42] All shareholders nonetheless need to understand better their obligations as trustees. They themselves are the beneficiaries of the wealth inherited from the past, from the hard work and skill put into that company over many years. Their duty is to preserve and, where possible, enhance the value of the company in which they hold the shares rather than milk it short term for their own narrow advantage.

Furthermore, at the heart of stakeholding is the principle that it is not just the shareholders who own the company. In many ways the concept of a company being owned by outside investors looks increasingly undemocratic and anachronistic. It values the physical above the human assets at a time when it is increasingly the 'human capital' that provides greater value to a company. In the stakeholder model, employees could be paid a share of the dividends when the company is performing well.

It is only just for a share of the surplus to be given to those who have contributed to earning it with their skills, rather than the dividends going solely to those who contributed with their money, most of whom have not, says Handy, 'paid any to the company itself, but only to the previous owners of the shares'.[43]

Beyond the company's own frontiers, they need to adopt much higher levels of responsibility. Milton Friedman, the father of monetarism, told the *New York Times Magazine* in 1970, that 'the social responsibility of business is to increase its profits'.[44] In the past, companies could plead innocence of their wider responsibilities, but no more, with all our understanding of environmental hazards, world poverty, inequality and unfettered consumerism. These issues have forced everyone to realise we are part of an interconnected world: if a company ever was an island entire unto itself, it is an island no longer. Much more needs to be done by business to demonstrate to the public that it is taking its wider responsibilities seriously: one poll from mid-2009, for example, showed that 71 per cent of respondents thought that businesses had not done enough to help create solutions to minimise global warming.[45] Companies that behave ethically can flourish. The Co-op, an impressively ethical company, saw a 70 per cent increase in profits in its finance division in 2009 despite a 60 per cent increase in write-downs in April. From climate change to fair trade, the Co-op is an industry leader; it offers a range of ethical consumer products, and feeds its profits back into local community projects in Britain and abroad.[46]

But companies were not incorporated to make the world a better place, nor to pursue environmental, social, and governance (ESG) considerations. Corporations have always been driven by competition and profit, and there is indisputable merit in the cost minimisation, efficient use of resources, and product innovation that this entails. Mirroring this motive, accounting and auditing methods have come to focus narrowly on the financial metrics of performance. Evaluation on the basis of 'intangibles' such as prudence has been marginalised, especially as a result of attempts to develop standardised international methods of accounting and auditing through Basel I and II. In

August 2009 Adair Turner criticised such a narrow priority and castigated the City for indulging in practices which were 'socially useless'. He even suggested a tax on banks' financial transactions to fund 'public good'.

There is now a renewed recognition of the value of non-financial imperatives and principle-based auditing which centres on values such as prudence. Companies thrive and make long-term profit when they preserve customer goodwill, handle risk responsibly, cherish, motivate and train their employees, as well as when they innovate to cut costs and improve product quality. In contrast, those companies managed by 'fly-by-the-night' bosses who focus too much on short-term profits are apt to borrow against their company's reputation. They will tend to under-train their employees, take reckless gambles, exploit consumers, and avoid innovation. Successful management calls for careful management of values and profits, and a balance between profits now and profits later. Indeed, Goldman Sachs views the integration and serious consideration of wider ESG responsibilities 'as a proxy for management quality'.[47]

There are already indications that non-financial measures and 'intangible' ESG values are becoming central, rather than incidental, to core business activities.[48] Stephen Green, chairman of HSBC and author of *Good Value: Reflections on Money, Morality and an Uncertain World* (2009), insists that the core question for all in banks and the corporate sector is: 'How does the business we do contribute to the common good?'[49] There remains nonetheless a minority of companies fully engaged in this approach. To catalyse this paradigm shift, the Department of Business, Innovation and Skills should devise measures to compare companies on the basis of the trust they inspire within the business community and the wider public, and for their commitment to ESG priorities. The Honours List rewards those in business who are successful, but far more could be done to highlight and celebrate individuals and divisions within organisations who act in ways that build trust within and beyond the company. We need to celebrate achievement other than the maximisation of profit.

Only intrinsic motivations will lead to an enduring change in finance and business and, for this to happen, we will need to have a different quality manifested in leaders, a new culture, and more training on ethics in business schools. CEOs and chairmen have a unique opportunity to build trust within their organisations. Unfortunately, like Prime Ministers and cabinet ministers, their place in the sun is often all too brief and frenetic for them to embody the deeper values and principles they no doubt hold dear. The imperative of the urgent takes over from the desirable but less insistent. Top business leaders must therefore take it upon themselves to build daily time for reflection into their lives: if they are true leaders and in control of events, they will be able to command their agenda, and will make the time available. They should have the humility to open themselves up to the frank comments of those who work for them, or to work with coaches, to ensure that they become more grounded and better able to articulate their core beliefs. Ken Rea works with CEOs and echoes what many coaches experience: executives have very little idea about the image they project to others. 'The first step is to help them to see themselves, and then to take control of how they come across. Once they start becoming more true to themselves, their authority will grow, as will the trust others have in them.'[50]

Figure 5.5: A stakeholder, not a shareholder, world[51]

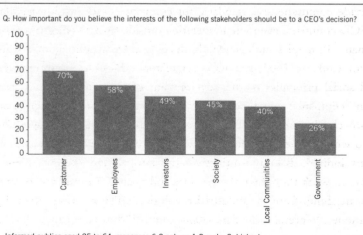

Q: How important do you believe the interests of the following stakeholders should be to a CEO's decision?

Informed publics aged 25 to 64; responses 6-9 only on 1-9 scale; 9=highest
Source: Edelman, 2009 Trust Barometer

The Edelman mid-year Trust Barometer for 2009 (Figure 5.5) shows an increase in demand for CEOs to take the lead in shifting the focus of their companies away from a shareholders to a stakeholder focus.

The demand for CEOs to have a vision beyond mere profit maximisation is likely to persist as the recession continues to be felt. 'Voluntary executive pay cuts and forfeiting of bonuses send a powerful message that leaders are in tune with the reality facing employees.'[52] Such actions would be in line with 'level 5' leadership, the highest level, championed by Jim Collins in *Good to Great* (2001). What characterises such leaders is personal humility and that 'their ambition is first and foremost for the institution, not themselves'.[53]

A trusting culture is facilitated by the way the leadership conducts itself and communicates honestly with all in the company. The bespoke culture will, in good Burkean terms, emanate from the traditions of the business, while being fully cognisant of the 21st-century world. Cultures are underpinned by effective ethical codes, often are derived widely from individuals across the company, and which move them closer to a sense of shared ownership. The codes can be guided by the Organisation for Economic Co-operation and Development's (OECD) Ethical Guidelines for Multinational Banks and Businesses, which provide comprehensive standards for companies with headquarters in OECD countries, even when operating outside OECD countries. The Equator Principles, independently developed by a number of private sector banks in 2003, provide a set of more rigorous environmental and social principles in the development of project finance. In this vein, companies need consciously to develop moral character, an approach advocated by Roger Steare, professor of organisational ethics, who works to help develop ethical approaches in business. To Steare, many individuals know instinctively how to behave, 'but when they come to work they leave those values and virtues at home and morph into machines from the industrial revolution'. The banking sector, he continues, 'represents the dark satanic mills'.[54] Most companies, despite all the money poured into head-hunters and recruitment specialists, are poor at identifying fully rounded talent when appointing and promoting staff. If we are to move beyond the industrial revolution, successful candidates for jobs need high ethical values as well as being good at their work. The culture will otherwise never change.

Much of the impetus for change can come through better training by business schools. The popular image is that they turn out Gordon Gekkos, the character in the film *Wall Street* (1987) played by Michael Douglas, who became the symbol of greed in the late 1980s and 1990s. Business schools in fact have a long tradition of trying to develop responsible business leaders. Wallace Donham, the second dean of Harvard Business School, spoke about the school's objective being 'the multiplication of men who will handle their current business problems in socially constructive ways.'[55] Hauk and Saez-Marti are unequivocal: 'Business school faculties and deans have an institutional responsibility to socialise students to a model of behaviour that inspires them to respect other institutions in society, especially the basic units of family and community, and to inspire students to accept the responsibilities and obligations that come with occupying society's most powerful positions.'[56] Many business schools do highlight ethical standards and wider responsibilities, but they need to give them far higher priority still, so that graduates place the companies they join under pressure to aspire higher. Most young people entering business are fully aware of global dimensions: John Browne, former chief executive of BP, used to say that new graduates were all keen to join the environment division, small though it was.[57] Business schools would be pushing at an open door.

British banks and corporations have a chance to become world leaders, not by dragging their heels on spreading stakeholding or on environmental and social responsibilities, but by making the weather and taking the lead. As the target of developed countries allocating 0.7 per cent of GDP to development purposes comes under threat during the recession, the scope for British companies to help development directly themselves is considerable. Companies need to look over their own fence and beyond their trade associations, and form partnerships abroad with governments and NGOs. Tesco shows the way with its Value Chain, which integrates international development with its business needs. The same can be said of its contribution to tackling climate change, by helping to develop clean energy and taking a leadership role in reducing its carbon footprint. Within the UK, companies can help build trust locally by embedding within local communities rather than being seen to be excessively centralised. Between 1995 and 2003, some 3,000 bank and building society branches closed in areas with high concentrations of low-income families. Relocalising our banking system is a solution favoured by Philip Blond, author of *Rise of the Red Tories* (2009).[58] The idea, which would include developing local capital, is also supported by the left-wing pressure group Compass, which favours reinvigorating the Post Office network. David Pitt-Watson, a trustee of the IPPR think tank and former City fund manager, argues for the introduction of a 'civil economy' where mechanisms are established to ensure that, to the greatest degree possible, those who handle our savings can be trusted to work on our behalf. He notes that research done by the RSA's Investor Project shows that 'most people just want to give their money to someone local they trust; they don't want the very costly system which so often characterises financial products'.[59] The idea of local savings through the Post Office meets this need because it is simple and organised through an institution which is trusted.

Rebuilding trust in the economy

Three final recommendations will build trust and trusteeship at the level of our national economy. The aim of the national economy has been and is almost everywhere today the maximisation of GDP. We need new measures to compare economies and measure how they are performing, as opposed to our obsession with growth. Data have been telling us for several years that there is little correlation between money and personal life satisfaction. Whilst levels of income are important at the lower end of the scale, the increase of income beyond a certain point does not lead to a continuing rise in life satisfaction. Figure 5.6 could not show more starkly the disjuncture between GDP per capita, or average real income per person, and life satisfaction: the former has almost doubled, while the latter stayed resolutely the same, with around 70 per cent of respondents saying that they are satisfied with their lives.

Figure 5.6: UK life satisfaction and GDP per capita 1973–97[60]

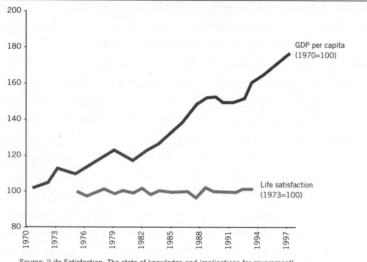

Source: 'Life Satisfaction: The state of knowledge and implications for government'
(Cabinet Office, 2003)

Are we pursuing the wrong goals? The Happy Planet Index (HPI), pioneered by the New Economic Foundation, considers the environment, society and happiness as key factors to be measured. Life satisfaction is typically measured with the following question: 'All things considered, how satisfied are you with your life as a whole these days?' The responses correlate very clearly with the size and strength of social networks, relationship status, level of education, presence or absence of disability, as well as material conditions such as income and employment. When countries enjoy higher life expectancy, more voice within government, higher levels of social capital and better standards of living, country averages tend to be higher.

Any measure for the economy has to also incorporate the trustee aspect of well-being. The HPI integrates this trustee element through a calculation of the ecological footprint necessary to sustain current levels of consumption. 'No moral framework would accept high well-being if it was at the expense of others living today and/or future generations.'[61] The British government led by Tony Blair, a late but powerful convert to climate change, gave the world a decisive lead at the Gleneagles G8 summit in July 2005, and it has given the country a powerful voice on the world stage. The British economy needs to lead the world in producing clean energy. In the nineteenth and twentieth centuries, Britain was a global power by dint of its empire and military might: in the twenty-first it can lead the world through moral authority, utilising our intellectual capital and industrial specialisms. Martin Rees believes that 'this goal is perfectly achievable, if the government gives it the priority. We have the technological base, we have the strength in universities, and it will confer great economic benefits.'[62]

According to the HPI measure the UK recorded an 11 per cent decline in its HPI score from 1961 to 2005.[63] Five years ago, the HPI would have been dismissed as new age: the work of the free-market think tanks was regarded by *The Economist* and by the status quo as similarly faddish until, almost overnight in the mid 1970s, they became the conventional wisdom.[64] New measures of international comparison need urgently to be further developed and widely promulgated; these must be attuned to trust and trusteeship. They could find themselves very quickly becoming the new norm, as indeed they must.

More needs to happen if Britain is to nurture and fully utilise its best human talent. Although there is some recent evidence that the UK may have reached the bottom of its decline in social mobility, access to society's top jobs and professions has become less, not more, socially representative.[65] The Panel on Fair access to the Professions, which reported in July 2009, said the reasons for this stagnation included the professions changing to select only graduates, declining rates of progression into professions from apprenticeships, and a greater concentration of professional and managerial jobs in London and the south-east. It concluded that 'the fact that the UK remains such a persistently unequal society is, in large part, the reason why social mobility is lower than in other less equal nations. Greater equality and more mobility are two sides of the same coin.'[66] Family wealth, private education and privileged access to university remained, it said, the principal routes to the professions.[67]

Change will occur only when the majority of the country believe that wide social differences and vulgar consumerism by the affluent are as socially unacceptable as racism, sexism and other forms of discrimination and exclusion. Government needs to 'level up', not 'level down', with state-funded schools doing far more to give the young from less advantaged backgrounds the same opportunities that independent schools give, or that grammar schools once provided. Universities are only too eager to take children from working-class backgrounds, but will never do so willingly until they merit their places from the quality of their teaching in schools. 'Positive discrimination' by universities in favour of disadvantaged children will detract from the schools having to improve, and lead to new types of unfairness: improving schools so they give pupils the right leg up is the key. Professions need to do much more to build pathways with children from less advantaged backgrounds; HSBC provides a laudable example through its enterprising Education Trust, run by Mary Richardson. Mentoring, role-modelling and paid internship schemes all have a vital role to play in reducing the unrepresentative composition professions currently have. Until there is a change within us, Britain will continue to be the divided, and hence mistrustful, society that it currently is.

Our final recommendation is to float the proposal that the government adopt positive employment policies. Having 2.5 million unemployed and inactive, and increasing police and welfare bills to meet the demands of that number, makes no sense.[68] The unemployed experience mental health problems as well as enhanced physical problems, as do their families, all of which detract massively from trust and social capital. Rather than accepting unemployment as an inevitable fact of life, government should proactively be working to create volunteer forces from the unemployed, for which they would receive marginally higher benefits, to build trust in society, for example, regenerating run-down areas, cleaning up Britain's waterways and beaches, and helping in schools and other social services. Building trust in society stretches to all sections and the waste of human life and ingenuity from unemployment must be addressed if our more trusting society is to be built.

'A kettle and a cup of tea will prove more powerful in building trust and cutting crime than kettling and a truncheon.' *(AFP/Getty Images)*

CHAPTER 6

TRUST IN THE POLICE, THE LAW AND DEFENCE

Every kind of peaceful cooperation among men is primarily based on mutual trust and only secondarily on institutions such as courts of justice and police.

Albert Einstein (1879–1955)

The most basic responsibility of any government is to protect its citizens against attack from abroad and from violence to persons or property at home. If the government fails to fulfil these core functions, the public become angry and lose trust. In this chapter we look at the armed services and the police, the buckling prison and detention system, and our lawyers. The public trust that dangerous criminals will be put in prison and be kept isolated, and they trust lawyers to counsel on the law in an honest and fair manner. These areas are not luxuries: a very high degree of competence, honesty and integrity in the execution of these responsibilities is taken as a given. For the system to work properly, it is necessary for there to be internal trust, i.e. for those in the armed services, the police and the prison services, to trust their leaders, and for their own leaders to trust them.

How trust has been lost

Trust is key within the military. The armed services receive low pay, work far from home, operate under extreme duress, risk their lives, and yet are given commensurately little public recognition when they are away fighting. The rewards are high comradeship, a sense of service and personal satisfaction, rather than pecuniary, material comforts or other perks. When Ipsos MORI asked which institutions in Britain people trusted most (or 'next most') around 29 per cent cited the military. This was still quite high, but behind the Church of England (36 per cent), NHS (47 per cent) and the BBC (50 per cent). However, there was little evidence of distrust in the military: only 15–16 per cent of respondents characterised it as their 'least' or 'next least trusted' institution, which was significantly below mistrust in big British companies (35 per cent), the media in general (44 per cent) and the government (65 per cent).[1]

The British public have great pride in the armed services; an Ipsos MORI poll in January 2006 recorded 87 per cent of respondents agreeing that 'the British armed forces are among the best in the world'.[2] That October, a YouGov poll found that 77 per cent of respondents were proud of the way armed forces were performing their duties.[3] Terence Blacker captures this new mood of admiration: 'It is as if, quite suddenly, the armed forces have come to represent the best of us as surely as other institutions – political, financial, law-enforcing, journalistic – reveal the worst.'[4] Within the army itself, trust levels are high, despite the large numbers of British soldiers killed during the campaign in Iraq (179 from March 2003 to February 2009)[5] and at relentlessly high levels in Afghanistan (204 from November 2001 to 16 August 2009).[6] Regardless of the dangers, the armed services have completed their duties on every occasion they have been asked.

Where trust is low, however, it is in the public's confidence in politicians and their strategy. The Army had prided itself on not losing a war for many generations. Initial enthusiasm for the operation in Iraq fell rapidly; by October 2006, 70 per cent of the public thought there was no clear strategy.[7] Afghanistan has seen similar loss of public support. In October 2001, 56 per cent thought the military campaign was very or fairly effective, a figure which had fallen to 38 per cent by July 2009.[8] During the four months from March to July 2009, reflecting the high number of British fatalities, people who thought the war in Afghanistan was not worthwhile rose from 15 per cent to 22 per cent.[9] A further poll in July found that 50 per cent thought the cause was just but not worth the loss of British lives, with twenty-two British dead that month alone.[10] Trust is also a problem between the military command and the government; many senior officers do not trust civil servants in the Ministry of Defence highly. A senior commander reflects that the current confidence of the senior military officials in the MoD is 'very poor', with paucity of resources, i.e. money and materials, at the heart of the mistrust.

The military's anger stems from the belief that the government expects them to fight with inadequate numbers and equipment, thereby endangering troops and damaging the prospects of success. The public are clear where they stand in the debate about whether current resources are sufficient – in July 2009, 71 per cent said they supported the military and believed the government to be providing 'too little, too late'; only 11 per cent of those polled backed the Prime Minister.[11] Completing this picture of lack of trust in the corridors of power in the MoD, the traditional rivalry between the three armed services is heightened because of the economic downturn, with the Army, Navy, and RAF fighting their corners for scarce resources.

Trust in the police seems to have fallen since the 1950s. However, we should be cautious in drawing conclusions about 'a public attitude' from the polls; Ian Loader and Aogán Mulcahy (2003) talk of 'the coexistence of a *diversity* of public registers' in visions of policing and identification with police.[12] Those who have encounters with the police, as suspects, witnesses or victims, generally have less favourable views, as do the young, ethnic minorities, males and the economically deprived.[13] The first set of data in Figure 6.1, taken from the Ipsos MORI Veracity Index (2008), measures 'telling the truth' as an indicator of police trustworthiness, rather than trust in the effectiveness of the police. It is a matter of obvious concern that the police, whose job it is to ascertain the truth when law-breaching occurs, have such an apparently low reputation for being truthful themselves.

Figure 6.1: Telling the truth as a measure of police trustworthiness[14]

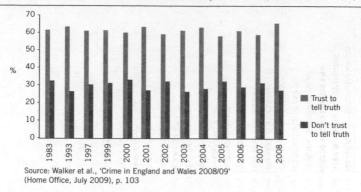

Source: Walker et al., 'Crime in England and Wales 2008/09'
(Home Office, July 2009), p. 103

The police fare a little better when we turn to public trust in their
effectiveness. The British Crime Survey, a household survey, has been
collecting data, including on public satisfaction, for more than twenty-
five years. Figure 6.2 shows a steady drop over the twenty-one years
from 1982 to 2003 in those who thought the local police were doing a
'fairly good' or 'very good' job, but then a rise in those who thought they
were doing a 'good/excellent' job.

Figure 6.2: Ratings of local police 1982–2005/6

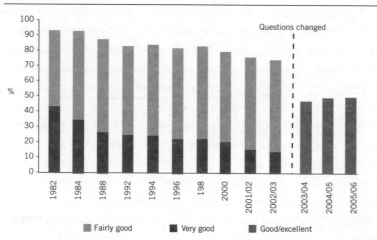

Source: British Crime Survey, 'Measuring Crime for 25 Years', p. 21

Figure 6.3: Trust in the legal system in European countries[15]

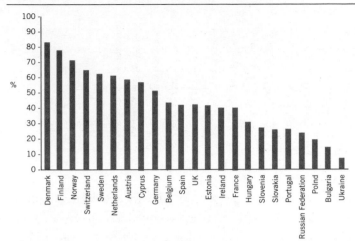

Source: European Social Survey Round 2 data (2004/5), Norwegian Social Science Data Services

Further data reveal that trust in the *local* police has, in recent years, risen steadily, with 67 per cent polled stating they were doing a good or excellent job in 2009, up from 63 per cent since 2006.[16] These are good figures for the police. But the rise in private security firms can be seen as a measure of the loss of trust of individuals and corporations in the capability of the police to defend their material and commercial wealth. The British Security Industry Association (representing more than 70 per cent of the industry) says that companies in their organisation currently employ 75,500 security officers and that there are an estimated 4.25 million CCTV cameras installed in the UK.[17] The global security market is set to rise from US $28 billion in 2003 to over US $170 billion by 2015, a sixfold increase in just twelve years.[18] The wealthy across the world are abandoning the free police service, as they have the free health and education services, and paying high prices for the privilege of this bespoke provision. Equally, they have more to defend than the average man. Are we moving towards a two-tier service?

We have been losing trust in our prison service from the mid-1990s, with the percentage believing prisons were doing a 'good' or 'excellent' job falling from 38 per cent in 1996 to 27 per cent in 2005.[19] Confidence in the justice system overall in Britain has similarly declined, from 65.7 per cent in 1981 to 49.1 per cent in 1999–2000.[20] The European Social Survey data show further that trust in the legal system is fairly low in the UK compared to some other European nations, with most of the countries to which Britain would want to compare itself enjoying higher levels of trust (see Figure 6.3).

The now familiar Ipsos MORI poll on Trust in the Professions found lawyers rated very poorly compared to other professionals, including doctors and head teachers. Only 13 per cent of those polled said they had a great deal of respect for lawyers and the job they did, 35 per cent had little or no respect. Doctors received four times this level of respect with 58 per cent, and head teachers three times the respect with 38 per cent.[21] The Committee on Standards in Public Life surveyed people's attitudes towards conduct in public life in 2008. They found that 82 per cent of respondents claim to trust judges, a figure beaten again only by family doctors and head teachers.[22] If judges are highly trusted, then the problem must lie elsewhere in the profession, presumably with barristers and solicitors. A survey for the Bar Standards Board appears to confirm this, with only 24 per cent expressing trust in lawyers, a result described by the chairman, Ruth Deech, as 'underwhelming'.[23] The discrepancy is likely to lie in the nature of the jobs: judges are impartial figures who mediate in a dispute, while solicitors and barristers represent one party within it and are fundamentally partisan, while their services are available only at a cost. It is conceivable then, that despite a negative impression of lawyers, clients of lawyers rate the service they receive highly, as 82 per cent of respondents to a Solicitors Regulation Authority Survey claimed at the end of 2008.[24]

Why have we lost trust?

It is easy to see, with Iraq and Afghanistan, why trust has become an issue for the British armed services. The army thrives on success, and failure often leads to a poisonous whirlwind of accusations. Complicating trust in both wars still further are the question marks over their legitimacy. Should Britain be fighting at all? It makes for a toxic brew. 'There's no doubting that our relationship with the public has been made harder because some see Iraq as a discretionary war and its genesis and prosecution were so mired in controversy, and in Afghanistan, while the American effort has been huge, we frankly have the minimum backing from other NATO countries,' said a senior British soldier, summing up a general view.[25]

Fighting in Northern Ireland for nearly forty years after 1969 did not provoke the same questions of legitimacy because the fighting was conducted on British soil, while the Cold War, which occupied the British forces for a similar period, was directed against a clear threat to the British public. In Iraq and Afghanistan, it is hard to argue that the troops are fighting to make Britain safer from terrorism, the greatest fear among the British public; the concerns are rather that the wars might *provoke* terrorists and make Britain *less* safe. Some 58 per cent of people interviewed by ICM after the London bombings in July 2005 felt that the terrorist attacks were linked to British involvement in Iraq.[26] A *Guardian/ICM* poll found that 6 per cent of all households in the UK had a member attend a march against the Iraq war in 2003, the biggest protest in British history.[27] Against that background, the surprise is that the protests have not continued, and that mistrust in the government's conduct of the war is not much higher.

The high levels of mistrust between the armed services and the Ministry of Defence can be explained almost exclusively by disagreements over the appropriate troop levels and materials which the military judges are necessary to win the war and to minimise casualties. The media have been supportive of the cause – the media like war, and see themselves as 'getting behind our boys' – which has further whipped up public discontent. The press made much of coroner Andrew Walker saying in 2006 that the death of paratrooper Captain James Phillipson was an 'unforgivable breach of trust' because he had inadequate equipment,[28] while the *Daily Telegraph* spoke out in July 2009 against forty-eight apparently 'avoidable deaths' in Afghanistan, more than a third of the total of British soldiers killed in action at that time.[29]

British military spending over the last ten years was based upon the assumption that there would be only one medium-sized conflict being fought at a time. Instead, concurrent fighting in Iraq and Afghanistan – both conflicts a little bigger than medium scale – meant inevitable shortcuts and economies, which damaged fighting capabilities. Public distrust has been directed at the civil servants in the Ministry of Defence, who respond that they are only trying to protect ministers. Gordon Brown himself is the principal target, especially because when Chancellor from 1997 to 2007, he was renowned for being no friend of the armed services. He was described by a former chief of the Defence Staff as 'unsympathetic' and was criticised for blocking defence spending which Prime Minister Blair had approved.[30]

The difficult relationship between the professional heads of the three services and the chief of the Defence Staff has led to some unsavoury counter-briefing, much of which has been made public through the press. The prosecution of war is always difficult and trust is hard to build in war – the history of D-Day, and subsequent operations in Europe, reveals lack of trust between the Americans and the British – but at no point since the Second World War has trust between military chiefs and politicians been lower than it is today. Richard Dannatt (chief of General Staff, 2006–9) was the most outspoken of the military chiefs. About Iraq, he said: 'The military campaign we fought in 2003 effectively kicked the door in.'[31] Shortly after his appointment he accused the government of breaking 'the military covenant' between soldier and country, and on his last visit to Afghanistan shortly before he was due to retire in August 2009, he said provocatively: 'Self-evidently, if I move in an American helicopter it is because I have not got a British helicopter.'[32] Yet Dannatt vented only a fraction of his frustration in public.

Harder to explain is why British servicemen kept fighting so loyally in Iraq, as they have done in Afghanistan, when they know they should be better equipped, and when their cause is unclear and disputed. The explanation has much to do with the soldiers' admiration for Dannatt and for their officers who (as casualties show) have led from the front, and with the high morale cultivated within the profession; there is much here to be learnt by other institutions. Not that the Army has always been free of guilt itself. Public trust was shaken by the investigation into the abuse of ten Iraqis in custody by British troops in 2003. Back at home, there is still a culture of cover-ups and bullying, which it has been alleged was a factor in four deaths among recruits at the Deepcut barracks alone within seven years.

It is puzzling why trust in the police is not higher, because the public – the vast majority of whom are law-abiding – should see them as allies who protect and assist them, rather than viewing them with suspicion. Trust in the police's honesty, oddly, is a bigger problem than trust in their effectiveness, with their integrity taking a bad dent in a series of very high-profile misdemeanours. The Stephen Lawrence case was the worst. In April 1993 Lawrence, a black teenager, was stabbed to death while waiting with a friend at a bus stop in Eltham, south London. His killers were not brought to justice by the police despite their having prime suspects and Lawrence's lawyer did much to publicise it as an 'impact case' which exposed police malpractice.[33] An inquiry led by William Macpherson, reporting in 1999 on the way police handled their investigations, suggested that errors in the taking of evidence and 'institutional racism' were jointly responsible for the failure to convict his murderers, with suggestions of corruption in the force and links between the accused and policemen.[34] An ICM poll taken in July 1998 found that 48 per cent of Londoners had less confidence in the Metropolitan Police in the light of the inquiry, with 75 per cent agreeing that deficiencies had been highlighted in Met procedures.[35] An Ipsos MORI poll conducted in February 1999 found that only a third of respondents felt less favourably towards the police in the wake of the investigation. Among black and Asian respondents, however, the proportion of those who looked on the police less favourably was nearer two thirds, at 59 per cent.[36] As of today, no one has been convicted of Lawrence's murder.

Distrust by ethnic minorities and the perception that they are being targeted by police is not surprising. Statistics printed in the journal *Criminal Justice Matters* suggest that the number of Asians subjected to stop-and-search powers by police increased following 9/11.[37] A 2003 BBC documentary made by an undercover journalist who joined Greater Manchester Police captured incidents of extreme racism and widespread use of pejorative racist terms among probationers. It was followed by the departure of several officers. In October 2008, Ian Blair, commissioner of the Metropolitan Police, resigned, a move which coincided with the escalation into the public domain of the internal race row at Scotland Yard. In 2008, Alfred John, chairman of the Metropolitan Black Police Association, reinstated the 'black boycott' of the police, first instituted in 2003, saying he would actively discourage ethnic minorities from joining a force he claimed had not reformed in the ten years since Lawrence's murder.[38]

The high profile killing of Jean Charles de Menezes on 22 July 2005, fifteen days after the London 7/7 suicide bombings, saw police error followed by accusations of deceit. Operating at a time of acute suspicion of terrorists, police mistakenly killed the innocent Brazilian man in an Underground carriage, but then compounded matters by trying to cover their tracks. Officers claimed they shouted 'armed police' before shooting him seven times in the head. Passengers on the Underground denied that this warning was ever given.[39] The jury accepted their evidence, rather than that of the police. Any damage to trust was short lived, as a poll two months later found that 86 per cent thought the Metropolitan Police had responded well in general to the attacks in July.[40] But doubts still rumbled on.

Concerns of heavy-handed police conduct reared up again during the G20 protests in April 2009, with their policy of 'kettling' (keeping protesters in tight, cordoned-off groups for a period to control them) particularly coming under fire after it emerged that many non-protesters were inadvertently caught up in the crowds and prevented from leaving. Ian Tomlinson, a member of the public, died following physical contact with the police, who initially claimed Tomlinson had collapsed and was being helped by police officers who were themselves under attack.[41] It was later suggested that Tomlinson had been attacked by a protestor 'dressed in police uniform'.[42] But the incident was caught on camera by members of the public and circulated on the internet for the world to see that the police's claims were wrong. Further skirmishes between the police and the people were captured on the cameras and mobile phones of the public, with one officer filmed slapping and hitting a remonstrating protestor with his truncheon. The footage also showed that officers had obscured their badges to avoid identification.

The police do a difficult job very well much of the time, and it is galling for them that it is the occasions when things go wrong which stick in public memory. But there are legitimate concerns about the tendency to close ranks in the face of external criticism. Had the police been candid and displayed the kind of leadership praised by Cicero and Confucius in probing the occasions in which errors were made, they would have won the public's sympathy, not its ire. They open themselves up to criticisms from liberals and the left. A report by the think tank Reform focuses on the 'accountability gap' in police hierarchy,[43] while *New Statesman* journalist James Macintyre writes that 'because of such long and sustained support from the governing classes, the police remain the *last closed shop in Britain today*. This lack of oversight has led to the tolerance of incompetence, violence and racism.'[44] But the police are now also being criticised by the right. Damian Green, the prominent Conservative frontbencher, was arrested in December 2008 for handling leaked Home Office documents. 'It's absolutely crucial that senior police look at the way they interact with normal, respectable people. The danger is of the police being on one side of the barricades and all civilians being on the other.'[45]

A breakdown in trust across the whole criminal justice system can be heard in comments made by Simon Reed, vice chairman of the Police Federation, who said in the wake of the G20 protests that the police were being blamed unfairly. He suggested that low morale among police was spread by the criticisms. 'The public has no faith in the system,' he said, 'the courts do not always convict, criminals continue to commit crimes, officers are growing disillusioned.'[46] Many of the problems the police face do indeed stem from factors beyond their control. In November 2006, a leaked document from the Prime Minister's Strategy Unit revealed the estimation that 80 per cent of the recent decrease in crime had been the result merely of more favourable economic factors.[47] 'Long-term trends in crime broadly mirror economic and social trends', concurs crime authority Marian FitzGerald.[48] To Robert Reiner, another leading writer on the police, societal problems – rising inequality, unemployment, diversity and declining deference – explain many of the difficulties police encounter.[49] For all their difficult circumstances, the perception of police dishonesty continues, among not just the liberal left but also the judiciary. 'They tell lies that would be unacceptable in any other public body. It is destructive to law and order when those charged with keeping it don't tell the truth themselves', said one senior judge.[50]

When Robert Peel founded the Metropolitan Police in 1829 he said: 'The basic mission for which the police exist is to prevent crime and disorder.'[51] The role of the police has widened, but their core purpose is still to minimise crime. Figure 6.4 shows the staggeringly dramatic rise in crime per head in the last century.

Figure 6.4: Indictable offences known to the police (per thousand population) in England and Wales 1900–1997[52]

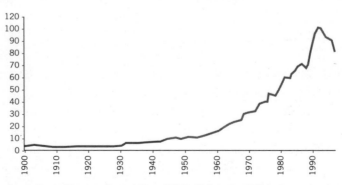

Source: House of Commons Research Paper 99/111, 21 December 1999, p. 4

According to Home Office crime figures, in 1950 there were 1,053 recorded offences per 100,000 people in England and Wales; by 2002/3 this figure had risen to 11,323 per 100,000. It has purportedly since dropped to 8,579 in 2008/9,[53] and the government claims that crime has been on the decrease for the last fifteen years. Figure 6.5 shows the number of incidents recorded by the police, and those reported to the British Crime Survey (which asks a representative sample of people about their experience and perception of crime in the last year, whether they reported it to the police or not). The survey paints an encouraging picture where crime peaked in the mid-1990s and has been falling steadily ever since.

Figure 6.5: Trends in BCS and police recorded crime 1981–2005/6[54]

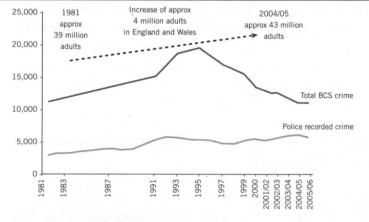

Source: British Crime Survey, 'Measuring Crime for 25 Years', p. 8

These optimistic figures have been contested, however, principally since the survey asks householders if they have been victims of crime, so excludes crimes such as murder and drug possession, and, prior to January 2009, those under sixteen years were not included in the survey. The police's own recorded crime figures, which have also shown a slight decline in crime recently, are thought to be less reliable because of fluctuations in victim reporting and police recording.[55] Many claim the target-driven culture of New Labour has pressured police to register crimes in as low a category as possible. Opposition parties who are critical of these figures argue that any decline there may have been in British crime is less than the EU average.[56] Whatever the truth, the public *believes* that crime has increased, with the proportion of those perceiving an increase in crime nationally rising sharply from the already high figure of 65 per cent in 2007/8 to 75 per cent in 2008/9.[57]

The public have mixed confidence in the police to clear up minor crimes, or to be there when they need them.[58] Public anxiety focuses on anti-social behaviour and juvenile crime rather than burglary, which people are less likely to encounter. They expect the police to capture criminals, but success rates have declined. Detection rates nearly halved in the fifty years after 1951, when 47 per cent of all crimes were detected, compared to only 26 per cent in 2004/5. Conviction rates also fell from 96 per cent in 1951 to 74 per cent in 2004/5.[59] Admittedly, crime rates have risen during the period as social inequality rises, but it is understandable that the public have become uncertain about the police's effectiveness, and as a consequence, many crimes are left unreported.

The knee-jerk reaction to any problem is often to reach for greater powers, and to resort to strong-armed extrinsic measures or greater accountability. One sees it in teaching all the time: 'We will punish the rotten lot of them' goes up the cry when some child humiliates a teacher. It is in the interest of the malign al-Qaeda, as of other terrorist bodies, that the governments they are targeting should so increase surveillance of their own people that it makes life in those societies intolerable for them. In the eight years since 9/11 and again after the 7/7 atrocities in 2005 in Britain, anti-terror laws have invested the police with a whole range of powers which even many on the right of politics now consider intrusive. Police surveillance has indeed reached extraordinary levels: in 2007, Privacy International declared Britain the most monitored country in Europe, and placed us in a special 'endemic surveillance society' category alongside Russia and China.[60] Libertarians believe anti-terrorism legislation is in serious danger of undermining the social contract in

Britain. Shami Chakrabarti, the director of Liberty, told *The Economist*: 'People were sold a lot of bad laws, in a hurry, on the basis that it would never affect them: it was going to be the bad guys.'[61] Home Office figures show a total of 42,000 people were stopped and searched under anti-terror laws in 2006/7, which increased to 124,700 in 2007/8 – only 1 per cent of those stopped were arrested.[62] The public mostly understands the job the police need to do to minimise the risk of a terrorist attack, and the sensitivities involved, but the police seem to have alienated large numbers of the general public in doing it.

The police themselves have been hampered by bureaucracy gone mad, which requires them to fill in a form every time they stop a member of the public in the street. The task takes the officer an average of seven minutes, plus untold amounts of time spent having to follow up the reports. All this administration takes the police still further away from solving crime and from interacting with the public. The reduction in number of familiar and approachable policemen from the street has been a final factor in loss of trust. In 1981, 49 per cent of the public said that they had had contact with the police in the previous year, whereas by 2005/6 the figure had fallen to 39 per cent.[63] The nature of the contact has also changed. Those contacting the police in 1981 were most commonly asking for directions; twenty-five years later it was to report a crime.[64] Research by Marian FitzGerald and others reveals that the public most want the police to spend time on foot patrol (58 per cent), compared to just 27 per cent who believe the police should spend more time on car patrolling.[65]

Lack of public trust in the prison service is straightforward to understand. What the public wants is for prisons to be effective in reforming prisoners, for the cost to be reasonable, and for the service to avoid sending back out into the world people who will commit more crimes. The prison population in August 2009 was just over 84,000, pushing its maximum capacity of 85,000 – an increase of around 10,000 inmates from early 2004.[66] Heavier sentencing, particularly as a result of the 2003 Criminal Justice Act, has been responsible for the upward pressure on numbers. It is widely argued that there has been inadequate recognition that the problems of many inmates – mental illness, learning difficulties and deprivation (half of all young offenders have literacy and numeracy levels below that of an eleven year old, despite an average age of seventeen)[67] – are not best served within prisons. According to the BBC, overcrowding led to the early release of some 50,000 prisoners between June 2007 and March 2009, who had been responsible for more than 1,000 alleged crimes, including murders.[68]

Very high reoffending rates do not suggest that the system is effectively reforming prisoners, and the popular belief that prison is the 'university for the criminal' has some justice: 67 per cent of those in prison in 2007 had previously served prison sentences, compared to 51 per cent in 1992.[69] Reoffending by ex-prisoners is estimated to cost £11 billion annually.[70] It seems that prisons are doomed to failure because they seek to achieve two objectives which are incompatible: punishment and reform. The latter cannot be achieved by segregation from the rest of society, and association with fellow, often hardened, criminals. A vast proportion of crimes are motivated by drug addiction and reform is hindered because so many offenders continue to use drugs while in prison. The public wonders how the drugs manage to come in past all the checks without complicity and lose trust in the prison service accordingly. Trust in the efficiency of the prison service is further unsettled when prisoners are seemingly able to continue running their criminal empires from behind bars. The riot at Ashwell in April 2009 was an unwelcome reminder of the riots that dogged prisons twenty-five years ago.

High trust in judges compared to generally low levels of trust in lawyers overall is hard to explain, especially when the press pillories judges who they believe have given too lenient sentences. The current *bête noire* is Judge Elizabeth Fisher, billed as Britain's most lenient judge. Many of her sentences have been appealed against and the sentences increased. In August 2008, Daniel Gordon, 22, attacked a woman in a bungalow in Birmingham and sexually assaulted her. Fisher gave Gordon four years. 'Wholly inadequate', said the Court of Appeal: 'it should not have been less than ten years.'[71] Low trust in barristers is likely to derive from a mixture of social exclusiveness, archaic dress and language in court (where they refer to defendants in the third person) and high fees. Concerns about solicitors include the level of their fees and their tendency to pursue litigation for pecuniary gain, which fuels a culture of blame between individuals, and companies and institutions. The adversarial nature of litigation means that the losing side is likely to blame the lawyer for the loss – moreover, an untutored public may associate the defence lawyer in a criminal, say murder, trial as amoral and pursuing financial gain alone.

We are becoming an increasingly litigious society, as is the case in the US, 16 per cent of whose nationals claimed in 2005 to believe in their justice system.[72] For lawyers to encourage individuals to take legal action where there has been gross negligence is justifiable, but unsettling authentic trust, which has made doctors, dentists, and other professionals overly cautious, is not.

The law is expensive to access. Cuts of almost £200 million in legal aid are currently being made and financial eligibility for it restricted.[73] With virtually no legal aid available for civil cases, it can be argued that employing the services of the law is increasingly the privilege of the rich. Those of lesser means feel little reason to trust a system that seems only to be run by, and to the benefit of affluent white people: the old quip that 'the law is open to everyone in the same way as the Ritz Hotel' holds true.[74] The Sutton Trust found that whereas more solicitors are beginning to come from state schools, the social exclusivity of judges and barristers has remained largely unchanged, with 76 per cent of judges and 68 per cent of barristers privately educated in 2004, little changed from the mid-1980s.[75] Judges are still overwhelmingly white, male, above average age and from well-off backgrounds. Justices of the peace or magistrates, who are unpaid, are disproportionately white, female and middle class. Although efforts are being made across the board to alter these demographics, the route to becoming a judge, which is still predominately via the Bar, militates against working-class children who cannot afford the expense of training. Barristers' chambers are reluctant to provide comprehensive funding as each barrister is self-employed and they gather in chambers only to share expenses.

Corruption is less a source of worry with lawyers than with the police and prison service, though incidents do arise and certainly cause concern, as with the case of 'Britain's richest solicitor guilty of exploiting sick miners for fees': this case involved the serious professional misconduct claim brought against two solicitors in November 2008 whose joint earnings were £23 million.[76] Lawyers have a long way to go before they are seen to be making law available to all – regardless of money – in a fair and straightforward way, and before the profession represents a cross-section of modern Britain.

How to rebuild trust

The core to rebuilding trust in the armed services, and within them, is to ensure that they are properly funded. The decision has been taken that Britain is to continue in Afghanistan: Dannatt's successor, David Richards, announced in August 2009 that Britain would be involved in Afghanistan for 'the next thirty to forty years'.[77] Securing that funding will be difficult, as it will mean allocating the military a larger share of the public expenditure budget, which is set to be reduced in 2010. If this money cannot be found, government will continue to come under fire for leading the country into a war but not being prepared to back it fully. Money needs also to be spent on looking after troops' housing, education and mental health better. Dannatt warned in 2007 that 'the tank of goodwill now runs on vapour; many experienced staff are talking of leaving'.[78] Britain's care for its troops lags behind the United States, which has a highly developed system of veteran care, and where far better provision is made for the armed forces while they are still in active service. Overall, the armed services merit the high levels of trust placed in them, but must continue to guard against informal malpractice, and be candid when it occurs.

Police practice has improved considerably in recent years, despite them operating in an extremely difficult environment, where public expectations are unrealistically high. But they fall short of the trustworthiness and example of the armed forces. For all the hard work and skills of many individual officers and their commanders, the police fail to achieve this same public recognition. They should merit high levels of public confidence in their honesty and proficiency; Peel spoke of the need for the police to 'maintain a relationship with the public that gives reality to the historic tradition that the police are the public and the public are the police'.[79] Having a trusted and highly esteemed police is entirely possible. Three changes are required to see trust rise: leadership, culture and strategy. Police leadership has improved. More graduates are joining the service, and many senior police staff have master's degrees or higher. But the search for better leadership needs to go still further. A Sandhurst-style leadership college is strongly opposed by the police, but might help develop a more independent-thinking style of police leader. Better pay would bring in a higher calibre of recruit. What the police service needs above all is a leader, ideally a succession of leaders, at its very apex who provide a new, Peel-style vision from top to bottom: a vision that the police are there to serve and the public are always to be treated with great respect. In this way the police would both support and encourage good citizenship. Where the police make errors, the service from now on will be fierce in its commitment to root out and communicate the truth.

The culture in the police is improving in many respects. A passion for service to the community and a sense of the high honour and privilege of working for the police, which is present in the best police officers, needs to permeate every pore of their work. The police have their codes of conduct, but they seem to have less impact than, for example, the Army's 'values and standards code', which highlights 'mutual trust'; it is taught to recruits, and is reinforced at every promotion, in training and throughout the year. The forces must demonstrate their commitment to create a genuinely diverse police force through recruitment. There are already some promising signs of this, as the growing number of openly gay and lesbian officers testifies. Forces must also be rigorous in disciplining those guilty of racism, or corruption: as the corruption expert Robert Klitgaard argues, examples need to be made to deal with corruption.[80] To help the police communicate in more friendly ways with the public, more time needs to be devoted to teaching them social skills and emotional intelligence. The hearts and minds of the British public are there for the winning over. With that will come their trust.

Community policing provides visible figures of authority whose presence offers the public reassurance about their own security and builds trust in the police. Moves towards neighbourhood policing and the creation of Police Community Support officers in 2002, heralded by professor in criminal justice Barry Loveday as 'overwhelmingly successful',[81] have gone some way to meet that need. The overriding attitude of the police needs to change from a presumption of mistrust to a presumption of trust in the public: the strategy must be 'positive policing' similar to the 'positive health' we advocate for the NHS. The main priority must be to deter crime from happening. As happens in the best schools, a highly visible presence with staff befriending pupils diminishes the likelihood of anti-social behaviour; the problems occur when the students are alienated by abrasive and surly teachers, and do not enjoy positive interactions with them. As in the best schools, graffiti and petty vandalism are not tolerated. New York in the 1990s under Mayor Giuliani, which saw a 75 per cent drop in crime from peak rates,[82] is an example of the success of the theory that by following up smaller crimes, one deters larger crimes. The approach has been tried in Britain, poorly branded as 'zero tolerance'. Ray Mallon, mayor of Middlesbrough, managed to cut crime rates by 20 per cent in nine months.[83] The initiative, entitled Raising Hope, focused on creating a clean and safe environment – allaying public fears of crime, reducing anti-social behaviour and regenerating run-down areas,[84] rather than relying on installing more CCTV cameras. A report commissioned by the Home Office in 2005 concluded that 'CCTV is an ineffective tool if the aim is to reduce overall crime rates and to make people feel safer'.[85] Surveillance, as we have repeatedly seen, does not build inner trust. Human contact does. To help bring the police down out of their police station citadels, police boxes should be erected all round cities and towns, as the Japanese have with *kobans,* usually manned by three to four officers who help with mundane enquiries as well as providing deterrence, reassurance and a quick response unit. A kettle and a cup of tea will prove more powerful in building trust and cutting crime than kettling and a truncheon.

A sadder and more counter-productive system can hardly be said to exist in Britain than the prison service, for all the dedication, skill and compassion shown by many within it. Does one simply accept the status quo in which prison is often a training ground for further crime, or is there a better way? Is trust helpful? 'Restorative justice' is centred around rebuilding trust, it is where victims, offenders and communities are brought together to decide on the response to a crime. Here, the criminal confronts the wider community, their own family and the victim's suffering, in a realisation of the advice of Richard Reeves, director of Demos, that 'our best defence against crime is not the police or judicial system, it's each other'.[86] Crime occurs largely when there is anonymity: soldiers do not like killing an enemy who they experience as a human being (brilliantly caught in Erich Maria Remarque's *All Quiet on the Western Front,* where hero Paul Baumer spends the night in a trench with a dying Frenchman he has stabbed). Neither do criminals, unless particularly perverted, like to engage with the individual humanity of their victims. Face-to-face contact makes harming another very uncomfortable because it reminds us of our common humanity. Trust and goodness are in all our cores, even those of the vilest criminals, albeit very deeply hidden. Where victims are willing, face-to-face encounters with those who have wronged them can heal not only the victim's distress, but also that of the criminals – the Restorative Justice Consortium finds that 27 per cent fewer crimes are consequently committed by those who undergo the programme.[87] It can pave the way for an apology from the criminal and even an all-important forgiveness from the victim, distasteful or repellent, though the thought might at first seem to them. It can help to reduce reoffending 'by fostering remorse, not fear'.[88] Projects such as 'community payback' and 'antisocial behaviour contracts', make the criminal immediately accountable to others rather than delaying this in favour of the shorter term solution of custody. Britain can learn from the Truth and Reconciliation Commission which operated in South Africa in the 1990s, and set up a similar body to adjudicate in such cases.

In the ultimate test of trust, more humanity can be introduced into prisons to help change the hearts of inmates (not even the most right wing of observers can believe that the current system is doing much to reform people and stop them reoffending). James Mill, father of the better known John Stuart, and his close friend Jeremy Bentham wrote about penal reform and punishment with his colleague Bhutan. Like Plato, they believed that the prime purpose of punishment was less retribution, deterrence or removal (of a dangerous person from the community) than reform; literally, they wanted to re-form the inmates through proper education so they would be safe to be released into society to build, not further detract from, trust. Prisons today are like zoos for caged animals, and need to be turned into museums. They should be rebuilt, with all inmates being located in small groups like houses in boarding schools, where they eat, sleep and work. These communities would consist of only thirty people, and they would not meet other prisoners outside, greatly reducing the opportunities for corruption and enhancing human scale. If we refuse to teach people right from wrong clearly, if our police continue to inspire suspicion rather than affection, and if we treat those who have offended against society as animals, trust will reduce, and we will all lose.

A similar principle can be applied to legal procedure. It is imperative that we move away, where possible, from court-based solutions. Court cases have become too long, expenses are huge and even the winning party can end up feeling they have lost when it comes to pay its court fees. Alternative means of dispute resolution, primarily mediation, should become the first port of call, particularly in civil cases. There are significant psychological benefits of mediation – both parties feel they themselves have achieved the solution, which leaves the chances of further dispute greatly reduced. Where cases do go to courts, judges could manage cases better by using the principle of 'equality of arms', which accords equal time to both parties, to set limits on the amount of money recoverable from the case and the level of legal expertise attainable, and to cap case length in advance. The profession is already seeking actively to make its demographic more representative, although this will take some time to filter through to judges, often appointed after the age of forty-five. The number of women training as solicitors nowadays often trumps the number of men, and access to the Bar for those with modest means has been much improved now that trainee barristers receive salaries during pupilages. However, the profession remains appealing for many for its high salaries. The avarice of lawyers must be restrained, through limiting lawyers' access to legal aid by capping the annual public funds a lawyer can receive, and in time we should move towards a fused system in which the casework of barristers and solicitors is no longer differentiated. Particular burden of responsibility for building trust must fall on those whose remuneration is so high.

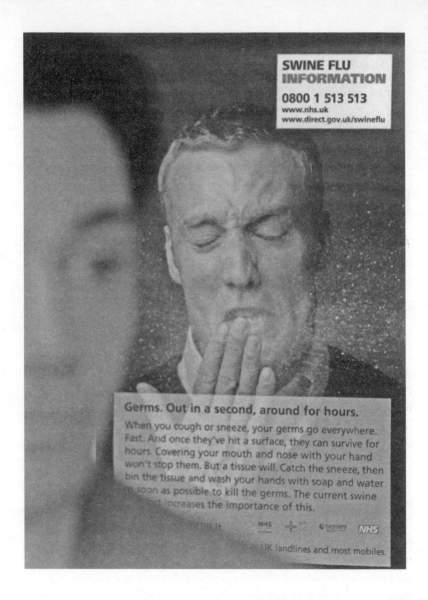

Public fear over swine flu repeatedly threatened to explode into widespread panic. The media spread fear like a virus, and the public did not know who to trust. *(Getty Images)*

CHAPTER 7

TRUST IN HEALTH, EDUCATION AND SOCIAL SERVICES

There is no higher religion than human service. To work for the common good is the greatest creed.

Woodrow Wilson (1856–1924), 28th US President

This chapter looks at services which provide for some of the most vulnerable people in society. Since the advent of the welfare state, the public has looked to government to provide these services, with only the affluent opting out and paying for private provision. In the 1940s and 1950s, people were reluctant to criticise the new services, but then followed a prolonged period of disappointment in them. Because of the vulnerability or youth of those who use these services, and because for most the state is the only provider, trust is particularly significant. 'Core to the trust relationship is the experience of vulnerability,' say Abelson, Miller and Giacomini in *Health Policy*, as it 'provides the impetus for placing trust, or seeds distrust, mistrust and resilience.'[1] Expert knowledge is central to public services: the professionals who deliver them have qualifications which instil respect, though their expert knowledge is increasingly being challenged by the internet, which has made an 'expert' of us all.

A barometer for testing faith in public services, as well as levels of disposable income, is the number of people who choose private provision:

according to the Association of British Insurers, those with some form of private medical insurance increased from 1.3 million in 1979 to 6.5 million in 2001 and 7.3 million in 2008,[2] for example, although these figures include those with corporate cover. The recession has seen some people move back to public services for financial reasons,[3] but the high political priority they have been given by Labour and the extra money pumped in have also been responsible for growing contentment. The British Social Attitudes report published in January 2009, for example, found that more than half (51 per cent) of the people surveyed in 2007 said they were 'very' or 'quite' satisfied with the NHS, an increase of 9 per cent since 2000 and 17 per cent since 1997.[4] The report stated: 'It is hard to resist the conclusion that massively increased NHS spending over the last seven years, enabling [the service] to increase its staffing considerably and . . . reduce waiting times to their lowest since the inception of the NHS, must have played a significant part in boosting satisfaction.'[5]

Has trust been lost?

Health, of all areas in this book, is the one where trust in the honesty and proficiency of the service is most important. We are entrusting doctors with nothing less important than our own lives, and those of our children. 'Our patients trust us with confidence and information. They trust us to apply up-to-date and effective technical skills to their problems. They trust us to care for them, medically and emotionally. Above all, they trust us to place their interests first,' says Mike Pringle in the *British Journal of General Practice*.[6] Doctors have been the most trusted professionals in Britain for many years: as Figure 7.1 shows, in 1983, 82 per cent of people trusted them to tell the truth and since 2002, over 90 per cent have consistently trusted them to do so. In 2008, the figure rose to 92 per cent.[7] The drop in trust after 1999 may have been attributable to the case of Harold Shipman, responsible as a doctor for the death of up to 250 patients.

Doctors and nurses are also trusted very highly for their professional competence, with nurses receiving scores of between 94 per cent and

96 per cent for public satisfaction in Ipsos MORI surveys from 1999 to 2004, and doctors rating between 89 per cent and 92 per cent.[8]

Figure 7.1: Trust in doctors to tell the truth[9]

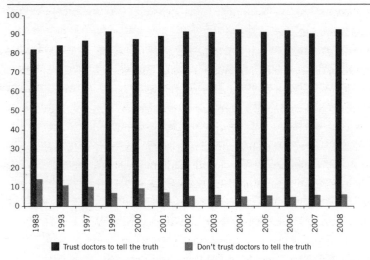

Trust doctors to tell the truth   Don't trust doctors to tell the truth

Source: Ipsos MORI, *Trust in the Professions: Veracity Index* (2008)

Doctors score very highly in polls compared to those in administrative roles, too. The Survey of Public Attitudes Towards Conduct in Public Life (2008) found 94 per cent trusted them to tell the truth (up from 92 per cent in 2004), over twice as high as the 44 per cent who trusted senior NHS managers (unchanged from 2004).[10] M. W. Calnan and E. Sanford probe this further and discover that 'the highest levels of distrust were found in relation to . . . waiting times and the consequences for the patient of cost cutting'.[11] The known and local individuals in healthcare, as in non-health sectors, are typically the most trusted. Surveys find a clear difference in the minds of the public between the 'national' health service that they read negative stories about in the press, and the 'local' health services which they, their family and friends use: 67 per cent agreed with the statement that their 'local' NHS was providing them with good service, compared to only 50 per cent for the 'national' health service.[12] On the national level, the Ipsos MORI *End of Year Review* in 2008 found, however, no doubt because of the economic downturn, most respondents believing that the NHS would get worse over the following few years.[13]

Public trust in the NHS is highest for 'providing care in an emergency' (94 per cent) and 'delivering babies' (87 per cent). At the bottom for trust is 'protecting from infection in hospital' (33 per cent), with the 'superbug' MRSA partly in mind, while 'care for the elderly' (41 per cent) is also clearly a concern.[14] Trust is greatest among the most frequent users of the NHS. Healthy males who use the service less tend to be less trusting and respectful than those who use it regularly.[15] For all the quibbles, however, 82 per cent of respondents in a 2008 BBC poll said that they were 'proud of the health service', and half claimed 'it was still the envy of the world',[16] support which manifested itself widely and publicly when the NHS was criticised in the summer 2009 debate over Barack Obama's healthcare proposals in the United States.

Figure 7.2: Trust in teachers to tell the truth[17]

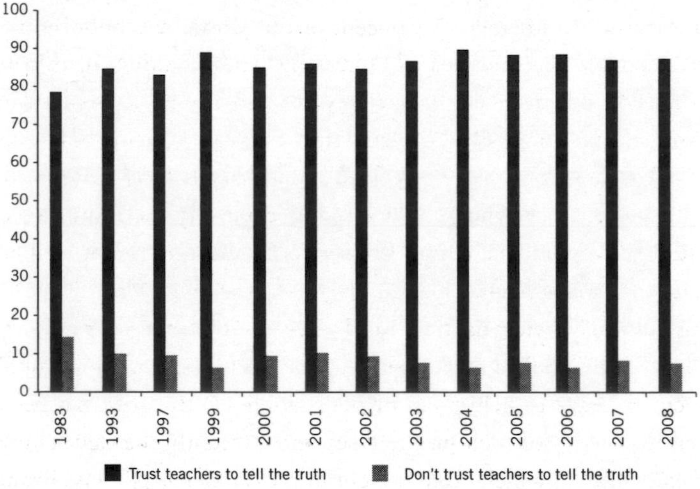

Trust teachers to tell the truth ■ Don't trust teachers to tell the truth

Source: Ipsos MORI, *Trust in the Professions: Veracity Index* (2008)

Information on schools is much scarcer. Head teachers have always rated highly: 83 per cent in 2008 said they trusted them to tell the truth in one survey, compared to 84 per cent in 2004.[18] But trust in teachers generally runs even higher: 87 per cent told Ipsos MORI they trusted them to tell the truth in 2008, up from 84 per cent in 1993, as Figure 7.2 shows.

Circumstantial evidence abounds of parents becoming less respectful of teachers' judgement, and the rise of the 'helicopter' parent who hovers over their child throughout their time in school, swooping down on any suspected slight or low marks. But parents still turn up to parents' evenings dressed smartly, and it is hard to find overall evidence of increased distrust. Schools fare less well in polls than heads and teachers. The British Social Attitudes Survey in 2007 found that, when asked about the standard of education in state schools, 3.9 per cent of people were 'very satisfied' and 37.9 per cent 'quite satisfied', compared to 26.4 per cent 'quite dissatisfied' and 6.5 per cent 'very dissatisfied', which seems rather pessimistic.[19] Some 57 per cent of people told Ipsos MORI in 2008 they would opt for private education, if they could afford it,[20] the highest level recorded since 1997, while the number of children whose parents actually pay for private education has risen slightly during the same period to just over 7 per cent of the school-age population[21] (and over double that number in London).[22] These figures are in part a reflection on the state sector, but they are also far more a reflection of means and ambition. One can still trust the state system, but want one's child to benefit from the perceived additional advantages of private schools. The number who would respond positively to being asked whether they would like a Ferrari, if they could afford it, might well be far higher than 57 per cent.

Trust in social services has traditionally been quite stable, with roughly two thirds of those polled by *Community Care* in 2007 saying they would trust social workers to help them or their families.[23] But trust has been knocked by a series of high profile cases, most recently the devastating Baby Peter episode, which came to light in November 2008. The infant died after seventeen months of intense cruelty by adults, revealing wholly inadequate care from those meant to be keeping an eye on the baby. Over 40 per cent of people said their opinion of child social workers had since deteriorated.[24] The Local Government Association has reported increasing numbers leaving the profession and significant difficulties attracting new candidates, while 93 per cent of councillors believe that the media's reporting of the case had a negative impact on the way the public perceive social workers.[25] Local authorities have borne the brunt for not doing more to improve social services, but this is not new: the British Social Attitudes survey found that a consistently large majority in 1984 and 1994 thought that government could have done a better job on social services.[26]

Why has trust been lost?

People's trust in public services in general, however, remains high. Where there has been distrust, it has often been because they have suffered from the general loss of trust in politics and politicians as their patrons, argues leading authority Howard Glennerster.[27] Government has certainly been responsible for engendering considerable distrust *within* the public services, not least by its growing monitoring since the 1980s. Stephen Harrison and Carole Smith argue that 'the policy drive to modernise health and social care is in danger of excluding trust and moral motivation' by privileging what Anthony Giddens called the 'accelerating processes of surveillance'.[28] Distrust begets distrust, and it has permeated throughout public services.

Turning specifically to health services, these have suffered from the rise in readily available information. More than 80 per cent of people now arrive at their GP or pharmacist with a diagnosis they have made themselves, according to a YouGov survey for Lloyds Pharmacy.[29] At the touch of a button, any individual has access to websites such as NHS Direct, Familydoctor.org and Net Doctor. Before home computers, the information was available in books, but the speed and comprehensiveness of the internet means the knowledge is far easier to obtain and to probe. The phenomenon is both good and bad. In theory, a large number of visits to the doctor could be rendered unnecessary:

straightforward problems can be diagnosed, fears allayed, and over-the-counter treatments bought from pharmacists. On the downside, patients scan websites, which are not all equally reliable, and find a formidable variety of reasons to worry about their health. The role of the medic is now evolving to include the interpretation of any information brought to them by patients, and they are required more than ever to keep up to date with the latest developments in their field.[30] The term *cyberchondria* has been in circulation for a decade, and it is on the rise. Researchers have found that although brain tumours affect only 0.02 per cent of us, the fact that around 25 per cent of sites thrown up by a web search for 'headache' mention them as a possible cause leads large numbers to imagine they might have developed one.[31] People suffer from 'base rate neglect', a propensity to believe something will happen to oneself, even though one knows the chances are very low. An American study by the Pew Internet Project revealed that although 80 per cent of us look to the internet for health information, 75 per cent of us do not check the source or the date it was created. 'If a healthy person under thirty-five has chest pain, it is unlikely to be related to the heart. But because there is so much on the web linking the two, they forget the low background probability,' says Eric Horwitz, a Microsoft research scientist.[32] Around three quarters of first- and second-year medical students suffer from so-called 'medical school-itis' where they believe they have a significant but imaginary disease they have been studying.[33] Now the general public has caught it. The MMR vaccine provides the classic recent example of the dangers of information circulating among those under-equipped to analyse it: concerns over the vaccine's safety have little basis in scientific evidence, but so great has been the public concern that the take-up has fallen, leaving a real risk of a measles epidemic. One GP told us that 'hopes and expectations aroused by the internet are seized on by the public that are almost impossible to manage; when we fail to produce the miracles, people get depressed and lose trust in us'.[34]

Scandals, such as the Shipman mass murders, have hit medicine as they have all other sectors. Less damaging to recorded trust levels, but still profoundly unsettling, were the events at Alder Hey Children's hospital in Liverpool. More than 2,000 organs were removed from 800 children in post-mortems without the consent of their parents, glands were removed during operations from living children and given to a pharmaceutical company in exchange for donations, and 1,500 foetuses were stored without consent.[35] Concerns that the scandal would adversely affect numbers coming forward for organ donations, however, proved unfounded. 'Bugs' have been more damaging of trust. In 2004, *New Scientist* magazine reported that deaths from the MRSA infection had gone up fifteenfold in a decade.[36] In 2006 the National Audit Office estimated that hospital-acquired infections contributed to some 5,000 deaths annually, which might explain why 31 per cent of people told the BBC they would consider avoiding NHS surgery for fear of catching an infection.[37] Figure 7.3, based on research from a BBC/ICM survey in 2008, shows that hospital infections became by far the public's biggest fear about hospitals.

Figure 7.3: Biggest hospital fears[38]

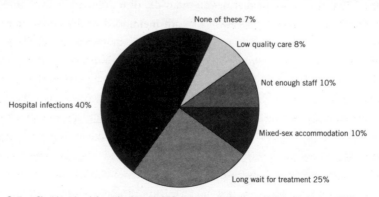

Source: Chart based on information from the BBC, 'Infections "the biggest NHS fear"', 30 June 2008

Doctors have mixed feelings towards the media – patients can set such great store by the health pages they read that doctors often have to allay inflated fears and dampen high expectations. However, while the sight of someone walking into a surgery with a newspaper article tucked under their arm may occasionally inspire dread, doctors are usually happy to discuss them with people, as it means a less paternalistic relationship, and provides an opportunity to build informed trust.[39] Many health journalists, such as Tom Stuttaford, a doctor, are reputable and have the public's interests at heart, but there are a large number who lack elementary medical training, alongside unscrupulous editors with a cavalier regard for the impact a story can have on its readers.

Swine flu appeared like a flash flood in the early summer of 2009. The media splashed front-page stories of swine flu death, including that of a supposedly healthy person who in fact had multiple health problems: the first fourteen deaths from swine flu in Britain all had underlying health problems.[40] The public's imagination was stoked to such intensity that when the National Flu Pandemic website went live in July 2009, it temporarily crashed due to an overwhelming volume of traffic, at one point witnessing 2,600 visitors per second.[41] The media exaggerates the fear of epidemics, to the detriment of more serious issues like smoking, which kills around 120,000 people in the UK annually but receives relatively little coverage:[42] the King's Fund claims that people who die of measles are 34,000 times more likely to have their cause of death mentioned in the news than if they die of smoking.[43] The media can also be extraordinarily capricious. A series of stories suggesting that drinking red wine in moderation is good for the heart, from which many draw succour, was followed by the claim that drinking just one glass of red wine a day could increase an individual's chances of developing throat cancer by an apparent (and absurdly precise) '168 per cent'.[44] Great harm is done to trust by the prominence the media gives to unrepresentative stories.[45] 'Only bad news is news,' says Glennerster. 'Researchers from TV programmes sometimes contact me on a story, but when I suggest it is not that bad or there is another side, they lose interest. The media has institutional incentives to focus on the critical, with insufficient constructive balance.'[46]

'Trust is built up over time through face-to-face contacts,' a doctor told us.[47] The physical and emotional intimacy of a relationship with a doctor is unlike that with any other in life, outside physical relations. A familiar face and smile give tremendous reassurance and boost morale and recovery. The quality personal time is, however, coming under strain in the managerial era. In nursing, some believe that from the 1970s the culture of selfless dedication to caring for the patient shifted towards one which was much more time- and money-watching. The European Working Time Directive, introduced from 1998, more factually has meant cuts in doctors' hours; a good development, but as a result patients in hospitals may no longer have the same exposure to a doctor they first bonded with on admission, or see the same nursing team before and after an operation, because they are all on tighter shifts.[48] We may have a more efficient NHS, but what is lost is incalculable.

The rise of the compensation culture has been one unintended consequence of the decline in personal relationships. We may be unhappy about suing someone we know, but feel less compunction doing it to strangers. The danger is that 'preventative medicine' (protecting the patient) is being taken over by 'defensive medicine' (defending oneself from litigation).[49] In 2008, solicitors suing the NHS received more than £91 million in costs, nearly three times as much as solicitors acting for the NHS, which has had to set aside a record £787 million in 2009 to cover the rising cost of litigation.[50] Typing 'clinical negligence' into Google brings up 390,000 responses, usually from solicitors with mouth-watering invitations for legal assistance from 'the most experienced personal injury firm in the UK' who are 'franchised by the Legal Services Commission to undertake publicly funded clinical negligence compensation claims'. If you type in 'no win, no fee', you receive around twenty million results, telling you all about the benefits of the conditional-fee arrangement. It was introduced by the Courts and Legal Services Act in 1995 and means that the lawyer will charge nothing if he loses a case, but collects his fees in full from the other side if he wins. Some websites even provide interactive body maps showing the potential compensation value of everything from an injured finger (£1,000 to £75,000) to serious brain damage (millions).[51] Dentists are coming under similar pressure and are equally fearful about litigation. It is good news for the insurance industry.

The drive for increased accountability has been particularly detrimental to trust in the health service. The *British Medical Journal* expressed the concern that doctors' 'internal motivation (the most important thing) is crushed, that their time is diverted into activities that are more bureaucratic than beneficial to patients, and that they resort to game-playing to buck the system'.[52] Targets were described as a principal reason for the 'appalling standards of care'[53] at Mid-Staffordshire NHS Foundation Trust between 2005 and 2009, notably for patients who were admitted as emergencies and suffered unexplained high mortality rates. The *Daily Telegraph* reported that NHS financial targets 'may have led to 1,200 deaths',[54] citing a Healthcare Commission's report which found that patient care suffered dramatically because of the focus on targets for cutting costs.[55]

Within the NHS, the criticism is directed principally at the bureaucrats. In March 2009, 1.36 million people worked in it – a rise of 27 per cent on 1999 – but the number of managers rose three times more quickly than the number of nurses and there are now 5,000 more managers than consultants, and 15,000 more managers than midwives.[56] A YouGov poll in June 2008 found that 78 per cent of respondents thought the NHS employed too many managers.[57] But it is the politicians who are more responsible than anyone for trust being an issue in the NHS. Both main parties have felt the need to chastise the quality of the NHS and public services in general to show that 'they' uniquely would improve them, if in power. Blair was particularly guilty for his use of negative language about the welfare state to win the case for public service reform, and the negative perception fed straight back into the surveys.[58] The public is concerned that politicians have not done more to reduce the uneven quality of care across the country, with some primary care trusts spending £118 per person on cancer treatment and others just £47 (even after adjustments for varying local needs).[59] Healthcare professionals overall are suspicious of the increasing politicisation of the NHS, notably of vote-catching initiatives in the run-up to elections.[60]

Loss of trust in the education sector is less specific in a profession where trust and public opinion have been placed less under the microscope. A principal concern remains the continuing gulf in performance between the state and private sectors. Blair raised expectations after 1997 when he promised to build a 'world class' state school system, so good that the middle classes would no longer pay for their children to attend independent schools. Gordon Brown went further, and promised in March 2006 to raise spending in state schools to the same level as that in independent schools, an extraordinary promise which he must have known would never materialise, even without the recession. Despite unparalleled attention from Downing Street since 1997, and an 85 per cent increase in spending per head in real terms,[61] the gap in performance between the state and independent sector has continued to grow. *The Observer* reported in August 2009 that '31 per cent of privately educated pupils achieved three 'A' grades [at A level in 2008], compared with 26 per cent of selective grammar school pupils and only 7.7 per cent of those in comprehensives. In the most challenging schools in the country – secondary moderns that neighbour selective grammar schools – only 1.7 per cent obtained three As.'[62] The state sector did improve very considerably under Labour from their base in 1997: there were many outstanding performers, including the 165 remaining grammar schools, and a large number of individual comprehensives such as Ninestiles in Birmingham and Thomas Telford in Shropshire, or sixth form colleges such as Greenhead in Huddersfield. State schools such as these outperformed all but the best independent schools in league tables (although this is only a narrow measure of a school's value).

Comparisons of access to the top universities, teacher: pupil ratios, qualifications of teachers, quality of facilities and co-curricular enrichment opportunities all show independent schools still to be streets ahead, however. A Sutton Trust report in 2007 found that of the 100 schools with the highest admissions rates to Oxbridge over the previous five years, eighty were independent schools, eighteen were grammar schools, and just two were comprehensives; together these schools accounted for a third of all admissions, despite representing less than 3 per cent of the total number of schools nationwide.[63] A further Sutton Trust report in 2009 found that, as a result of the number of applications made and other factors, 'a student with the equivalent of ABB at A level (including at least one "core academic" A level) who attended an independent school had a 79 per cent chance of entering one of the 500 most selective degree courses, compared with 70 per cent for a similar student attending a state maintained school.'[64] The failure of state schools to reach the overall standards that had been promised by New Labour's two Prime Ministers, together with continuing evidence of social exclusion (noted most recently in the Milburn Committee's final report in July 2009)[65] have inevitably eroded trust.

Trust has been lost in the examination system, particularly with grade inflation, which has seen the numbers of 'A' grades at A level rise from 17.68 per cent in 1998[66] to 26.7 per cent in 2009.[67] The number of state and independent schools abandoning A level in whole or in part for the International Baccalaureate (IB) in the sixth form has risen to 190 in Britain.[68] This is an expensive and to some extent a risky move for the schools, but is undertaken because of the individual schools' lack of trust in the quality and integrity of the A level exam. Similar questions are being asked about GCSE, and concerns about possible 'dumbing down' led to the Tories commissioning a report under former Imperial College director Richard Sykes, in August 2009. Some schools are so concerned about GCSEs that they are abandoning them in favour of IGCSEs, or, far more radically, the IB's Middle Years Programme.

Questions are also being asked about British universities. They too have seen grade inflation, with the proportion of graduates earning first-class degrees increasing from 8.2 per cent in 1998 to 13.3 per cent in 2008, along with a slight rise in the number of upper second-class degrees over the same period, a subject of concern in July 2009 to the House of Commons Select Committee.[69] Undergraduates appear to be less happy with the quality of their university lives, with 19 per cent of more than 220,000 final year students telling the National Student Survey that they were dissatisfied or ambivalent about their courses, a rise of 1 per cent on 2008.[70] Student loans, declining lecturer:student ratios, and anxieties about the job market after graduation have all contributed to the concern. In August 2009, Manchester's vice chancellor, Alan Gilbert, said that universities had been fighting a long battle, and that extra money from student loans had failed to keep pace with teaching and research needs.[71] Three months before, undergraduates rebelled at Bristol University in what has been described as the most significant student revolt for a generation.[72] Dissatisfied students have been opting out of British 'state' universities less to attend the independent university at Buckingham than to travel to university abroad, principally in the United States, which has seen a steady, if unmeasured, rise in interest from British students.[73]

Social workers' roles are wide-ranging, and cover childcare and protection, adult care, elderly care, and helping those with disabilities and mental difficulties. They work with and on behalf of the least advantaged members of society, but have no powerful voices to support them, and their role is often of little interest to the public[74] and the media.[75] The well off do not go near social workers voluntarily, and when something goes wrong, as it will given the problematic lives led by those they work with day by day, the press swoops. Social workers are thus on the defensive, which is never a good starting point, but they have also been guilty of some terrible errors which have damaged the public's trust.

In February 2000, the eight-year-old Victoria Climbié was severely abused and then killed by her guardians in Haringey, north London, both of whom were convicted of murder. 'Blindingly incompetent' was how the judge at the trial described the failure of social services from several local authorities, the police, the NHS and NSPCC – all of whom had contact with Victoria – to investigate the abuse properly.[76] The inquiry into the case by Lord Laming offered 108 recommendations to improve child protection, from which emerged the Children Act of 2004. As happened after the Shipman fiasco, many new regulations were introduced to social services, which collectively led to a further erosion of trust. Reforms by the General Medical Council after the former will not prevent a future Shipman, because he was trusted by his patients, and the latter did not stop Baby Peter being killed in the very same London borough of Haringey seven years later. In April 2009, the daughter of an 86-year-old woman, Betty Figg, who suffers from dementia, took her out of a nursing home so she could care for her herself. The police then arrived at her home with a battering ram to escort her mother from the property, with a warrant alleging that Betty was being mistreated or neglected. They then placed a blanket over her head as they took her back to the nursing home.[77]

Such incidents do little to improve the public's view of social workers, but their relative rarity should be stressed. With precious few voices speaking up for them, high staff turnover, and a sense they are overworked, social services are at a low ebb. The accountability ethos has meant that they now spend three quarters of their time on paperwork, leaving much less for the face-to-face encounters that can make a difference.[78]

How is trust to be built?

Trust is running at high levels across much of the NHS, so the question is how to build further trust. The next few years will be difficult for healthcare because public expenditure will have to be cut, yet life expectancy and the costs of medical equipment continue to rise. The Office of National Statistics predicts that by 2031 the number of over-75s will have increased from 4.7 million to 8.2 million.[79] While 17 per cent of the under-40s have a long term condition, 60 per cent of the 65-and-over age group suffer from one or more.[80] The challenges will be vast for the NHS, and will require a shift from health and treatment plans to social care – especially in old age – so that people can live longer and happier lives rather than hospitalised ones.[81] Several of the current concerns relating to trust are being addressed, such as the multi-million-pound 'deep clean' to rid hospitals of MRSA, and more attention is being paid to patient psychology in medical and nursing schools. But none of these initiatives goes far enough.

Major changes need to be introduced to boost trust further: to culture, role models and the sense of ownership. The required change in culture is profound; we need to stand thinking about health on its head. The NHS is often outstanding at dealing with ill-health once it has occurred, but is less impressive at preventing the problems occurring in the first place. The culture must be changed to 'positive health', where every person is taught from earliest childhood onwards about taking responsibility for their bodies and minds, and about how to live their lives to minimise the risk of damaging them. At present, the NHS deals with patients who have fallen over the edge of a waterfall, whose bodies or minds are damaged or broken. We should be working much harder to prevent them falling over the edge in the first place. Many illnesses, physical and mental, are avoidable, or could be significantly ameliorated if only personal responsibility for health were taken more seriously. Our bodies are like cars that we are given at birth. At present, too many – most, even – drive these cars with insufficient care, secure in the knowledge that they can have endless free repairs and services. A more enlightened way of thinking comes from our trust model. We should see our bodies and minds as something that we are entrusted to protect, for our own benefit and for others; many do not fully consider the anguish their personal disregard causes their friends and family, who can only watch as their loved ones abuse their bodies and willingly shorten the time they have together. If we are taught properly from the earliest age up how to look after ourselves, and if we take our responsibilities seriously, we will live much healthier and more fulfilling lives.

Doctors, as part of their code, should 'walk the talk'. If they are obese, drink too heavily or smoke, they should come before a peer or patient group, since they are role models. Ara Darzi, in his enlightened 2008 report into the NHS, favours a positive approach of leading from the front, and is a strong advocate of well-being.[82] He would not have been pleased by the national audit of NHS staff habits in August 2009 finding high ratios of smoking (20 per cent), obesity and absenteeism.[83] At present, doctors have little incentive to be the role models they need to be, and patients have little to model their own behaviour upon. Is it surprising that we are not a healthier nation? Change 4 Life (the public health campaign which started in January 2009) is a move in the right direction, advocating wholesome eating and exercise, and encouraging medics to be role models.[84] We denigrate trust if we abuse our bodies with excessive food, alcohol, drugs or lack of exercise, and expect the same rights from the NHS as those who have become unwell involuntarily. Parents need to be much better examples to their children, who learn deep and lasting lessons from them: if the parents worry and are stressed, their children will too. If they overeat, drink too much, smoke, take drugs, do not exercise or cannot relax, their children may well follow suit. Being a trustworthy role model and acting as a trustee of one's own body are the keys to sorting out the health service.

The health service must build itself from the ground up based on human scale and face-to-face interactions. Much illness is psychological and can be improved by a positive state of mind. Nothing is more powerful in achieving this than the reassurance and love that comes from personal relationships. Julia Abelson speaks of the importance in healthcare that the 'truster' know the 'trusted',[85] while Calnan and Sanford found that the 'extent to which the doctor is patient centred' is fundamental to the building of trust.[86] Regardless of a doctor's personal views on faith, they should all be taught about spirituality, and keep abreast with it, the better to minister to and understand their patients.[87] The length of time that doctors have to spend form-filling takes time away from patients, and means that even when patients visit their surgery, the doctor's eyes will be as much on their computer screen as on the patient themselves. Nurses, too, should be better paid and should be given back wider powers to run their own profession as capably as they once did. Bureaucratic intelligence has been allowed in the last twenty-five years to trump emotional intelligence, yet the latter is the better way to care for patients.

Ownership in the NHS needs to change. The public needs to be trusted and to be far more involved in the health service from top to bottom. They are the *raison d'être* for the NHS; its objective is not to provide a comfortable living for managers and health workers. The more patients are involved, the more they will trust; the more they trust, the more they will listen to professionals and take their own health seriously.

What does giving the public more ownership of the NHS mean? County government should run healthcare, with elected members having key roles, and more members of the public should be on the boards of hospitals and primary care trusts: the Royal College of Pathologists has paved the way in calling for greater representation of patients on governing bodies. Patients should be given much more information about the cost of treatment and the options available to them, including the damage they will do to themselves through unhealthy living. The insights of positive psychology, which is a powerful tool in combating depression, should be made widely known; optimism and emotional resilience can be learnt.

Paternalists down the decades have said that the public neither wants nor understands choice; the Darzi report, however, quotes the British Social Attitudes survey of 2005, which shows that it is the poorest and least well educated who most desire greater choice.[88] The new-look NHS website now provides patients with the information to make informed decisions about which of their local facilities to use, which doctor to see, and what treatment to choose.[89] These steps to empower and enlighten patients should prove beneficial for trust and are to be welcomed. Such changes must take place on a personal level, too, as Martin Marshall argues in the *British Journal of General Practice*: GPs must be more proactive in their roles by acting as 'the patient's guide through the morass of information available to them and the complexity of the health system'.[90]

Schools should be places overflowing with trust and gratitude. It is not surprising that the satisfaction levels measured in the 2007 British Social Attitudes Survey were not higher, however, when most parents have little effective choice over their children's school, when they hear in the media that exams are being devalued, when their own opportunities for involvement are so restricted, and when the performance of the independent sector seems so much stronger than state schools. By the end of the twentieth century, 'factory schools' were the norm in the state sector: large institutions offering little variety from a common norm, overseen by a tight inspection and regulation regime, with their principal objective being to ensure that the children who initially walked through the doors left at the end of the assembly line with target grades in public exams. Schools became increasingly narrow largely because of the imperative that the students performed well in these exams, and the school showed progress in the league tables. The accountability and target regime's role, when it came in during the 1980s and 1990s, was to help root out poor teaching and develop a more academic focus, and it achieved much in these areas that enhanced children's learning and opportunities in life. But the targets, as we have seen everywhere, became so dominant that they changed what education was about. Alan Smithers wrote that 'while results may have gone up, the narrow focus has inflicted collateral damage',[91] a view supported by Peter Hyman, the deputy headteacher of Greenford High School in west London, who wrote in *The Observer* in August 2009 that 'too many lessons do not get beyond information-giving and that's often because exams test knowledge and some understanding but not a lot else. That means much of a child's education is spent on low-level thinking. The result is, sadly, that the imagination and potential of too many children are dulled.'[92] Hyman had in an earlier incarnation worked as a senior aide in Number 10: the pity is he could not have reversed his career positions.

The way ahead is for a presumption of trust to be the guiding principle at every level of the education system; only when the trust is shown to be unjustified should it be retracted. Parents need to be trusted to choose the school for their child: choosing means we take an active interest, while a lack of choice often leads to a lack of involvement. Parents are perfectly capable of discriminating and choosing the right school, as they do in health. Choice will encourage schools to become more diverse, and parents to become more active. The more involved a parent is with the school, as long as they show appropriate trust, the better a child performs. Unit size of schools needs to be much smaller. The independent sector flourishes with senior schools usually teaching between 500 and 900 students. No secondary school should exceed 1,000 pupils in size, and all children should be known individually. Schools would thus become engines of civic and educational regeneration in the twenty-first century.

Teachers must be trusted to teach what they want to teach, and in the way that they think is best for the children. The national examinations and inspection regimes have introduced a dull conformity, for all their impact in reducing bad practice, and have squeezed the lifeblood and creativity out of too much of learning. Jonathan Smith, author of *The Learning Game* (2002), says 'it was driven by fear, and it made teachers fearful of being imaginative and of making mistakes.'[93] In the first chapter we discussed the continuum between individuality and the collective; in schools, the pendulum has swung far too far in the direction of the latter. Schools themselves should be trusted more, not least to choose their own curriculum and examination system. Schools should be largely self-governing, with governors derived widely from across the community. Students should also be trusted much more; children even more than adults respond well when they are shown respect, and act anti-socially when they feel that they are not being trusted. As an example of mistrust, Stockwell Park High in London was reported as having installed almost 100 CCTV cameras to combat truancy, prevent vandalism and protect teachers from false accusations. A hundred schools across Britain are introducing similar measures, which are also said to be used to film lessons and expose poor teaching.[94] Ample opportunities for leadership should be available; all older pupils should be given such roles. They themselves should draw up their own 'honour code', which older students help enforce in the school. In lessons, they should be given more responsibility for their own learning; they should also have 'Harkness tables' in the sixth form, which are oval tables designed to stimulate group discussion and debate, where the students are actively engaged in taking the initiative.

To educate the young to be fully aware of their civic and trustee responsibilities, and to encourage them to live life to the full, education at school and university needs to be much more holistic. We have a mechanical and old-fashioned notion of what 'intelligence' means, associated with the development of the intellect and its ability to perform certain tasks in certain measurable ways. The American psychologist Howard Gardner has argued for 'multiple intelligences', and says: 'Don't ask how intelligent a child is:

ask rather, how is the child intelligent?'[95] Every child and adult can be said to have eight intelligences or aptitudes, comprising four pairs: the logical and the linguistic, the creative and the physical, the personal and the social, the spiritual and the moral.[96] The job of the school or the university is to develop all eight of these aptitudes with the clear understanding that what is not brought out in a person's youth (the word educate comes from the Latin *educere*, 'to lead out') may well remain dormant for the rest of their life. Children from more affluent families will have more opportunities for this kind of wider enrichment at home: for children from less advantaged backgrounds, it is imperative that the *school* provides the wider education. Universities, too, should have a broader and more generous vision of their responsibilities for teaching their students to live full and trustworthy lives. One reason for the growing interest in American universities is the perception that they take holistic education more seriously than higher education does in Britain.

The job of social workers is too serious to be given the low priority that it currently receives. The general public and the media should do more to recognise the altruistic, difficult and often dangerous tasks that social workers undertake. For the role to attract dedicated and trustworthy people in greater numbers, social work must be afforded similar respect to that which we bestow upon doctors, nurses and teachers. The wide-ranging role of social workers needs higher profile, so that their job ceases to be viewed as a mystery, or – as much of the media would wrongly have us believe – the preserve of the heartless and incompetent. Such judgements weaken the already fragile morale of people who, while often honourably serving those less fortunate than themselves, receive little of the recognition they deserve from society.

Some specific policy recommendations along these lines are contained in *Facing Up to the Task – The Interim Report of the Social Work Task Force*,[97] published in July 2009. Other than that, we suggest that, if the other proposals in this book are taken seriously and applied, the bewildering and seemingly endless nature of social work will become more manageable, and trust in it will blossom.

Robert Oppenheimer, father of the atomic bomb, famously quoted from
the Hindu text *Bhagavad Gita* 'I am become death, the slayer of nations',
when witnessing the detonation of the first atomic bomb test in Los Alamos,
New Mexico. Man survived the nuclear bomb in the twentieth century,
but will he survive global warming, population increase and food shortages in
the twenty-first? *(Getty Images)*

CHAPTER 8
TRUST IN SCIENCE, RELIGION AND IDEOLOGY

Science without religion is lame, religion without science is blind.

Albert Einstein (1879–1955)

Trust takes a new turn when we move into the beliefs we hold – or not – in ultimate questions. We have a choice in life to believe and therefore to trust in God, or to believe religion has no meaning or value, and to believe in an ideology such as humanism or Marxism. All can choose to make science an active reference point in their lives or not. A religious person will trust not only in God's existence but also have a determination to act out the will of that God in their daily lives. A Marxist will, in a very similar way, trust in their ideology and try to manifest it in their lives, but a humanist will not 'trust humanism': Humanism does not rest on a model of 'divine' or 'enlightened' commands, but rather the hope, if not expectation, that we can identify universally shared human values by which to live. Religion claims to deliver absolute truth and so do some ideologies, but science does not (though the public continues to believe that science is a body of knowledge which is absolutely true).

Religion has been on the defensive since the Enlightenment offered scientific explanations for much that had hitherto been left to the mysteries of religion: Matthew Arnold in the poem *Dover Beach* (1867) wrote about hearing the 'melancholy, long, withdrawing roar' of the 'sea of faith'. Religion has had to accept much from science about evolution and the claim that God did not create the universe in 'six days' (though many religious people continue to believe in the literal truth of their ancient texts). But many humanists have continued to believe that science has rendered religion redundant and even ridiculous. We need to trust science, more so now than perhaps than in the past: we depend upon it to find cures for the pandemics, population increase, climate change and food shortages which will make their impact increasingly in the future. Science explains much about life, but not all: it has not told and cannot tell us the full nature of human consciousness, nor provide us with a moral compass, nor rationalise the existence of selfless love. Trillions more dollars will be spent at CERN in Geneva and elsewhere, but the answers to these three questions will always elude science. No subject so arouses passion as the three topics covered by this chapter, and it will be necessary to tread warily.

Have we lost trust?

Trust in scientists has increased in the last ten years, rising from 63 per cent in 1997 to 72 per cent in 2008 according to the Ipsos MORI Veracity Index.[1] Astronomer Royal Martin Rees believes 'scientists are trusted – what the public is wary about is the applications of science running away without adequate controls', a subject which he writes about at length in his *Our Final Century* (2003).[2] The persistence of large numbers who believe in creationism – 22 per cent in a BBC *Horizon*-commissioned poll in 2006 – in flat contradiction to everything scientists tell us,[3] reveals much about how people will accept only those aspects of science which suit them. The greatest public problem with science is our individual inability to discern the weight of competing arguments. Ipsos MORI found in June 2008 that 60 per cent of people believed that 'many scientific experts still question if humans are contributing to climate change', which is indicative of unwarranted scepticism, if not ignorance, of the scientific research.[4,5] Research commissioned by the

Royal Society found the scientific issues most causing concern were biological weapons (74 per cent), global warming (70 per cent), genetic modification (60 per cent), diseases such as BSE/CJD (55 per cent) and nuclear power (53 per cent).[6]

Fraud and deception, which are castigated by Onora O'Neill in her Reith Lectures,[7] are a serious problem amongst scientists and medical researchers, and undermine trust. A report from Edinburgh University in June 2009 based on anonymous surveys found a third of scientific medical researchers admitted to scientific fraud, nearly three quarters saying they had witnessed deliberate warping of data to achieve desired results.[8] Author of the report Daniele Fanelli said: 'I had naïvely assumed that scientists would be principled [but scientists] are human beings driven by their interests, hopes and beliefs. Given opportunities to cut corners by falsifying data, they may well do so.'[9] The science journal *Nature* estimates that approximately 1,000 incidents of fabrication, falsification or plagiarism in scientific research go unreported every year in the US, while Mike Farthing, chairman of the Britain's Committee on Publication Ethics, estimates major institutions will see at least one case of seriously fraudulent research each year, meaning there will be around fifty nationwide.[10] However, despite the apparently widespread nature of this fraud, it does not seem to have fed into public mistrust of scientists. It is conceivable that the sheer volume of medical journals publishing each year and the immense mass of data are making it increasingly difficult to unearth such fraud.

Whether trust in religion in Britain is increasing or falling is hard to discover. Figures for non-Christian faiths are often not collated, and information on Christianity is difficult to verify and interpret. In a poll, 37 per cent of Britons polled said they 'tended to trust' religious institutions, a long way below Denmark (74 per cent) and Italy (55 per cent) but above Catholic France (33 per cent) and Protestant Sweden (21 per cent):[11] overall Britain's institutions are marginally less trusted than the average of European nations. Richard Harries, former Bishop of Oxford, said: 'The 1960s saw a big move away from attendance. With more consumer goods and more leisure, people in the West have plenty of good and amusing ways to spend their time, and religion often does not rate high up their agenda.'[12] The first time Britons were asked about their religious denomination (as opposed to if they went to church) was in the 2001 census. It was a voluntary question, yet 92 per cent replied to it: of these, only 16 per cent said they had no religion, 78 per cent identified themselves as Christian, 3 per cent as Muslim and 3 per cent other (Jewish, Buddhist, Hindu, Sikh, and smaller religions). That figure differs markedly from a *Guardian*/ICM poll of December 2006 to which 63 per cent replied that they were not religious, half of whom nevertheless described themselves as Christian. There is a significant difference between being *of* a religion, and *practising* religion.

Attendance at churches, and the extent to which it can be interpreted as a proxy for trust in organised Christianity, seems to be in decline overall. This is particularly so among the young, with exceptions such as the evangelical Alpha course, which has been taken by two million individuals with an average age of twenty-seven.[13] From 1980 to 2000, the Church of England saw a 27 per cent decline in membership with a similar decline in the taking of Mass in Roman Catholic churches.[14] In half of the Church of England's 16,200 churches, the congregation each Sunday is below fifty people. Regular Sunday attendance is estimated at 871,000.[15] The Religious Trends survey estimated the following decline: 48,300 churches of all denominations in 2005 would decline to 27,500 by 2050, the current 35,300 ministers would reduce to 26,100. Ruth Gledhill wrote in *The Times* in May 2008 that a 'God-shaped hole will lead to loss of national sense of identity' and concluded that 'with thousands of churches facing closure, there is something unbearably sad about the plight of Christianity in the country. It feels as if the soul of Britain is dying.'[16] The Church of England defends attendance figures by saying that there are different patterns of worship and that people are expressing their faith in other ways. Any decline, it says, is less than in other institutions such as membership of trade unions and political parties. Here again, the evidence suggests there was never a golden age, and that the cavernous Victorian churches were rarely full. Belief in a devout Victorian Britain is undermined by the 1851 census which shows great numbers not declaring themselves Anglicans.

The Christian churches which are flourishing today are the evangelical and charismatic congregations, with Holy Trinity, Brompton in London, a conspicuous example of expansion. Membership of such churches has reversed the decline in church attendance, specifically in London, where Anglican churches experienced a 3 per cent increase in attendance in the 1990s, and Baptist churches 11 per cent.[17] Pentecostal and other predominately black churches are also growing: 44 per cent of people in church on a Sunday in London are Afro-Caribbean, and 14 per cent are non-whites of another descent, according to *Economist* editors John Micklethwait and Adrian Wooldridge.[18] Polish and other nationalities new to Britain are also responsible for boosting the numbers attending church. In line with the long-term decline in church attendance, trust in the veracity of clergy and priests to tell the truth has declined over twenty-five years, with 85 per cent in 1983 saying they could be trusted, down to 74 per cent in 2008, according to the Ipsos MORI survey on the most trusted profession.[19]

Polls nevertheless suggest that Britain resolutely remains a nation which believes in divinity in some form, but that people are turning increasingly to outlets other than organised religions to give expression to their spiritual quest. Britons now follow more than 170 different faiths or belief systems.[20] Whereas the modern onslaught on faith may not have dented this growing spiritual interest, it may have had an impact on the image the public has of the positive contribution that religion can make: 82 per cent see religion as a cause of division, and 76 per cent said they believe 'religion often stands in the way of open debate between people across the world'.[21] The use of faith by militant Islamists and other extremists as a motivation for murder may also have coloured these responses. Curiosity was fuelled by the degree of media coverage given to the 'atheist summer camp', a branch of the American Camp Quest held in Bath in July 2009, which aims to give young people an enhanced understanding of evolution, 'pseudoscience' and critical thinking. The available data on whether atheism and attachment to ideologies are on the increase are inconclusive. Intellectually, however, liberalism is the doctrine which has triumphed in the West. William Gladstone would have been pleased: 'Liberalism is trust of the people tempered by prudence; conservatism is distrust of the people tempered by fear.'[22]

Why has trust been lost?

The public believes science to be the facts or truth about the universe, which it is not. Science is a method of understanding the world (the word 'science' derives from the Latin *scientia*, meaning 'knowledge'), from which can be derived a body of evidence which is testable. Scientific conclusions can have high degrees of probability, but never provide the absolute truth and certainty that the public seems to want. The public become frustrated when they receive conflicting evidence, as over genetically modified plants and animals or stem cell research. When they do not receive the certainty that they want from scientists, they become disillusioned. The sheer complexity of science compounds the problem: much of what C. P. Snow said fifty years ago in his famous 'The Two Cultures' lecture in 1959 remains true today. There is still a wide gulf in understanding between those with a background in the arts and those in the sciences. 'It is nearly impossible to provide the layperson with a fair account of the state of knowledge regarding, say, the role of word meanings in syntactic processing,' writes Jason Zevin in an article entitled 'The Perils of Popularising Science'.[23]

Communicating science thus becomes difficult when there is such great public interest in so many new discoveries, but its findings are complex and nuanced. A high figure of 85 per cent of the public believed in 2002 that science needed to improve the way it communicated its research findings though the media.[24] Figure 8.1, from 2005, shows that nearly half those asked believed it was 'very important' for the public to be informed about new developments. Yet when scientists like Steven Pinker or authors like Bill Bryson try to popularise science, they can be attacked by scientists for oversimplification.

Figure 8.1: Importance of informing the public about new developments[25]

Q: Using this card, how important, if at all, do you feel it is for the general public to be informed about new developments in science and technology?

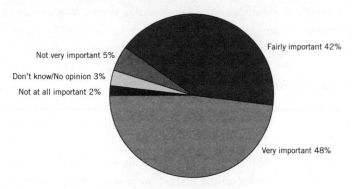

Not very important 5%

Don't know/No opinion 3%

Not at all important 2%

Fairly important 42%

Very important 48%

Base: All respondents (1,966), Fieldwork: 20-25 October 2005
Source: MORI

Ara Darzi believes that 'communication is the big problem with British science. Americans communicate their science much better, with a much more positive approach in their press.'[26] The responsibilities for communicating science, the public believe, lie first with the government (51 per cent), newspapers (39 per cent), followed by television (32 per cent) and industry (21 per cent).[27] Better communication clearly needs to be achieved.

The public is fearful, as Martin Rees has said, about where science might lead. It sees extraordinary developments coming from science, including television, mobile phones, keyhole surgery and cheaper, safer cars. But, as the Royal Society survey showed, it fears biological weapons, GM and nuclear power, all of which are created by man. The internet has accelerated the conventional media's ability to spread alarm: as noted throughout, it is much easier to spread mistrust than to develop trust. When new discoveries are being applied for the first time, public apprehension is often a phase that has to be negotiated: it happened with heart transplants, atomic power, and IVF/sperm donation. GM technology and stem cell research are two of the leading current concerns. When CERN began to operate the Large Hadron Collider in September 2008, predictions were made that it could lead to the end of the world. The popularity of futuristic science films like *Terminator* or Dan Brown's *Angels and Demons* heighten apprehensions that scientists might indeed make discoveries, which will change their lives adversely, or even precipitate the end of the world. With the decline of organised religion, it is as if the public look towards scientists to provide the protection and security which hitherto they had looked to their religious institutions to provide.

High profile cases of scientific fraud also eat away at the public's confidence. In 2005, Hwang Woo-Suk was found by Seoul National University to have been guilty of publishing material, which fabricated results for nine out of eleven stem cell lines. Previously celebrated as Korea's top scientist, he had in the previous seven years received £23 million for facilities and research. His stem cell work had been heralded as a breakthrough, opening up hope of cures for degenerative diseases. Dismay worldwide was profound. The highest profile case in the UK came in 1994 at St George's Hospital, London, when a consultant obstetrician alleged he had successfully reimplanted an ectopic pregnancy, which doctors had previously been unable to achieve. Again, high hopes were aroused, only to be crushed. The media inevitably gives great and unbalanced attention to such cases, though the widespread reported incidents of fraud suggest that the public is right not to have blind trust in the veracity of scientists.

Scandals have been a significant reason, too, for loss of trust in religion. Between 1995 and 1999, twenty-one Catholic priests, out of the 5,600 in England and Wales, were convicted of child abuse.[28] The damage was made much worse by the clear reluctance of the Catholic Church to be candid and pursue the victims, leaving the widespread impression of a cover-up. Cardinal Murphy-O'Connor, then Archbishop of Westminster, was himself damaged when it emerged that he had appointed a man convicted of nine sex attacks to the position of chaplain at the same airport where he had previously attacked a boy.[29] The Vatican in Rome, and the Catholic Church in Ireland, which has itself been enormously damaged by the number of cases uncovered, have also been widely criticised for failing to have a more robust attitude towards child abuse. The result has been an inevitable growth of checks and inspections, which has been corrosive of natural trust throughout the entire Christian church. Volunteers in parishes have to be checked, and bureaucracy at every level has increased. In religious institutions, which are predicated upon loving goodwill from one to another and a presumption of trust, the new regime is particularly alien.

God is supposed to be uniquely good, and those who follow him are trusted to behave well. Yet people claiming religious justification have been killing, torturing and imprisoning each other throughout modern history in extravagant numbers, with Britain unable to claim the high ground when its own civil war between Catholics and Protestants in Northern Ireland ended so recently. Extremists acting in the name of Islam have spread fear across the world in the last ten years, in particular since 9/11. Such actions have been readily seized upon by authors including Richard Dawkins and Christopher Hitchens to show that religion is inherently divisive and even evil: they have done much to popularise the idea that it is the religions themselves, rather than the malign interpretation of it by followers, that are the issue. It is easy and comforting for many to believe what such powerful and persuasive minds say, and to probe no further.

Consumerist society in modern Britain provides opportunities unknown seventy years ago to fill every spare minute with engaging and rewarding activities. The weekends are particularly busy for many families, and finding the time to attend mosque, synagogue, temple or church can be challenging with so many other diversions. Periods of loss and unhappiness have often been a 'wake up' call to look for God, but with anti-depressants, drink and luxuries to numb pain, the search may well not even be begun. Religious attendance is often highest amongst the poorest in any society and weakest amongst the most affluent, as it has been throughout history. What is the need to trust religion's promise of a better life in the future when life is so full, and science appears to provide so many answers?

Failure by religious authorities to connect with their communities is the most important ground for mistrust. The human race has a deep hunger for meaning in their lives, for lasting love and for profound peace. One cannot be human and not, deep down, desire these. But religious institutions have not connected well enough with these aspirations. Those religious groups that do thrive, as with the evangelical churches in Britain today, do so with a very strong binding philosophy that they are the righteous ones and the saved, and only by following their path will others be saved too. Exclusivity and notions of 'the saved' are powerful motives for religious faith, but they are not for all. Many find evangelists of all faiths intellectually and emotionally distasteful: how can a small group possibly claim monopoly of truth? Religious exclusivity boosts trust within the fraternity but engenders an attitude of mistrust to outsiders, as do exclusive clubs such as the Freemasons or Mafia. People hunger for those whom they can believe in and who will inspire them – the Obama syndrome – but instead they often find in religions warring factions, petty politics and disputes which merely reinforce accusations of anachronism and irrelevance in modern society. Persistent internal wrangling over equal rights for women and gays instils a deep mistrust of the church after decades of rapid social change and liberalisation across Britain. Not since William Temple was Archbishop of York from 1929, and then all too briefly of Canterbury (1942–4), was there a figure of national stature in the Church of England. Rowan Williams, Archbishop of Canterbury since 2003, is one of the weightiest religious figures in Europe. The media has not always been charitable to him, but the real problem is not his beard or his razor-sharp intellect: but his difficulty leading the church through a period of moral division, and still more to find a language that connects, beyond the intellectually adept and the spiritually minded, to the masses.

Francis Fukuyama wrote in *The End of History* that what we are witnessing is 'the end point of mankind's ideological evolution and the universalisation of Western liberal democracy as the final form of human government.'[30] Politics in Britain since Thatcher departed in 1990 has, for all the protestations to the contrary, become decreasingly ideological. Marxism has been discredited, and although a new portmanteau ideology may be thrust upon us in the future, for the time being it is hard to say that Britain would be a better place with one.

How do we regain trust?

Building trust in science must begin in schools, where young people need to be taught what science is. Children should have the natural curiosity for science which they all possess nurtured and stimulated, and not have their nascent curiosity crushed by the tedium of facts and complex formulae beyond their comprehension. The emphasis should be on experimentation and active involvement in making discoveries. The new style GCSEs and A levels currently being introduced in British schools shift the focus away from the learning of facts and onto 'how science works'. The International Baccalaureate has a still better approach to science for children of all ages between six and eighteen and further insists that all students in the sixth form continue with science – in contrast to the worrying trend for physics and chemistry to decline as a proportion of subjects studied at A level.[31] Parents are a key part in the mission to promote scientific understanding, but are not well equipped generally at answering their children's questions on science. All children ask questions about the way the universe works and if parents respond that they 'don't know', it can stunt their curiosity. A website – sciencesowhat. direct.gov.uk – has been created to answer the questions children most frequently put to parents, such as why the sky is blue, where bees go in winter and what causes waves on the sea. In all these ways, the young will absorb a better understanding of what science is and can do, and trust will grow from solid ground.[32]

Science communication is improving in Britain, albeit slowly. The Royal Society has been working hard to spread the public understanding of science, and is encouraging articulate scientists to speak out. The ablest of all is one who cannot even speak, Stephen Hawking, awarded the Presidential Medal of Freedom in August 2009, while Susan Greenfield and Richard Dawkins serve science well by being such eloquent communicators. Most effective of all are those like David Attenborough in his television programmes and books, and the new 2009 television series *Bang Goes the Theory*, which is based on experiments and interaction with young people, in contrast to *Tomorrow's World* (1965–2003), which focused more on new discoveries.

Science festivals, as in Manchester and Cheltenham, and Jodrell Bank Observatory's use of Twitter to communicate with the public are exemplars for the future. The government's chief scientific advisor, John Beddington, is working to improve communication between the science community, business and government, but much more needs to be done. Britain has some of the best university scientists in the world, and it has some of the strongest small and medium-sized science companies, but they could still communicate much better. Over the last fifty years, 40 per cent of scientific studies in the world have come out of Britain, and no country has been better at new discoveries. Where it has been weaker is in the delivery of these inventions to the market. MRI scans were developed by Peter Mansfield in Nottingham in 1968, but it was the USA who first introduced them and they were not available in this country until the late 1980s. Clean energy is another area where British universities have the scientific expertise, and British business the technical capacity to make it a world leader.

The press should be encouraged to communicate science in a less sensational and more informed way. The journalistic ethic of equal and balanced coverage often leads media outlets to give wide and sustained coverage to often widely discredited scientific claims which thus portraying scientific 'controversy' where in fact none actually exists. As Chris Mooney, author of *The Republican War on Science*, argues: 'Reporters need to understand better how science abusers exploit the journalistic norm of "balance" . . . and adjust their writing accordingly.'[33] Critical to this, newspapers and media outlets must turn to scientific experts to write not only their comment sections but their mainstream news articles on scientific discoveries. Too often they rely on journalists who are non-specialists with the consequence that much of the nuance of scientific research is lost, and the calibre of differing scientific claims unsubstantiated.

Building trust requires a significant reduction of fraud and plagiarism, which can be addressed by more peer review and cross-checking claims against other research. The motivations for scientists to cheat can be powerful: to advance university careers, to achieve further funding, to make money commercially, and the problem needs more candour in tackling it. The Standing Committee on Responsibility and Ethics in Science advocate the intrinsic motivation that we have consistently endorsed: '[The] ethical responsibility of the scientific community is ultimately borne by the individual scientist . . . the ethical awareness of the individual scientist is of utmost importance.'[34] The personal integrity of scientists is also called on to build trust in one final area: the public fear of scientists leading us sleepwalking into disaster. More open debate with the public, and the emergence of many more scientists of integrity with public faces to debate issues on television may be all one can do. A malevolent scientist unleashing a biological weapon in a crowded city is always a possibility and being honest with the public about the risks is the only course that will build trust. Science, technology and astronomy are wonderfully exciting and enriching to all: with better teaching, communication and investment to allow our best scientific ideas to blossom, there is no reason why science cannot be where it should be, one of the most trusted and treasured facets of Britain.

If science explores the physical world of material, religion explores the spiritual world within us. Whereas the scientific method depends upon experimentation and the accumulation of evidence from which one builds a testable hypothesis, religious faith will always remain a personal matter, which can never be tested or seen. It is not about knowing something about the material world which can be communicated to others. This is not to deny that many people who may not have a deep personal faith will nevertheless still trust their religious institutions and derive meaning from them – as a source of cultural identity, social network and moral code, often deepening the bonds with their own families who have belonged to the same bodies. But with faith, it is personal experience alone which motivates an individual to hold trust in what they see as a supernatural power or person. Arguments from militant atheists can be met with counter-arguments from philosophy for the existence of God, but such debates are ultimately arid because trust and belief in God is not about intellectual arguments but conviction.

For public trust in religion to grow, it has to be seen to be practising what it preaches. Where scandals occur, as they are bound to, religious authorities have to be scrupulous in doing everything they can to investigate the problem, and communicate the truth to the public. We will always expect religious professionals to behave better than we do ourselves, and those who opt for the religious life have to accept that responsibility. What some priests and others have done to innocent children will scar those children for life, and their actions have spawned powerful waves of mistrust: but the deeper corruption is that the powerful people in authority hid the truth because they were worried about their own reputations and that of their own institutions. Of all the preachers of trust described in this book, their conduct ranks as the worst.

The indifference to religion that comes from affluence and consumer goods may yet turn to religion's advantage, as people find that material goods do not provide them with the depth of meaning they seek in life. The spiritual, which includes the sense of wonder in nature and the arts, of love, and of awe at creation, is far more deeply satisfying than anything materialism and intellectual conviction can provide. The three Abrahamic religions have been often suspicious of young people turning to the mysticism of the East, including meditation, and some church groups have banned yoga from their premises. Yet it is those who are turning to contemplation and meditation who may well be doing more to try to align themselves with divine purpose than those who have gained powerful positions in religious hierarchies. As Karen Armstrong argues in *The Case for God*, religion is not something we simply believe in, but rather it is something we *do* through liturgy, ritual, prayer and meditation. Moreover its appeal lies in its ritual and the gathering, over and above the belief.[35] The novelist and commentator Bidisha adds: 'Prayer is a type of moral philosophy, an active process in which the individual interacts . . . with what Plato would have called the good or the just . . . But a prayer it is, because it involves a moment of self-awareness and world-awareness, the both together.'[36]

Five hundred years ago the Christian church split in two because leading reformers thought that it had lost touch with its founder. Five hundred years on, a new reformation is needed to meet the widespread yearning of people for spiritual nourishment. John Gray talks about the 'irreducible reality of religion',[37] but religion's relevance and appeal hinges on its ability to satisfy spiritual need free from the constraints of hierarchy and exclusive and dogmatic claim to truth. The old-style Protestant and Catholic churches are dying before our eyes, as are many of the religious hierarchies of other religions. The institutions are not the religions, yet we have all come to believe that they are. No one knows what Moses, Buddha, Shiva, Jesus and Mohammed would think of those institutions and people who preach in their name. Radical change is needed in the twenty-first century so that people at large can feel again the strength of connection with their religious traditions.

'The almost weekly stories of some tragic death are always rooted in
the community in which the incident took place.'
(Universal Images Group)

CHAPTER 9
TRUST IN COMMUNITIES, FAMILIES AND CHILDREN

It takes a village to raise a child.

(Traditional African proverb)

A trust-filled childhood, belonging to a trustworthy family, and living in a trusting neighbourhood are a crucial grounding for a life which will be happy and worthwhile. To enjoy these benefits requires neither wealth nor privilege, yet will confer advantages that money can never buy. Those experiencing a childhood not characterised by trusting relations, a family which is not trustworthy and a community which is atomised will be more likely to lead a life full of suspicion and anxiety. In society's drive for personal gratification and gain, we have given insufficient time and trust to these three areas.

Have we lost trust?

Images of an increasingly fragmented society, memorably caught in Robert Putnam's depiction of America in *Bowling Alone* (2000), which had considerable influence on Blair's thinking about community, are not always corroborated by polls closer to home.[1] In 2004, 82 per cent of respondents told an Ipsos MORI poll they were 'fairly satisfied' or 'very satisfied' with their local neighbourhood as a place to live, while only

11 per cent were 'fairly dissatisfied' or 'very dissatisfied'.[2] Moreover, 95 per cent of those polled in the same year by YouGov claimed they knew who their neighbours were.[3] But being 'satisfied' with and conscious of your neighbours is not the same as trusting them. More significant is the response to the question: 'Do you trust the ordinary man/woman on the street to tell the truth?' After falling from 64 per cent to 52 per cent between 1993 and 2000, the number who said 'yes' has since remained relatively stable at around 50 per cent.[4] Britons know on average just nine neighbours by name, and only fourteen neighbours overall.[5] A report by the Prince's Trust in 2008 found that almost one in ten Britons failed to meet others socially on a weekly basis, and 15 per cent did not speak to their neighbours more than once a week. A high 65 per cent of respondents thought that people in the future would have more contact through the internet than they would 'face-to-face'.[6]

Throughout human history, man has learnt to rely on cooperation with others in order to survive, and many have concluded that man is 'hard wired' for trusting relationships with his neighbours.[7] Richard Layard sees trusting relations with neighbours as fundamental to individual happiness; yet numbers claiming to believe that others 'could generally be trusted', which stood at 60 per cent in the late 1950s, fell to 44 per cent in the early 1980s and had fallen even further, to 29 per cent, by 2003.[8] Richard Reeves, director of Demos, commented: 'We're not just talking about being happy to chat in the lift. What we're talking about is that people believe most people can't be trusted most of the time and it is difficult, but not impossible, to trust someone whom you don't know well.'[9]

We value our families highly. In a BBC poll taken in 2007, 69 per cent said they were 'very happy' with family life, and 94 per cent described themselves overall as 'happy' with it. The pleasure is not shared equally by all ages: in the same poll, 73 per cent of respondents said they were 'most happy' when spending time with their families, but 42 per cent of 18–24 year olds said they were 'most happy' being with their friends instead (one might have expected this figure to be higher). While 70 per cent of respondents to the survey thought that family life was 'less successful' than in their parents' generation, 76 per cent nevertheless professed to be 'optimistic' about the future facing their family.[10] Whatever the truth about trust in the community and family, it is certainly the case that trust levels could be higher.

Why is trust not higher?

The last fifty years have not been easy for community life. A series of factors have eroded the stability and cohesion of the patchwork of villages and towns which once made up Britain. Even if the England of 'long shadows on cricket grounds, warm beer [and] invincible green suburbs'[11] was always more the stuff of legend than reality, community identity has undoubtedly suffered over time.

The decline in opportunities for shared experiences has been a strong factor detracting from community cohesion. The 'Pals battalions', made up of men who enlisted from the same towns to fight in the First World War, such as the 'Grimsby Chums' and the 'Accrington Pals', could not have been more significant in binding those communities together. When their young men died, the villages, towns and cities had a common source of grief. The war memorials that spread across the country in the inter-war years, and the services of remembrance, provided the communities with a tangible and emotionally charged shared folk memory. So too did the Second World War, with a new set of names, smaller in number, chiselled lower down onto the same memorials. Putnam believes that trust levels of 1950s America might have been higher because many felt a deep bond created by their experiences during that war.[12] The evocation of the 'Dunkirk spirit' and the sense of a common enemy gave communities a common reference point, and VE Day in May 1945, with its street parties, fêtes and bunting, was perhaps the high point in the last hundred years of shared community activity. Even terrible adversity has a silver lining: we shrink from it when it happens, but it binds us together because it forces us to rely on each other and to acknowledge something bigger in our lives than our own daily worries and needs. The fiftieth anniversary of VE Day in May 1995, and the sixtieth anniversary of

D–Day in June 2004, were occasions when local communities organised events together. But if these anniversary celebrations continue into the future, will they still have the same resonance? Will Remembrance Day services, which provide opportunities for communities to congregate and reflect, continue to have the same potency as we journey deeper into the new century? The deaths, within a week of each other in summer 2009, of Harry Patch and Henry Allingham, the last surviving British veterans of the First World War, signalled the end of a human link to an event which so profoundly affected every family in Britain last century. Do we need wars and a common enemy to nurture our communities? It would be sad if we did.

Sports teams can provide opportunities for an upsurge of collective spirit against opponents, though teams are now rarely local. An underdog football team reaching the late rounds of the FA Cup is the highest expression of this local sporting pride. But only a fraction of communities have the chance to be swept up in such euphoria. Richard Harries, the leading churchman, believes Britain is now so splintered into different sub-groups that it has virtually 'no unifying set of symbols, myths, or language, except the vestiges of monarchy'.[13] Royal events do indeed provide significant opportunities for communities to join together; it is rare that people above a certain age do not have memories of events organised locally across the country to mark the Queen's coronation in June 1953. The royal wedding of Charles and Diana in 1981 provided another occasion for national celebration and local festivities. But that occurred thirty years ago.

Dwindling too is the number of locally based institutions, which impart a sense of community. Occold, in Suffolk, is fondly promoted as 'an old, traditional, rural village that has always had some kind of communal point' by its residents. Yet the village no longer possesses the post office, local shop and pub that it did five years ago.[14] Out-of-town shopping centres, boasting large stores capable of satisfying every need at a cheaper price, have drained the lifeblood out of village shops and town centres. Convenience and consumerism have conquered community.

British pubs were closing at a rate of fifty-two a week in the first half of 2009, a third more than during the same period in 2008, the quickest rate of closures since 1990, when the information was first collated.[15]

In growing numbers, local libraries are closing and amalgamating into larger complexes. Wirral Council is proposing to close twelve libraries, and replace them with a smaller number of centralised, multi-function facilities.[16] Churches are emptying, and public transport in rural areas is dwindling. In October 2007, the Post Office announced its intention to close 2,500 branches out of its network of 14,000; by October 2008, nearly 1,800 post offices had closed.[17] Decline of local employment, including mining, manufacturing and agriculture, the high price of city and town houses, and speed of transport mean that even more people work away from their communities. Some heartening signs counter the trend to centralisation, including NHS walk-in clinics and community policing. But the overall drift is centripetal. A 2009 YouGov survey found that 'the waning community spirit of younger Britons is explained in part by more transient, urban lifestyles. Many young people say they see "no point" in getting to know their neighbours.'[18] By contrast, in Scandinavian countries, where there are higher levels of trust between strangers, the population is less transient; possibly of greater significance, they are also more homogeneous, which, given Britain's history of empire and of immigration, may render the Scandinavian countries a somewhat moot comparison.[19]

Communities, more and more likely to contain people of mixed origins, have to work far harder to develop trust because they *lack the* common reference points which fast-track trustful relations. Bobby Duffy of Ipsos MORI argues: 'We are less likely to be trusting in areas where people are more mobile and where it's more ethnically diverse . . . People like and trust people who are like them.'[20] England's population is set to grow by 9.5 million by 2034, with 70 per cent the result of immigration. Racial antagonisms and inter-racial distrust has led to 'white flight' as the indigenous population moves out of certain areas perceived to be no longer ethnically suitable.[21] These apprehensions have fuelled increased support for the BNP, itself a powerful engine of mistrust. Trevor Phillips, head of the Commission for Equalities and Human Rights, has warned of the dangers of British schools becoming ever more racially segregated, and universities 'colour coded'.[22] Building trust in areas of high racial mixing is fraught, as is finding a way of addressing Muslim extremism which avoids alienating the whole Muslim community. A 2009 report, *Stronger Together*, warns that the government's current 'PREVENT' scheme to address Muslim extremism is proving to be counter-productive, and stresses that it needs to be extended to all extremism.[23]

Crime has taken its toll on trust in communities. We may ideally want to live in a community where we can leave our homes and cars unlocked, walk outside at night without glancing around us, and have our dropped wallets returned, but more often than not, to do so would be an act of unwarranted blind trust. In August 2009, the Audit Commission warned of a surge of drug addiction, alcoholism and domestic violence as the recession continued and unemployment grew. It suggested that most areas are likely to witness increasing social problems, and councils would have to prepare for more fly-tipping, abandoned cars and even stray dogs.[24] The actual crime figures may be falling, but it is the rising fear of crime that damages trust. The almost weekly stories of some tragic death are always rooted in the community in which the incident took place. Certain episodes stick in the mind: Garry Newlove died in August 2007, after being kicked in the head by a gang of youths whom he confronted for vandalising his wife's car; Nick Baty was killed by a seventeen year old in February 2008 whilst trying to help an unconscious youth.

Fear has done much to erode trust within family life also. In *Paranoid Parenting* (2001), Frank Furedi argues that almost everything is now considered dangerous: the cot, babysitter, school, supermarket and park.[25] Fearful parents breed fearful children. Parents may think they are doing their best for their children, but it is their fear of something dreadful happening – statistically very unlikely – which shapes their actions. Images of Jessica Chapman and Holly Wells, murdered in Soham in

2002, or the disappeared Madeline McCann, float in their subconscious. Parents are fearful of letting their children take risks, whether playing in the park unsupervised or climbing trees. According to the Children's Society's 'Good Childhood Inquiry' (2009), 39 per cent of adults went out unsupervised before their eleventh birthday, but only 17 per cent of the same adults believe today's children should be allowed to do so.[26] The charity Living Streets reported in August 2009 that half of all 5–10 year olds had never played on their own streets, whereas almost nine in ten of their grandparents had done so.[27]

The result, says relationship counsellor Suzie Hayman, is that 'children who are overprotected trust neither themselves nor the outside world. If parents don't train their children to be self-reliant, they won't develop the skills to make their own judgements'.[28] Child protection policies have arguably done more harm than good to the development of psychologically healthy young people, and have fostered an atmosphere where, as Furedi writes, 'adults feel uneasy about acting on their healthy intuition and feel forced to weigh up whether, and how, to interact with a child'.[29] If we constrain people's natural human instinct to nurture and protect others, we make unnatural what should be natural. The balance when it comes to children has tipped too far towards a presumption of mistrust. We are becoming a 'sick society' and creating 'mass mutual distrust', says Jenni Russell in the *Sunday Times* in August 2009. 'First, children were warned about adults; now adults are being warned about children . . . the effects of this coldness and detachment will be worse for those who need adult guidance and contact most.'[30]

Parents, who may not have had the benefit of good parenting themselves, do not give their children the space and respect that they need, if they are to grow into autonomous adults. Letting children make mistakes, including getting drunk, holding parties that get out of hand, and having relationships, are all parts of the rite of passage. If parents are too heavy handed, their child will never feel that they are supported in piloting their way through the difficult terrain of adolescence. Many parents look furtively through their children's computer activities on Facebook or

Bebo, or purchase packages like the Internet Babysitter, which will record all internet contact, chat room usage and websites their children visit.[31] Some have even resorted to hiring private sleuths, such as the Surrey-based Answers Investigation, or employing undercover 'teenagents' to spy on their children. 'The relationship between parents and adolescent children has broken down,' concludes paediatric psychologist Dr Nick Barlow, and 'it isn't just the children who are at fault: the parents are partly to blame.'[32]

The break-up of the traditional family has compounded problems of trust. Britain has the worst record in the world for family breakdown, and boasts the highest levels of divorce and lone parenting in Europe. Although divorce rates have been falling, around one in three children still experiences divorce or separation before the age of sixteen.[33] Marriage rates are at their lowest level since 1895, according to *The Economist* in July 2009, falling by 40 per cent between 1970 and 2000, with births outside marriage rising to four in ten.[34] Numbers of single-parent families have risen significantly, and the effects have not been happy for children: lone mothers are often poorer, more likely to suffer from stress and health problems, and may have more problems interacting with their children.[35] Cohabitation, where couples live together without being married, increased from 9 per cent to 14 per cent in just ten years, from 1996 to 2006.[36] Yet, as a Civitas report found, children living with cohabiting couples do less well at school and are more likely to suffer emotional problems than those with married parents.[37] There are many superb single or cohabiting parents, and equally many exceptionally poor parents in traditional nuclear families, but evidence overwhelmingly demonstrates that traditional family structures, and their stability, are enormously significant in the formation of trust in children. The *Good Childhood Inquiry* blames excessive individualism for family break-up and many of the other problems children face.

Trust has been eroded, finally, because of the ubiquitous temptations of modern consumerist society. 'You use your wealth to free yourself of the inconvenience of other people,' said former Number 10 staffer David Halpern.[38] 53 per cent of respondents told the BBC that they ate a main meal with their family every day, but this might entail the most perfunctory gathering and quick dispatch of food, while mobiles are simultaneously checked, with little conversation or interaction.[39] 'Television has had a terrifically negative effect,' says Putnam. 'If you walk down the street in any English or American town you'll see a blue glow coming from the window. People are watching television rather than being connected with each other and that is making them more mistrustful.'[40] It is not just television; computers are the bigger problem. At least families can share one television screen together; only with difficulty can they watch the same computer screen. Instead, the family scurries off to their own terminals to pursue their own separate lives, watching films and television, visiting social network sites, catching up on e-mails and listening to music. 'Everyone is increasingly desperate for attention,' says India Knight, 'and yet we spend more and more of our leisure time . . . ignoring live humans and doing things alone online.'[41] More money has meant that drinking, smoking and drug-taking become more affordable. These activities are often disapproved of by parents, but with the consequence that children become more secretive and, in a vicious cycle, trust evaporates further.

How can we regain trust?

It is individual, family and community resilience in the face of great adversity which most strikes me, rather than apocalyptic visions of a broken society. Trust, nevertheless, could be and must be higher within communities and families, and with children.

Rebuilding trust in communities provides a rich concoction of ideas; here we begin small scale and work up. Greeting neighbours and strangers, and showing good manners to all, should become ingrained in our national culture. How does one achieve this? A national Good Manners Day, held in 2003, was the right idea, but the wrong vehicle. The 'Young Foundation' published a booklet, *Civility: Lost and Found* in 2009, searching for how to cultivate a more civil society, with more respect, kindness and decency. Its authors, Geoff Mulgan and Alessandra Buonfino, argue that civility is best understood as a set of norms and rules first learnt in childhood.[42] We absorb these manners principally from parents, then school, the media and, least importantly but still significant, from leaders in all spheres. Children whose parents teach them to be polite and respectful themselves rear children who are polite and respectful. Local communities could promulgate their own codes of good manners, but more important is to inculcate civility through education, role models and the good example of others. Holding doors open, giving up seats on buses and trains, learning the importance of saying 'thank you' and asking those who look lost if they want help should all be passed down and become second nature. Learning how to speak clearly, and how to listen, are also fundamental. Predictability is a vital ingredient of trust, and clear understandings and expectations of norms between people would allow neighbourliness to flourish. Older people are typically disconcerted by the lack of civility of the young; a clearer understanding of civil conventions would reduce the mistrust between adults and young people.

Civility needs to be manifest on our roads. 'Shared space' is a novel, some say tricksy, concept which encourages good manners and personal contact between drivers and pedestrians by removing the 'extrinsic rules' of traditional road vocabulary, such as traffic lights, road signs and kerbs, thus making vehicular traffic fully integrated with other human activity. Drivers and pedestrians must have eye contact and communicate with each other to avoid accidents, rather than responding to impersonal instructions. 'We're losing our capacity for socially responsible behaviour,' says the scheme's promoter, Dutchman Hans Monderman; 'the greater the number of prescriptions, the more people's sense of personal responsibility dwindles.'[43] In Norrköping in Sweden, accidents and traffic speeds fell after zebra crossings and traffic signs were replaced by aesthetic improvements to the area and benches.[44] Similar schemes have been operating in Australia, Germany and the Netherlands, and have been trialled in Britain in Ipswich, London and Brighton. In Ashford in Kent, the accident rate has fallen dramatically, and locals speak positively about a new sense of community and courtesy. A more modest scheme on Kensington High Street in London saw a similar reduction in accidents.[45] With the car and motorbike such an integral part of daily life, and satnav making cars even more hermetically sealed, this attempt to 'humanise' the motorised vehicle should not be dismissed lightly.

Public transport possesses many opportunities for boosting conversation and community. Art and poetry on walls, sobering music and plants in bus, underground and rail stations, and the encouragement of live music and drama performances, will all bring people together. Waterproof pianos could be placed in bus and rail stations to develop a sense of community and break down barriers. Such a scheme has been trialled in São Paulo and in Sydney, where thirty pianos were distributed during the Sydney Festival 2009. Not to be outdone, London placed thirty-one pianos in suitable locations in June 2009. The organisers believe it encourages trust among the public because they avoid vandalising the instruments or stealing the laminated songbooks.[46] Oval Underground station in London already has a 'thought for the day' and music, helping to make the capital less of an 'unreal city' of lifeless people, and more one buzzing with human beings connecting with each other.[47]

Communities could become cleaner and greener. Rapid attention to abandoned vehicles, litter in the streets and derelict buildings, which are an eyesore, improves behaviour and spreads communal pride. In the place of ugliness, we need beauty. Plants and trees should make the whole of the country the 'garden of England'. For fifteen years, Trees for Cities has been campaigning for tree-planting around the world; they claim that 98 per cent of Londoners want to see more trees in the capital.[48] 'Brownfield' sites need to be reclaimed, green parkland constructed in their place: a minimum of 20 per cent of land in all urban communities (not including private gardens), should be devoted to green space for gardens and recreation – a feasible target, readily exceeded by Vienna which manages a figure of 50 per cent.[49]

We need food daily, yet very few living in cities understand how it grows. Much more space should be made available for allotments; residents of Camden in London have a forty-year waiting list for such space.[50] All children should have ground where they can grow food or flowers, as giving them a tangible connection with the earth will help develop their understanding of nature, as is happening at the instigation of Alice Waters in Berkeley, California with her idea of the 'edible schoolyard'.[51] The National Trust supports this cause, and in its own scheme, at Minnowburn in Northern Ireland, aims to 'give people with no gardens the chance to nurture their own green space, grow fresh produce and build a sense of community'.[52] Britain's rivers and canals are slowly breathing their way back to life, but much more could be made of them in our towns. Travellers from France, which invests more in creating beautiful towns and villages, must recoil when they arrive at Newhaven or Dover.[53]

Communities need to introduce or reinvent locally based organisations and activities which give people opportunities to belong, to give trust and to learn how to be trustworthy. Scouts, Guides and similar youth organisations should be available in every community, because they have the building of trust at their core. Police, fire stations and social services should all open their doors much more to the public, and provide increased opportunities for volunteering. Every community should possess sports facilities, including swimming pools, tennis courts, and pitches for rugby, hockey, football and cricket. Local arts activities should flourish. Every community could have its own choral, theatre and dance groups, with classes in art and creative writing. The growth of 'book groups' in the last ten years suggests the need for creative stimulation. To help provide a communal highlight, every community should have its own annual festival at a time of year and of a nature entirely of its own choosing. The continent organises such festivals much better, because they are locally inspired: the attempt by Basildon Council to have a St. George's Day celebration, in honour of England's patron saint, is not the way to do it.

Economic vitality needs to come back into town centres and communities. Local businesses of all kinds, offering local employment and catering for local needs, require support from central and local government. Retailers who have outlets in out-of-town shopping centres should be required to have proportional outlets inside the town. Generations of well-meaning town planners and local politicians have made a mockery of our towns and villages, as have national politicians, who sacrificed community life for national economic objectives. The

Liberal Democratic Party has for many years led the way on talking up communities, and it is good that now all the main parties are following suit, aiming to reverse years of damage they caused when in power.

National politicians need to shift genuine power downwards to local level, as discussed when we looked at government. 'Power to the communities' is the mantra at Westminster, but will it lead to devolution of power? Communities themselves must assume responsibility for their own future. 'We have become demanders, not citizens,' says Julia Neuberger; our notion of trusteeship requires that we instead feel a personal duty to leave what we encounter in better shape for future generations than we inherited it.[54] Every community should have elected officials to represent it and to oversee all strictly local issues. To widen participation still further, citizens' juries, consisting of between twelve and twenty jurors selected from the public, should be extended. They were first introduced in Britain, following the experiences of Germany and the USA, in Bristol in September 2007.[55] They hear from a range of experts on a variety of topical issues, and their views are then submitted to local or central government. They could be extended far more for use in local areas, and also involve specific groups, for example the elderly.

'Transition towns' exemplify many trust-building features by strengthening community ties and mutual support. Originating in Totnes in Devon in September 2006, other communities are now in various stages of embracing the thinking, including Lewes in Sussex, Bristol, Stroud in Gloucestershire, and Brixton in London. Started by entrepreneur Rob Hopkins, the idea embraces the thinking of 'give a man a fish and you feed him for a day; give him a rod and he will feed himself for life'. Efforts are made to 're-localise' food, energy supply and transport. Totnes have introduced their own currency to be spent in their local shops, and workshops are run to give the local community skills in growing fruit, making bread and repairing clothes.[56] Experience of shortage during the Second World War was an inspiration, when communities were forced to be more self-sufficient. Global warming will make this need increasingly apparent in the future.

Uniting all these ideas on rebuilding trust in the community is our idea of the 'trust footprint'. Every individual and community has a responsibility, year on year, to ensure that the total quantity of trust they generate has increased. An action which damages trust has to be balanced by actions which promote trust and trusteeship for the future to an equal degree. Each town, village and borough in the country should hold annual prize-givings for those members and institutions that have done the most to build trust. In schools, prize-giving ceremonies prove to be powerful unifying forces, which help identify to all role models who have contributed the most, and the approach could apply equally happily to civic life. National exemplars, in the form of a panel of a thousand celebrities and high achievers, who would agree to serve for five years as role models, would be invited to give away the prizes. These one thousand will all have received much from society in fame and money, and this is an opportunity for them to balance their 'trust footprint' by giving back to the community.

Volunteering at all ages builds trust and makes us feel happier. It also reduces blood pressure and cholesterol levels and extends life.[57] It builds trust in both the volunteers and those served.[58] Dame Elisabeth Hoodless, the head of Community Service Volunteers (CSV), says, 'The nation needs more of the love, skills and time that volunteers offer, to tackle child abuse and home care for the frail elderly, to raise reading levels and protect the environment. Volunteering builds trust across society.' As in France, Germany, Israel, Italy and the US, every school leaver should be offered the chance to serve full time for a year. Research suggests 86 per cent would volunteer, if they could work with their friends.[59] The scheme would be made up of four equal components: training with the army and experiencing physical and mental character-building challenges; practical work to improve the environment, including cleaning beaches, towns and countryside of rubbish, repairing fences and walls, and creating new parks and playing fields; working on community programmes to help the elderly, the physically and mentally sick and the vulnerable; and learning social and practical skills, including making clothes, growing food, building furniture, leadership and emotional intelligence. National service would develop all eight of the aptitudes that reside in each human being, not just the intellectual intelligence tested at schools and universities. It would reduce youth crime[60] and teenage pregnancies[61] and would be a rite of passage, as in Israel. Two MPs in particular, David Blunkett and Frank Field, support the concept: in 2008 Blunkett took a plan to the Prime Minister.[62] David Cameron and Steve Hilton, his strategist, have spoken positively about a more limited six-week programme. We need to be more ambitious: as the gap between rich and poor widens we need to strengthen our communities by harnessing youthful energy.

A national service programme would not be cheap – but far less expensive than doing nothing. Youth crime, teenage pregnancies, poor parenting and low reading levels, leading to unemployment and environmental neglect, combine to cost the nation substantially more. Would such a scheme strengthen the democratic process? Certainly. CSV's 'Agents 4 Change' and Barack Obama's election campaign demonstrate the positive impact of 'giving people something to do'. Young people identify increasingly with causes, not political parties.[63] They want to generate change and explore how to achieve it. This energises them to engage with the democratic process, building on their compulsory citizenship education. Politicians need to harness this energy by listening and assisting citizens to take action. Half of the UK's population volunteers and eleven million people tell researchers they would 'if only they were asked'.[64] Volunteer numbers have risen sharply since 2008. The need is for more opportunities, as many voluntary agencies are at capacity.

Government at all levels should 'open doors' to welcome the public's help in hospitals, schools, national parks, libraries, child protection, the police and emergency services and the judicial system. There are outstanding beacons of excellence nationwide. It can be done, but leadership is needed to overcome inertia and fear. The recession has caused many to rethink their values. Schools are increasingly recognising the value of curriculum-related service; it raises both attendance[65] and attainment.[66] CSV mobilises over 200,000 volunteers annually – and over 70,000 on its 'Make a Difference Day' – and 64 per cent are still volunteering six months later.[67] Broadcasters should develop storylines featuring 'unsung heroes'. Government should also review the 'vetting and barring' regulations, which discourage volunteers and give young people and children the sense that no one should be trusted. It would be the making of a more trusting and trustworthy Britain.

Families are the core building blocks of society; they are where children develop 'a sense of self, security and self-esteem . . . and an inner code of conduct'.[68] Figures on the decline of marriage and the rise of sole and cohabiting parents suggest that the mix of government policies and societal norms over the last forty years have not been sufficiently effective at stemming family decay. Still more needs to be done to ensure that children have a home where they encounter trustworthy adults, from whom they can absorb their core lessons for life. The vicious cycle of bad parenting needs to be broken, or the problems of untrusting and untrustworthy children and adults will deepen. The desirable outcome is that only adults that are emotionally mature enough, and practically able to offer a serious prospect of giving their children twenty years stable love and care, should have babies. To get to this state, we all – individuals, schools, media and government – have responsibilities. A change of heart within individuals is the only way that we will be able to build a more trustful society which endures. It is easy to ignore our own responsibilities, through neglecting our own relationships within the families we were born into, and with the families we choose to have. Schools need to provide young people with considerable family and sex education, and with an education that gives them a sense of self-worth and of belonging, to reduce the risk of a void in their lives, which they might be tempted to fill by having a child. The media needs to give a more responsible message about having children and how best to rear them. Society has been too keen to defend the rights of parents, however ill suited they are to have children, and insufficiently mindful of the rights of the child to have stable and trustworthy parents. Finally, government should give clearer signals and benefits to sufficiently mature parents, and disincentives to those who are not ready.

We need to nurture our children better, which can best be achieved while setting firm boundaries and a framework of duties and responsibilities for them to fulfil: children flourish best not with indulgence but with clear structures. The young in Britain have seen levels of depression and distress rise; the UNICEF report, although contested for its reliability, ranked Britain bottom in five of six categories for child well-being among twenty-one industrial countries.[69] More love and stability at home, and emotionally intelligent schooling, will best support children. Pets can further help them develop their trustworthiness, and can provide a happy relationship for them to enjoy.

Forming good relationships and giving trust comes naturally to some, but to many others it does not, and must be learnt. The Relationships Foundation in Cambridge is a leading body studying relationships within families and institutions. Its findings are very clear. For optimum communication, participants should be face to face. Trust is cumulative in relationships, and grows with each successive encounter, so continuity of relationships is all-important. We need background knowledge and understanding of whom we are communicating with to maximise benefits. All these three factors speak of the importance for families to be stable, to be loving and accepting, and to spend time with each other.[70] We have seen how much Chinese society gains because of the great respect families have for their older generations. Family history projects, which involve the young interviewing their more elderly relatives, can build bridges between generations and help the young form a new appreciation of the old. Families are sacred, and no time in life will ever be better spent in the building of trust than families spending time together.

Communal and family life needs to become the bedrock of people's lives, rather than an add-on, as it had become for many by the year 2000. We may dispute the ways of achieving these goals: the ideas contained above may appear too far-fetched, or socially authoritarian, for some tastes. We speak with real conviction though when we say that the pendulum has swung too far towards self-obsessed individualism, and is beginning to swing back, to the great enrichment of us all.

The media has many diverse motivations. Giving the public a balanced and representative view of what has happened is rarely high on its list.

(Reuters/Andrew Winning)

CHAPTER 10
TRUST IN THE MEDIA, CULTURE AND SPORT

You cannot hope to bribe or twist
(Thank God!) the British journalist.
But, seeing what the man will do
Unbribed, there's no occasion to.

Humbert Wolfe (1885–1940), poet

In this final chapter, we turn to three areas which all have vital roles because of their extensive impact on our lives, in breadth and depth. We look first at the media, and later consider sport and culture. Sport appears to have a deeply embedded cheating culture, and we examine some recent cases of corruption. But sport also provides quite exceptional opportunities, as do cultural pursuits, for rebuilding trust and trusteeship.

Have we lost trust in the media?

Claims of a 'collapse of trust', as we have repeatedly seen in this book, have been exaggerated. But if only 19 per cent of respondents in a recent Ipsos MORI poll[1] said that they 'trust journalists', and if tabloid journalists came out bottom of the 2008 Public Standards trust survey with only 10 per cent of the population saying they believe them,[2] then is there a genuine crisis of trust in the media? Cases of journalists, newspapers and media companies behaving poorly are numerous. Concern about it has sparked a number of analyses: Onora O'Neill spent some considerable time in her 2002 BBC Reith Lectures[3] discussing trust in the media; Robin Aitken published *Can We Trust the BBC?* in 2007;[4] 2008 saw the publishing of Adrian Monck's *Can You Trust the Media?*[5] and Nick Davies's *Flat Earth News*;[6] while Tony Blair spoke with passion at the end of his premiership about his view of an untrustworthy media. The relationship between the media and public life in Britain, he said, was so damaged that it was sapping 'the country's confidence and self-belief; it undermines its assessment of itself, its institutions; and above all, it reduces our capacity to take the right decisions, in the right spirit for our future'.[7] Jeremy Paxman described trust in his MacTaggart lecture as 'the defining problem of contemporary television'.[8] Is trust the defining problem of the media at large?

Distaste with the press certainly has a long history. 'I cannot understand how an innocent man can touch a newspaper without convulsing in disgust', French poet Charles Baudelaire wrote in the nineteenth century,[9] while Charles Dickens complained that the press was 'so filthy and bestial that no honest man would admit one into his house for a water-closet doormat'.[10] 'There was no golden age,' insists Brian Cathcart: 'I am not aware of any time when newspapers were really trusted.'[11] The polls support the idea that mistrust in the media is not new. Trust in journalists, low today at 19 per cent, is at exactly the same level as in 1983.[12] Richard Sambrook, director of BBC Global News, concludes that trust has declined no more in the media than anywhere else in society.[13] However, only 43 per cent of all people polled by YouGov in 2008 said they trusted journalists from upmarket newspapers to tell the truth, which contrasts with the 65 per cent who did five years earlier. Over the same period, trust for journalists working in mid-market papers dropped from 36 per cent to 18 per cent, but we do not yet know if this is a long-term trend. [14]

It is more revealing, therefore, to look at public trust in particular sectors of the media. The picture here is clear: national television news rates highest, broadsheets less high and tabloids lowest. Figure 10.1 depicts the results of a 2006 Globescan poll.[15] Blogs are the least trusted news source (there are now thought to be over 200 million), with only 24 per cent of UK respondents saying they trusted them.[16] Puzzlingly, websites are the third least trusted, though these are the fastest growing source of information internationally. In November 2008, there were estimated to be over 150 million websites – and that figure continues to expand at a rate of approximately 10,000 an hour.[17] Google claims there are over one trillion unique web pages.[18] One can only assume that people trust the sites they use most regularly, and the mistrust is directed at the millions of unofficial or bogus websites, which explains why one in two claimed to be 'undecided' in this category internationally. 'International papers' are trusted by only 35 per cent of British respondents – presumably because they are written by 'foreigners' whom we do not know.[19] Distance, we have seen, is fertile ground for distrust.

Figure 10.1: Trust in different media sources

Q: Which professions do you trust to tell the truth?

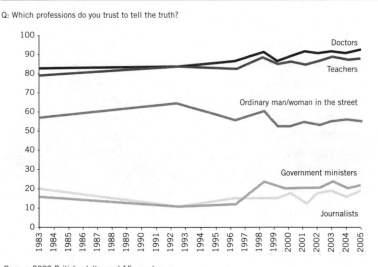

Base: c.2000 British adults aged 15+ each year
Source: Ipsos MORI

The public's trust is therefore higher for radio and television news, than for the print media.[20] Looking just at broadcasters, trust in the BBC outstrips that for the other outlets by a considerable degree. An Ipsos MORI poll in December 2007 found that 56 per cent of those asked said they trusted the BBC most to tell them the truth; only 12 per cent chose ITV, 10 per cent Sky and 9 per cent Channel 4.[21] The BBC also ranks highly compared to other institutions in Britain. In January 2008, as Figure 10.2 shows, the BBC was placed just above the NHS as the most trusted institution in Britain, and significantly above the Church of England and the military. The BBC had roughly four times the trust of the media in general, government and British companies. Only 7 per cent said they trusted the BBC least out of the institutions they were asked to consider.

Figure 10.2: Most and least trusted organisations

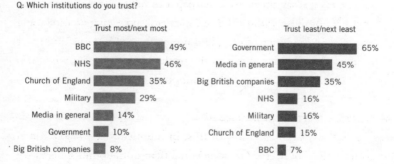

Q: Which institutions do you trust?

Trust most/next most		Trust least/next least	
BBC	49%	Government	65%
NHS	46%	Media in general	45%
Church of England	35%	Big British companies	35%
Military	29%	NHS	16%
Media in general	14%	Military	16%
Government	10%	Church of England	15%
Big British companies	8%	BBC	7%

Base: All respondents (1,070)
Source: Ipsos MORI poll commissioned for the BBC. Jan 2006

Consistently least trusted are tabloid newspapers, whose opinions, boldly stated, have always been considered to be amongst the most influential. The tabloids and mid-range papers such as the *Daily Mail* are courted just as eagerly as the broadsheets by party leaders because they are not only the highest-selling newspapers but are also read by those considered to be less highly educated, and therefore presumably more impressionable as to being told what to think. One expects that within the tabloid world, the *Daily Sport* would be the least trusted: indeed, one would have to ask about the judgement of the reader who did think that this paper was reflecting a balanced view of the world.

Questions of trust in the media are complex, because it seems to matter little whether or not people do 'trust' the media. As Onora O'Neill says of institutions in general: 'The public *claim* to mistrust them — *but still demand their services*.'[22] Monck goes further: 'Not being trusted never lost anyone a reader or a viewer. Editorial cock-ups and journalistic frauds are not followed by dramatic drops in circulation or ratings.'[23] That said, 28 per cent of UK respondents in the Globescan poll claimed to have stopped using a media source after it lost their trust.[24] But only 30 per cent of *Sun* readers say they trust their paper to tell the truth (as opposed to 90 per cent of those who read *The Guardian*), suggesting that for some readers, trust, and no doubt truth, do not rank high.[25] We can laugh that off, but if citizens do not care about the truth, nor recognise it when it is presented to them, a trusting society cannot be built.

Why have we lost trust in the media?

Looking at the reasons for a loss of trust in the media as a whole, or in particular sections of it, is more conjectural than in the other spheres we have analysed, as it is debatable whether or not we *have* lost trust. But we will hazard some explanations.

The sheer grind of having to turn out 24-hour news in multiple outlets, many of which seem to be barely read or listened to, plays its own role in sacrificing quality to quantity; Raymond Kuhn calls it 'the banalisation of the media'.[26] 'If journalism is really capable of changing for the better, of becoming more ethical and rigorous, or less hysterical, or less hypocritical, it will not happen in the midst of this desperate scramble to fill 100-page magazines, alongside 80-page news sections, and 20-page sports sections,' says Brian Cathcart.[27] Outlets fall over each other to compete for stories, and distort the truth of those they do obtain. *The Daily Telegraph* milked the MPs' expenses story over the summer of 2009 to maximise sales and advertising revenue. Charlie Beckett, director of the Polis think tank, criticises the paper for claiming the high moral ground when doing so, despite breaching the unwritten ethics of its own industry by using 'chequebook journalism' as a means to secure information for the story that was, arguably, obtained illegally.[28]

Overworked journalists frequently lift stories directly from the Press Association, the Associated Press, or Reuters news agencies. A team of researchers from Cardiff University found that over a two week period, 60 per cent of articles from *The Times*, *The Guardian*, *The Independent*, the *Daily Telegraph* and the *Daily Mail* consisted wholly or mainly of wire copy or PR material, and a further 20 per cent showed heavy influence from the same two sources. Only 12 per cent – and this is from the top end of the market – was generated by the reporters themselves.[29] But this phenomenon is not new. Seventy years ago, Sir Joseph Ball, the director of publicity for the Conservative Party in the 1920s and 1930s, taught party officials at headquarters how easy it was to write a press release that would then find its way directly into national newspapers, because journalists would be too lazy to probe the information.[30] Many wonder what percentage (2 per cent?) of the tens of thousands of words in a multi-section Sunday paper are in fact read by the average reader, and equally question the point of reading editorials and opinion columns when all too often we know what the writers will say. It is unsurprising that the sanely brief periodical *The Week*, which succinctly summarises the previous week's journalism, has so many admirers, with its circulation rising 189 per cent between 2002 and 2008.[31]

Hype and sensationalism have corroded not only trust in the press, but also in politicians, institutions and belief systems. The media's role in spreading panic, whether over petrol or the run on Northern Rock in 2008, with a cumulative 'snowball effect' as news channels out-sensationalise each other to attract viewers, is not trustworthy. The media circus around the death of Princess Diana, from the initial pursuit of the paparazzi to the Channel 4 documentary in June 2007, which included graphic images of the crash, despite pleas from Princes William and Harry not to do so, did not build trust. Nor did the media's exploitation of the Madeleine McCann story, following her abduction from Praia da Luz in May 2007; instead, it exhibited the worst episode of media dishonesty in the last decade. But we would be wrong to see sensational and irresponsible reporting as new. 'Early in life I had noticed that no event is ever correctly reported in a newspaper,' said George Orwell, who himself wrote some fine journalism.[32] What is new is the technology and ubiquity, which provide opportunities undreamt of by earlier generations.

As a consequence, 'Britain is a more cynical country than it once was', Polly Toynbee concludes.[33] Cynicism destroys trust in those in positions of authority or influence and it is powerfully corrosive. The media is significantly responsible for an increase in cynicism, especially among the more impressionable young, who know less of life. It is much easier to get a reaction through negativity than being positive: it is our one-in-twenty rule in action. Programmes like *The Thick of It* and *Have I Got News For You* and *Mock the Week* claim to be satire, and satire has a long and respectable history going back to the ancient Greek playwright Aristophanes, through Jonathan Swift and Orwell to the present day. Satire punctures the pomposity of the powerful and arrogant, and alerts us to the danger of blind trust. Cynicism is much easier and more disruptive, and leaves us wondering what, if anything, the cynic believes in. Too much media output claims to be satirical, but lacks the artistry to be so, and is plain cynical and cheap.

Corporate greed, the desire to maximise the audience size and drive for profits, has undermined quality and innovation and has, more obviously, damaged trust. The sense of corporate and moral responsibility that is present in the best companies in other industries seems to be largely absent from the media sector. The media has to rely on advertising but has not always displayed judgement and honesty in doing so. There can be a nasty smell about its relationship with advertisers, with even some news channels biased by the piper calling the tune.[34] 'From a commercial perspective trust is a worthless asset for media owners,' concludes Monck.[35] Restructuring of the industry initiated by the Conservatives before 1997 and continued by Labour, has also played its part in the loss of quality, with obligations removed from independent television to produce 'public service programmes'. In place of the great regional companies with distinguished records like Granada, Jeremy Paxman believes we now have 'one unstructured mass'.[36]

For all the enormous respect the BBC commands, it has not escaped criticism. The BBC likes to see itself as the drag anchor guaranteeing independence and sanity in a fast-moving world. 'But the drag anchor has been dragged along itself,' says Toynbee: 'it often takes its agenda from what have been recent stories in the press that day or the day before.'[37] Some are uncomfortable with how far the BBC has drifted from the high-minded, public service ideals set out by its founder, Lord Reith, and see its enthusiasm to become a multinational company, selling products around the world, as evidence of the profit motive's triumph. Others see it as a pragmatic response to the 21st-century world, and the surveys do not suggest that fears of commercialisation of the BBC are widespread.

The behaviour of powerful proprietors has regularly aroused concerns because of the extent of their influence. Media moguls are not new to Britain: Max Beaverbrook, William Camrose and Brendan Bracken dominated the press in the middle of the century, as did Lords Northcliffe and Rothermere before them. It is common to blame Rupert Murdoch of News Corp for lowering the moral tone and for taking his outlets downmarket in search of a mass market. But in terms of any interference and manipulation, he is an *ingénu* compared to some of these earlier press barons. Alastair Campbell is another favourite exhibit for the prosecution: indeed, he bullied the media and manipulated government information in a way that compromised the trustworthiness of both government and media. But such heavy-handed media management from Number 10 is not new either. When Neville Chamberlain was appointed Prime Minister in May 1937, the aforementioned Joseph Ball would give highly partisan press briefings, ostensibly on behalf of the government as a whole, but really in favour of Chamberlain. When Anthony Eden resigned as Foreign Secretary over appeasement in February 1938, Ball slipped to his boss that he had 'taken certain steps privately' to ensure their own version was the one the press would represent.[38] Not even Campbell or Damian McBride stepped so low as purchasing and running their own newspaper to boost support for the Prime Minister, as Ball did with *Truth*. Its politics were, Richard Cockett writes, 'notoriously pro-German and anti-Semitic'.[39]

How to regain trust in the media

Our aim is ambitious: to bring trust in the media up to previously unseen levels. Our recommendations start with the individual and finish with society as a whole.

Each of us should behave in a more trustworthy manner in our relations with the media. The reason newspapers keep belting out images of Madeleine and Kate McCann is because we like to see them. Without us, there would be no *Daily Sport*, no *Heat*, no *I'm A Celebrity: Get Me Out Of Here*, nor any of the other offence-giving reality TV shows. Kant speaks of our obligation not to deceive, of the need not to treat others as lesser mortals,[40] and wrote that it is natural to feel good when bad people get what they deserve. It is equally true that some feel good when good people get what they do not deserve. Something in the brain is excited by pain, the discomfort of others and violence. We can make a choice to nourish that sensation, as when we choose to drive exceedingly slowly past car crashes. It is *Schadenfreude*, pleasure in the suffering of others. It is not attractive, and without greater aspiration from the public to be higher minded, the media will continue to nourish those baser instincts. Buddhists have a concept of *mudita*, which is happiness in the good fortune of another, the opposite of *Schadenfreude*. 'Readers and viewers must themselves take responsibility for what they see and watch,' says one media commentator, because, as with politicians, 'we get the media we deserve.'[41] Our trust model places high responsibility on the individual, and without this aspiration to be more trustworthy, trust will never be built.

A new commitment to high standards of professional integrity needs to be made by journalists themselves. Perhaps former editor of *The Sun*, Kelvin Mackenzie, was speaking tongue in cheek when he described 'ethics' as 'a place to the east of London where men wear white socks',[42] but many still wondered what his ethical principles were, as with those of many of his fellow editors. Because of the reach of the media, the opportunities that journalism offers for doing good and spreading trust are incomparable. A doctor might see twenty patients in a day, a teacher interact with 150 children, but the work of a journalist can reach thousands and even millions of people. The potential to do harm through deliberate falsification, carelessness, being unrepresentative or manipulative is extensive. Journalists need not only to conduct themselves in their work to the very highest ethical standards; they need high standards throughout their lives. The popular perception of journalists is that they are hard-drinking, cynical and with uncertain moral values. It would be surprising if the pen and the life they lead were totally disconnected. Many journalists admit how shoddy the ethical standards are within their own profession, yet they carry on regardless: 'We journalists keep telling people that there is nothing to be done about it, or that it is all innocent fun, or that the victims are asking for it, or that it is a regrettable but necessary by-product of freedom of speech,' writes Cathcart.[43] Journalists themselves need to strive for the highest ethical standards.

Some have seen increased transparency as the catch-all solution to cleaning up the media. It will achieve no such thing, because increased visibility will never totally solve the problem of corrupt journalists and unethical programme makers. Transparency, we have argued, can encourage more devious forms of deception: it is not an intrinsic way of enhancing trust. O'Neill writes that transparency destroys secrecy but may not limit deception, and to restore trust, it is deception and lies which need to be reduced rather than secrecy.[44] Visibility is at least a step in the right direction. It prevents journalists hiding behind anonymity: until the late 1960s most articles were written in the press without by-lines.[45] Visibility certainly encourages people to take responsibility: the anonymous diarist hiding behind his cloak is the close cousin of the cyber bully.

Journalism should be taken seriously as a proper profession. Teachers require a specialist degree, or a post-graduate qualification, and are regularly appraised and monitored. If they want to become a headteacher, they have to pass a further professional qualification. Lawyers and accountants follow a similar route, with demanding exams. Doctors and dentists train for several years and then operate under the strictest of codes. Yet one can work in broadcasting, or become a journalist, an editor or a media executive, with no formal training or qualifications. Continuous professional development is further ingrained in the whole profession of teaching, medicine and law. It is not in journalism. Journalism must become a full profession such as teaching, into which only those who pass, and pass well, through university courses are admitted, and they should then be appraised and monitored as meticulously as doctors. A code, equivalent in impact to the values code in use in the army or doctors' Hippocratic Oath, should be introduced. But codes can still easily be flouted, as is the National Union of Journalists' code, which advocates 'avoiding plagiarism' and doing nothing 'to intrude into anybody's private life . . . unless justified by overriding consideration of the public interest.'[46] A more binding code for all in the media should be introduced, to be policed in the first instance by the media outlets themselves.

Improving the social diversity of journalists would enhance trust by allowing the British public to see a fairer, better representation of different ethnicities and social classes in the profession. Few factors cause more mistrust than the sense of 'us and them'. The drive to professionalise journalism will cut straight across this broadening objective unless considerably more money is put into grants and bursaries for those from poorer backgrounds. At present, the number of bursaries to pay for journalism courses has been reduced.[47] Roy Greenslade is one of many to argue that there must be greater effort to 'recruit more working class journalists'.[48] The growing realms of citizen and public journalism, facilitated by the electronic revolution, allow another route for the media to become more open to those of all social and ethnic backgrounds. Commenting electronically on articles has been possible for readers for more than ten years, and non-studio audience participation in programmes such as *Question Time* and phone-in radio shows for much longer. Open access forums such as network journalism and Wikipedia allow the public to write the scripts. But open participation does not necessarily build trust, as shown by the Edelman investigation that found only 27 per cent of 35–64 year olds considered Wikipedia 'credible',[49] despite a 2005 study which found it to be 'about as accurate as the Encyclopedia Britannia'.[50] Too much direct public participation, unless carefully monitored, can be detrimental to trust.

Enhancing accountability is never going to be a foolproof way of building trust in the media, any more than more regulation will in any other sphere we have examined. The best measures of accountability are those overseen by the organisation itself. So we should have good reason to trust that the board and senior executives of newspapers and broadcasting companies have the ethical beliefs and professionalism to ensure the highest standards prevail.

Accountability to external bodies is less desirable but, given the culture and behaviour of parts of the media, it is necessary until media outlets show that they are fully trustworthy without outside oversight. The Press Complaints Commission (PCC), which is funded by the media industry and draws half of its members from it, is often perceived as weak. For a transitional period, the PCC needs strengthening and made more independent, with a duty to investigate unprofessional conduct rather than merely reacting to complaints, as at present. 'On the larger floors of the national media, the PCC is strangely silent', wrote Magnus Linklater, 'and it is here that the standards of what passes as acceptable behaviour have become so grotesquely distorted.'[51] Alan Rusbridger warned in 2003 that 'if the PCC is not seen to be open, independent and effective, there is little doubt that the courts will intervene'; this is exactly what has now happened, with the courts, rather than the PCC, developing their own precedent-based law.[52] But with legal aid extremely rare, only the rich such as J. K. Rowling and Max Mosley are able to hold the press to account in court. Peta Buscombe, the PCC's chairman from April 2009, promises that, under her, it will have real teeth.[53] It certainly has a job to do to build trust in the press and in itself. Broadcasting regulation is generally better done. Ofcom, established in 2002, launches its own investigations and fines those in breach of the broadcasting code, with ITV having to pay a record £5.7 million levy for its part in a phone-in scandal.[54]

Relations between the media and government need to be improved, and dramatically. The battles between both since Labour came to power in 1997 have served no one. Mark Thompson, director general of the BBC, describes the relationship as 'vituperative,'[55] while Richard Sambrook describes 'an unbreakable cycle of distrust, whereby politicians can't be honest because they get crucified',[56] and John Lloyd sees a 'theatrical distrust of politicians' by the media.[57] Everyone agrees there is a problem: trust, which was often present in the postwar era, as during 1970–74, has been lost. No one agrees on a solution. Both sides have been guilty of terrible errors of judgement, and raking over the past is pointless. What there has to be is a *presumption of trust* on both sides. The government from top to bottom needs to appreciate that the media has a duty to inform the public, which is to pump out stories twenty-four hours a day, and is inevitably, in a free market, locked into competition with other outlets to provide 'better' stories. The media in its turn needs to appreciate that government has a difficult job; it cannot always say what it is doing or why it is doing it, and the pressure under which it has placed government has been largely responsible (though not totally) for the latter's resorting to 'spinning'. Whatever the new system adopted – more filmed press conferences given by the Prime Minister, a much more liberal Freedom of Information Act, or an end to the current lobby system – matters less than the commitment by both sides to change the culture and to begin a mature relationship together. Most other countries, including Germany and Australia, manage the relationship far better. There is nothing uniquely manipulative about either the British government or the British media, and there is no reason why a new era cannot begin, based on trust, rather than a presumption of mistrust.

Newspapers should be reclassified so that tabloids no longer immediately fall into that category, and only merit the privileges of being called a *newspaper* if they meet certain high standards. In the US, tabloids are not classified as newspapers,[58] and are fairly innocuous, though the 'supermarket tabloids', specialising in gossip, astrology, celebrity news and bizarre stories, would be more immediately recognisable to their British cousins. Finally, the industry itself, and individual outlets, should place far more emphasis upon positive stories that promote morality and feature human nature at its best rather than at its worst. Awards could be given amongst papers for those who make the strongest positive contribution to the outlet and to the industry, and produce the most elevating and inspiring output. As Martin Seligman noted ten years ago in his field of psychology, the focus was morbidly on the dysfunctional, the sick, the depressed, rather than the life-enhancing, the uplifting and the positive. The individual can transform his or her life by *learned optimism*. The journalist, the newspaper and the television channel can transform their outlooks, and by doing so, can change the world.

The media is only a reflection of ourselves: it is what we see when we look in the mirror. If we are petty, mean and obsessed by cruelty, then this is what our media will indulge. If we are compassionate, imaginative and concerned for the common good, as well as our own good, then that is what we will find the media becomes. The more we ourselves, and journalists, move into the second category, the more quickly we will move away from the media we deserve to the media we can trust.

Sport

'Of all the woeful cases of cheating in professional sport that have come up in recent years, none is more pathetic than the case of Harlequins rugby union team and the player who fiddled a substitution by means of a fake blood capsule,' wrote Simon Barnes in *The Times* in August 2009.[59] This incident, along with the club's attempted cover-up, has damaged the good opinion that many people had of a sport which (justly or not) always prided itself on its integrity. Dean Richards, the former England player and Harlequins head coach, was banned for three years for his part in the affair.[60] 'The fact is that rugby's integrity is dead,' Barnes continued. 'Victory is much more important than anything else.'

His words are a sad echo of Baron Pierre de Coubertin's, the founder of the modern Olympic Games: 'The important thing in life is not victory, but the fight; the main thing is not to have won, but to have fought well'.[61] Sport – like life itself – should be about the means and not the end, an ideal which has been forgotten in the high-stakes world of professionalism and intense competition. At its best, sport spreads friendship and trust; it transcends cultural, social and linguistic boundaries; it provides great pleasure, good health for those who play, and a vital release mechanism for those who just watch; it fosters teamwork and leadership, and teaches lessons that can be usefully transferred to other areas of life. Too often, however, the sport that we witness is so far removed from this description that it is barely recognisable, bound up in cheating, drug-taking and match-fixing, with violent fans, racism and badly behaved sports stars who offer no kind of role model on or off the pitch.

As elsewhere, 'there is a danger of seeing sport as having been in a golden age from which it is now in decline, but that's not the case. Sport had its origins in tricky behaviour, and has always had a complex relationship with honesty and trustworthiness,' says Ed Smith, the former England cricketer, now journalist and author of *What Sport Tells Us about Life*.[62] A fleeting glance at sporting misconduct throughout history suggests that he is right: even back at the Ancient Olympic Games in 388 BC, a boxer named Eupolus of Thessaly bribed his three opponents to let

him win, but he was caught and all four men were fined.[63] Smith explains
how even cricket, thought to epitomise sportsmanship and decency, was
tied up in gambling and match-fixing during the eighteenth century,
and it was only the Victorians who gave the sport its 'moral backbone'.[64]
In 1904, the American Fred Lorz won the marathon at the Olympics
in St. Louis, and was almost presented with his gold medal before it
emerged that for some 11 miles he had been driven by automobile.[65]
We can safely say that cheating in all its forms is as old as sport itself, and
while the ever-increasing amount of money and attention we pay to
sportsmen and women today may not suggest a loss of trust, our cynicism
has nevertheless grown proportionately.

Sports stars' recent behaviour has certainly not helped, especially since
their fame makes them important role models to so many. When players
like Zinedine Zidane are seen headbutting others in the final of football's
World Cup in 2006, or when in 2009 England hero Steven Gerard is
caught up in allegations of drunken brawling in bars, or when numerous
Bath rugby players are tainted with the suspicion of cocaine use, the
detrimental effect they have on fans, other players and the concept of
sport itself is lamentable.

For many people, the rise of gamesmanship and professional fouling
is the most regrettable aspect of modern sport. It is now unusual to watch
a football match without seeing players diving, appealing for throw-
ins they know they don't deserve, or deliberately fouling a player to
prevent them from gaining an advantage. Players in all sports know deep
down whether or not they are guilty of an offence, but the culture is
categorically not to admit to it. That was what made Australian cricketer
Adam Gilchrist seem a 'freak' when he walked off the field after being
caught in the 2003 World Cup against Sri Lanka: the umpire didn't give
him out, because he didn't believe the ball had touched his bat, but
Gilchrist knew and walked.

Perhaps the fact that the debate on honesty and trustworthiness in
sport is complex shows just how far we are from a sporting ideal. As
Smith points out, 'different people draw different lines':[66] one person's

clear-cut example of cheating is blurred for another in the grey areas of legitimate gamesmanship or competitiveness, and changing circumstances inevitably have a large part to play, too. 'You can't generalise with trust,' he says. 'Players are far more at liberty to act honourably when things are going well for them or their team . . . in the heat of a close match, with a borderline decision that could have a serious effect on the game, it's a lot harder.'[67] Nick Greenslade, deputy sports editor at the *Sunday Times*, adds that it can be more difficult to maintain individual integrity in team sports, where a personal decision to act honestly (such as Gilchrist's) could simultaneously let down all of your team-mates.[68]

Even if cheating occurred in the days of amateur sport, professionalism has created new imperatives. Greenslade explains: 'The stakes are a lot higher in the professional era – what they are playing for now is a lot more serious than in the past. Sport has become so intense that players are pushed right to the boundaries of cheating, and inevitably some of them go over the edge.'[69] Former Australian cricketer John Inverarity's opinion is clear: 'Money is an evil in sport. Real sport – the engagement of people for amusement, entertainment or character-building – is tarnished by money because winning becomes more important than those things. This desperation to win means that vile practices enter the sport.'[70]

Taking performance-enhancing drugs is one such practice that has seriously damaged the reputations of sports such as athletics and cycling. British sprinter Dwain Chambers tested positive for them in 2003 and was banned from the Olympics for life;[71] while the winner of the 2006 Tour de France, American Floyd Landis, became the first victor in the event's history to have his title stripped for drug-taking.[72] In 2006, the five-medal heroine of the Sydney Olympics, Marion Jones, tested positive for drug use and was stripped of all medals dating back to 2000 and imprisoned for six months.[73] The culture is so ingrained in the minds of athletes as necessary for success, it seems, that in a 1997 survey, when a group of elite Olympic athletes were asked if they would take performance-enhancing drugs to win, knowing they would not be caught, 98 per cent said 'yes'.[74]

To rebuild trust in sport, we recommend furthering the reach of mentoring programmes, which some of the most affluent football and other sports clubs already offer. These bring young people into contact with professional sportsmen and women role models, creating the face-to-face relationships which can be such a powerful force for good, and crucially reminding players of just how their example filters down into society. Codes of sportsmanship need to be embedded from the youngest ages and the smallest sports clubs upwards. Good values at school, as we have seen so often, need embedding. Inverarity says: 'Children should be taught about honour, and playing both *within* the rules and *in the spirit* of the rules.'[75] Many more awards should be created for individuals and teams who play in a particularly sporting fashion, not just those that win. Cheating and deception in any form should be treated with disdain by all in the media, not tolerated – journalists are often too afraid of doing this, Greenslade says, because they are worried about losing access to the players they criticise.[76] The media should also be encouraged to celebrate quiet heroes who set a good example, like the rugby player Jason Robinson or athlete Kelly Holmes, and either take the spotlight away from sportsmen like Cristiano Ronaldo, who flaunt their money without any principle, or have the courage to reveal how shallow such people are.

Children and adults must be taught to respect referees, and the media could educate the public better about how difficult it is to apply the rules of the game in the heat of the match. Finally, although improved technology will increasingly help to support referees taking difficult decisions, the enduring change we seek is for the players and the spectators to act with integrity themselves, and to have greater ends in mind than the winning of a match, their subsequent career prospects, and the weight of their purse.

Culture

Trust in the arts is generally high, not least because most actors, musicians, dancers, writers and artists are known to be on poor salaries, and rarely have full-time jobs. Most works of art are known to be genuine, and fraud is comparatively rare. The British painter Tom Keating (1917–84) claimed that he forged 2,000 works of art by one hundred artists, which found their ways into many galleries, although he always placed 'time-bombs' or clues in his paintings, knowing that x-rays or experts would reveal the deceit.[77] A greater concern to many is restoration, which purists see as destroying the integrity of the original work of art, be it painting, sculpture or architecture: the 'Ship of Theseus' paradox concerns the question of whether an object which has had all its component parts replaced remains fundamentally the same object.[78] Robert Hewison has written widely criticising the heritage industry, which he says is re-creating an idea of British culture and history which never existed in the past.[79] Britain has at least been spared the master rebuilders of some countries, whose restorations, as in the medieval French town of Carcassonne, 'improved' on the past with their own idiosyncratic additions.[80] The public does not seem troubled by ahistorical restorations, as testified by the growing numbers flocking to see arts and heritage sites: it may even be true that the public prefers the falsely dressed up to the weather-worn original.

The significance of trust in relation to the arts is not the public's trust in them, but rather the opportunities the arts provide for enhancing trust and trusteeship. Iris Murdoch, in *The Sovereignty of Good*, spoke of the unique contribution that the arts can make in elevating human beings to a higher level, and revealing our own natures to us. Brian McMaster reached a similar conclusion in his 2008 report on the arts in Britain: 'excellent culture goes to the root of living, and is therefore relevant to every single one of us. . . art has never been so needed to understand the deep complexities of Britain today.'[81] Accessing the arts should not depend on social class. So all schools should provide compulsory classes in the history of art, offer opportunities for playing in ensembles and listening to classical music, for acting in plays and going to the theatre. High culture need not be a world apart from the experience of all children. Ken Robinson, chairman of the 1999 National Advisory Committee on Creative and Cultural Education's report *All Our Futures*,[82] has repeatedly shown that creativity is innate in children, but schools and life knock it out of us. Our recommendation is unequivocally clear: cultural exposure and participation should be the right of all children at school, and government money should not only facilitate it, but should also be made available for far more art regionally and locally. The power of art to deepen and civilise is beyond the imagination of many in government, but not beyond the aspiration of every man and woman in the country. Through art, we come to know ourselves, a subject we explore further in the Conclusion.

CONCLUSION
TRUST IN OURSELVES

You must be the change you wish to see in the world.

Mahatma Gandhi, 1869–1948

The *leitmotif* of this book is that we will never see the decisive change towards a more trusting and trustworthy country until we stop pointing the finger at other people and start taking responsibility for our own actions. A month of fervent indignation at MPs was spent over their expenses; but are we completely honest with our own? We were outraged at the bonus and high-risk culture during the financial crisis; but are we never greedy and foolhardy? We despair at the media for its sensationalisation of trust; but do we never distort it in what we report? We are appalled at the breach of trust when doctors, social workers, the police and sportsmen behave unprofessionally, cover up or cheat; but are we never guilty of being unprofessional, clouding the truth and cheating to gain an advantage in our own lives?

From the moment we are born, we look to our families for our needs, and to the state to provide welfare. When adversity strikes, we want to know what 'they' – the government, officials, the police and the schools – are going to do about it. We assume we have an entitlement to whatever we want. We fail to see our life and this world as a gift, as something unique and wonderful, for whose care and nourishment we are, ourselves, utterly responsible. We consume far more than we need, and barely heed a fraction of it, as our minds are already rushing on to sampling the next attraction.

In our core natures, we are trusting. It is our cores which are, as Donne wrote, connected one with another. But we lose touch with our centres. As young teenagers, we begin to adopt a persona which bears little relationship to the person who each of us is at our heart. We create it to defend our true self from being hurt, and to present an image which we think will make us liked and maximise our potency. As we grow older, we rarely find time to be entirely with ourselves, and when we do, it can be unsettling and even frightening letting go of the outer rings of personality and reconnecting with our true nature. Many of us become uncomfortable doing so, and resort to a variety of tactics, such as overwork, alcohol, drugs and diverse sexual partners, to provide the distraction we require to prevent us from just being ourselves. The years pass, the lines increase, the energy fades, a whole life can pass with little or no time spent with ourselves. It can be much easier to keep moving. When we are living in our personas, life is more predictable and judgemental. We have a clear sense of 'us and them'. 'Them' equals the ones who are mucking everything up, who have no idea how to do things, and 'us' equals the ones whose life is being stunted by their incompetence and malign intent, and the failure to treat us with the respect we deserve.

The path back to sanity begins with getting back in touch with our centres. To achieve this, personally and professionally, we should adopt a 'presumption to trust'. This has to begin with trusting ourselves, so we can be the change we 'wish to see in the world'. But how? Therapists and coaches who work with leaders and managers commonly talk about the task being one of helping them to let go of their baggage – emotional, physical and mental. Discovering oneself runs counter to what we commonly do throughout life, which is to accumulate; trusting is about letting go. With young people, 'trust exercises' can help them to make contact with the authentic person underneath: even simple routines help build trust. One method is to have people working in pairs, and to have one person falling backwards into the arms of the other, knowing that person can be trusted to capture them and prevent them falling to the ground.

The only way to reconnect with our cores is to spend time with ourselves, hence the recommendation throughout this book for leaders, but not only leaders, to spend ten minutes of silent reflection a day, reading poetry, meditating, praying, breathing deeply or just being. We have heard in these pages how people can adopt completely different personalities at work, and how they can leave kindness behind when they close their front door, becoming ruthless in the belief that this is the only way to be, and the only way to succeed, at work.

It can often take a crisis for people to realise how much trust and support there is for them, and this can allow them to access their inner authentic self. When a person speaks from that true self, others wake up. It is indefinable, but it helps other people to let go and to reach deep within themselves. It can seem as if trust is the 'add-on', but in fact it is always there under the surface, and we need special events, or special people, to remind us. Trust is the natural state for human beings. Life is a journey, and we can either choose to travel in the direction of aggrandisement and personal gain, or in the direction of letting go, rediscovering our natures, and living in a state of trust with other people.

The widespread concern with the levels of trust which this book has examined, and the many areas where it could beneficially be much higher, points to the need for a profound rethinking, spiritually, of the way we are. The approaching crises of climate change, population increase and food and energy supply make this not a luxury but a necessity.

Chapter 1 began with the story of the man building a wall. I spent years thinking about that man, and how foolish he was to be building that wall of mistrust. Only now, years later, do I realise that the man building the wall has been me.

ACKNOWLEDGEMENTS

My principal thanks go to the members of the 'inner team', who worked flat out with me for seven weeks researching and writing the book. They are my co-author Kunal Khatri, Matthew Fright, Alice Mosby, Rachel Patton, Zenobe Reade, Jessica Seldon, Andrew Stevenson and Conor Turley. They worked seven days a week, and usually twelve-hour days, were extraordinarily assiduous, determined and capable. The 'outer team' all contributed in a wide variety of ways with research, ideas and helping to type the text. They are Rob Alderson, Emma Alywin, Rob Costelloe, Tom Edwards, Lara Greer, Luke Holbrook, Christina Moorhouse, Adam Seldon, Ed James and Hester Sunderland. All of them displayed a fierce determination to help make the book as good as it could possibly be.

I would like to thank those who read the book, Tony Buzan, Paul Fairclough, John James, Mark Lovett, Joanna Seldon and Raine Walker. Like everyone on this book, they were operating under conditions of great pressure, yet they produced many valuable ideas and corrections.

My thanks also go to those who read one or more chapters, or who gave interviews for the book: Charlie Beckett, Chris Bellamy, Vernon Bogdanor, Tony Buzan, Brian Cathcart, Ara Darzi, Laurence Evans, Frank Field, Pam Giddy, Howard Glennerster, Nick Greenslade, Nina Grunfeld, Andrew Haldenby, Lisa Harker, Richard Harries, Brian Harrison, Stephen Harrison, Gavin Hayes, Louise Hayman, Suzie Hayman, John Helliwell, John Inverarity, Dennis Kavanagh, Mike Kenny, Jill Kirkby, Raymond Kuhn, David Kynaston, Richard Layard,

Julian Le Grand, Sue Lipscombe, Geoff Lucas, Tim Kasser, Matthew MacGregor, Tony Manwaring, Nic Marks, David Marquand, John Micklethwaite, Michael Milner, John Mitchell, Adrian Monck, Martin Moore, Alan Moses, Hermann Mulder, Lord Norton of Louth, James O'Shaugnessy, Ben Page, Dr Nick Patton, Jules Peck, Robert Philips, David Phillips, David Pitt-Watson, Raymond Plant, Ken Rea, Patrick Reade, Martin Rees, Robert Reiner, Peter Riddell, Nick Ross, Richard Sambrook, Dominic Sandbrook, Peter Sinclair, Carole Smith, David Smith, Ed Smith, Roger Steare, Gerry Stoker, Matthew Taylor, Peter Taylor-Gooby, Justin Thacker, James Thomas, Russell Tillson, Polly Toynbee, Tony Travers, Michael Trend, Guy Williams, Shirley Williams and Colin Wright.

I would like to thank in particular Robert Philips of Edelman, whose inspiring interview in June helped start us on the book. I would also like to thank the following for helping supply information for the book in a wide variety of ways: John Ashcroft, Pat Carroll, Janice Clark, Jill Dillon, Dr. Francesca Gains, Louise James, Marie Keyworth, Jennifer Kivett, Dr Sue Lipscombe, Jennifer O'Brien, David Oosthuizen, Henry Porter, Michael Pooles, John Sabapathy, Antonio Sennis, Dr Adam Smith, Ian Summersgill, Michael Trend, Laura Trotter, Cari Tuhey, Michael Williams and Ben Wright. Fred Lancaster's help with team trust exercises was also invaluable.

At Wellington College, a large number of colleagues helped with the book in many ways: Matt Albrighton, Robin Dyer, Paul Fairclough, Sandra Hughes-Coppins, Nick Maloney, Paula Maynard, Susan Meikle, Michael Milner, Ian Morris, Lucy Pearson, Ant Peter, Angela Reed, James Thomas, Jamie Walker, Raine Walker and Guy Williams.

At Biteback, I would like to thank Iain Dale, Jonathan Wadman and James Stephens.

Finally, I would like to thank my wife, Joanna, and my children, Jessica, Susannah and Adam, for their contributions and forbearance.

BIBLIOGRAPHY

Books and Articles

Aaronovitch, David, *Voodoo Histories: The Role of the Conspiracy Theory in Shaping Modern History* (London: Jonathan Cape, 2009)

Abelson, Julia, Miller, Fiona A. and Giacomini, Mita, 'What does it mean to trust a health system? A qualitative study of Canadian health care values', *Health Policy*, 91 (2009), pp. 63–70

Adonis, Andrew, 'The People's William', *Prospect*, July 2009

Aitken, Robin, *Can We Trust the BBC?* (London: Continuum, 2007)

Allen, Gill, 'Andrew Walker: the coroner the MoD couldn't gag', *The Times*, 11 April 2008

Apple, Emily, 'Can the police give up confrontation?', *The Guardian*, 23 July 2009

Appleyard, Bryan, 'A guide to the best 100 blogs', *Sunday Times*, 15 February 2009

Aristotle, *The Politics*, revised by Saunders, Trevor (London: Penguin Classics, 1981)

Arlidge, John, '"I'm doing God's work." Meet Mr Goldman Sachs', *Sunday Times*, 8 November 2009

Armstrong, Karen, *The Case for God: What Religion Really Means* (London: Bodley Head, 2009)

Ashcroft, John and Schluter, Michael, 'Influencing, Assessing and Developing Relationships', Relationships Foundation Strategy Unit Seminar 3 (March 2009)

Bailey, Shaun, 'What and Who Is It We Don't Trust?' Joseph Rowntree Foundation, 9 October 2008

Bakewell, Joan, 'Resist the cultural vandalism: don't let them close our precious libraries', *The Times*, 20 February 2009

Bakir, Vian and Barlow, David, 'The End of Trust?', in Bikar and Barlow (eds), *Communication in the Age of Suspicion: Trust and the Media* (Basingstoke: Palgrave Macmillan, 2007)

Bamberger, M. and Yaeger, D., 'Over the edge', *Sports Illustrated*, 14 (1997), pp. 62–70

Barkham, Patrick, 'Stephen Lawrence case Q & A', *The Guardian*, 23 February 1999

Barnes, Simon, 'Integrity is at the heart of Arsene Wenger's code', *The Times*, 17 August 2009

Barnett, Steven, 'On the road to self-destruction', *British Journalism Review*, 19:2 (2008), pp. 2–13

Bassett, Dale, Haldenbury, Andrew, Thraves, Laurie and Truss, Elizabeth, 'A New Force', Reform (February 2009)

Batty, David, 'Alder Hey report on use of children's organs', *The Guardian*, 30 January 2001

Batty, David, 'Catholic Priesthood told to target child abuse', *The Guardian*, 17 September 2001

Baudelaire, Charles, *My Heart Laid Bare* (1887)

BBC, 'Bank reform "needs to be radical"', 1 August 2009

BBC, 'Climate scepticism "on the rise"', 7 February 2010

BBC, 'Damages "hitting" NHS care', 30 June 2009

BBC, 'Early prison releases top 50,000', 31 March 2009

BBC, 'Economic crisis boosts Dutch Calvinism', 10 July 2009

BBC, '"Forty year wait" for allotments', 10 August 2009

BBC, 'Historic Figures: William Beveridge, 1879–1963'

BBC, 'How Leeson broke the bank', 22 June 1999

BBC, 'HSBC global profits halve to $5bn', 3 August 2009

BBC, 'Infections "the biggest NHS fear"', 30 June 2008

BBC, 'Inquiry into Climbie officials', 12 January 2001

BBC, 'ITV hit with record £5.68 million fine', 8 May 2008

BBC, 'Miliband backs US-style primaries', 7 August 2009

BBC, 'Q&A bank bonuses', 9 February 2009

BBC, 'Race row police told to "shut up"', 28 August 2008

BBC, 'RBS boss does "the right thing"', 18 June 2009

BBC, 'Richards banned for three years', 17 August 2009

BBC, 'School safety "insult" to Pullman', 16 July 2009

BBC, 'Schools "letting down UK science"', 13 August 2006

BBC, 'Shock as woman returned to home', 22 April 2009

BBC, 'Speaker quits for "sake of unity"', 19 May 2009

BBC, 'The new capitalism', 8 December 2008

BBC, 'UK ghettos claim shocks ministers', 19 September 2005

BBC, 'UK has lost trust in neighbours', 25 May 2004

BBC, 'UK is losing 52 pubs each week', 22 July 2009

BBC, 'Who cares who wins?', 29 April 2002

BBC, 'Why more inmates are reoffenders', 30 January 2007

BBC, 'Wikipedia survives research test', 15 December 2005

'Best PMs revealed', *BBC History Magazine*, 29 August 2006

Beckett, Charlie, 'MPs' expenses and the media: chequebook journalism pays for political lessons', *Polis*, 10 May 2009

Ben-Shahar, Tal, *Happier: Learn the Secrets of Daily Joy and Lasting Fulfilment* (London: McGraw-Hill, 2007)

Bettelheim, Bruno, *A Good Enough Parent: A Book on Child Rearing* (Toronto: Random House, 1987)

Bidisha, 'An atheist's prayer', *The Guardian*, 17 August 2009

Bingham, John, 'Britain's richest solicitor guilty of exploiting sick miners for fees', *Daily Telegraph*, 11 December 2008

Blacker, Terence, 'The new British way of mourning', *The Independent*, 18 July 2009

Blair, Tony, 'Feral Beast', speech, London, 12 June 2007

Blair, Tony, 'Our Nation's Future: Time for proper debate on law and order', speech delivered 23 June 2006

Blastland, Michael, 'How to understand risk in 13 clicks', *BBC News Magazine*, 11 March 2009

Blond, Phillip, 'Rise of the Red Tories', *Prospect*, 28 February 2009

Bloomfield, Jon, 'Controlling, Cajoling or Co-operating? Central governments' policy approaches towards local government on the issues of performance and cost-effectiveness', *Council of European Municipalities and Regions*, May 2006, pp. 10–11

Bok, Sissela, *Lying: Moral Choice in Public and Private Life* (New York: Vintage, 1999)

Booker, Christopher, 'Lt-Colonel Rupert Thorneloe and Trooper Joshua Hammond should not have died', *Daily Telegraph*, 4 July 2009

Bowers, Helen, Macadam, Alison, Patel, Meena and Smith, Cathy, *Making a Difference through Volunteering* (London: CSV, 2006)

Bradley, R. L., 'K-12 Service-learning Impacts: A Review of State-level Studies of Service-learning', in Kielsmeier, Jim, Neal, Marybeth and McKinnon, Megan (eds), *Growing to Greatness 2005: The State of Service-learning Project* (St Paul, MN: National Youth Leadership Council, 2005)

Buonfino, Alessandra and Mulgan, Geoff, *Civility Lost and Found* (London: Young Foundation, 2009)

Burke, Edmund: *Reflections on the Revolution in France* (New York: Oxford University Press, 1999)

Butterworth, Myra, 'Britons know just nine neighbours by name', *Daily Telegraph*, 25 November 2008

Cain, Bruce, Dalton, Russell and Scarrow, Susan (eds), *Democracy Transformed? Expanding Political Opportunities in Advanced Industrial Democracies* (Oxford: Oxford University Press, 2003)

Calnan, M and Sanford, E., 'Public trust in health care: the system or the doctor?', *Quality and Safety in Healthcare*, 13 (2004), pp. 92–7

Carswell, Douglas and Hannan, Dan, *The Plan: Twelve Months to Renew Britain* (Great Britain: Douglas Carswell, 2008)

Carvel, John, 'Takeoff time for guilt over air travel', *The Guardian*, 28 January 2009

Cathcart, Brian, 'Trust us, we're journalists', *New Statesman*, 5 February 2007

Cathcart, Brian, 'Journalists: they can't live without us', *New Statesman*, 25 September 2008

Chakrabarti, Shami, 'Shami Chakrabarti on human rights', video interview, *The Economist*

Cicero, Marcus Tullius, *Pro Sestio*, translated by Gardner, R. (Cambridge, MA: Loeb Classical Library, 1958)

Clark, Michael, *Paradoxes from A–Z* (London: Routledge, 2002)

Coates, Sam, 'Sarah Wollaston selected to fight Totnes for Tories after open ballot', *The Times*, 5 August 2009

Cockett, Richard, 'Ball, Chamberlain, and Truth', *Historical Journal*, 33 (1990)

Cockett, Rickard, 'The Party, Publicity and the Media', in Seldon and Ball (eds), *Conservative Century: The Conservative Party since 1900* (Oxford: Oxford University Press, 1994)

Cockett, Richard, *Thinking the Unthinkable: Think-Tanks and the Economic Counter-Revolution 1931-1983* (London: HarperCollins, 1995)

Coffin, Charles (ed.) *The Complete Poetry and Selected Prose of John Donne* (London: Modern Library, 1994)

Collins, Jim, *Good to Great: Why Some Companies Make the Leap. . . and Others Don't* (London: Random House, 2001)

Confucius, *The Analects of Confucius*, translated by Huang Chichung (New York: Oxford University Press, 1997)

Confucius, LunYu, 2.3.

Crabtree, James, 'Citizenship first: the case for compulsory community service', *Prospect*, 1 March 2009

Crabtree, James, 'The *Prospect*/YouGov poll', *Prospect*, 1 March 2009

Curti, Elena, 'Does Nolan go too far?' *The Tablet*, 25 May 2002

Curtis, Polly and McVeigh, Tracy, 'State or private: still the key factor in shaping life for our schoolchildren', *The Observer*, 16 August 2009

Dalton, Russell, *Democratic Challenges, Democratic Choices: The Erosion of Political Support in Advanced Industrial Democracies* (Oxford: Oxford University Press, 2004)

Davies, Nick, *Flat Earth News* (London: Chatto & Windus, 2008)

Dávila, Alberto and Mora, Marie T., *Civic Engagement and High School Academic Progress: An Analysis Using NELS Data* (Medford, MA: CIRCLE, 2007)

Davis, Stephen, Lukomnik, Jon and Pitt-Watson, David, *Towards an Accountable Capitalism*, IPPR and Friends Provident Foundation (March 2009)

Dawkins, Richard, *The God Delusion* (London: Bantam Press, 2006)

De Tocqueville, Alexis, *Democracy in America*, ed. Heffner, Richard C. (New York: Signet Classic, 2001)

De Tocqueville, Alexis, *The Old Regime and the Revolution* (Chicago: University of Chicago Press, 1998)

Dodd, Vikram, 'Ali Dizaei, Metropolitan police commander, jailed for four years', *The Guardian*, 8 February 2010

Donham, W. B. 'The Social Significance of Business', *Harvard Business Review*, 5 (July 1927)

Donovan, Nick, Halpern, David and Sargeant, Richard, 'Life Satisfaction: The state of knowledge and implications for government', Cabinet Office Strategy Unit (2003), pp. 406–19

Einstein, Albert, 'Science, Philosophy and Religion: A symposium', 1941 Conference on Science, Philosophy and Religion in Their Relation to the Democratic Way of Life, Inc., New York, 1941

Eliot, T. S., *The Waste Land* (New York: Boni & Liveright, 1922)

Elliott, John and Quaintance, Lauren, 'Britain is getting less trusting', *Sunday Times*, 18 May 2003

'Family breakdown: a key factor', *Daily Telegraph*, 15 November 2006

Fanelli D, 'How Many Scientists Fabricate and Falsify Research? A systematic review and meta-analysis of survey data' (Public Library of Science, 2009)

Fanning, Evan, '"Walking Junkie" Chambers reveals full extent of his drug use', *The Guardian*, 2 March 2009

Finkelstein, Daniel, 'Car wrecks and Hutus: a guide to good conduct', *The Times*, 16 May 2007

FitzGerald, Marian, Hough, Mike, Joseph, Ian and Quereshi, Tariq, *Policing for London* (Cullompton: Willan, 2002)

FitzGerald, Marian, 'Massaging the crime figures', *The Guardian*, 20 July 2009

Flores, Fernando and Solomon, Robert, *Building Trust: In Business, Politics, Relationships, and Life* (Oxford: Oxford University Press, 2003)

Flores, Fernando and Solomon, Robert, 'Creating Trust', *Business Ethics Quarterly*, 8 (1998), pp. 205–32

Forbes, Clarence, 'Crime and Punishment in Greek Athletics', *Classical Journal*, 47 (1952), pp. 169–203

Fox, M., Forrest, S., Ling, A. and Lynch, M., *Global Food & Beverages: Integrating ESG*, Goldman Sachs (2007)

Freedland, Jonathan, *Bring Home the Revolution: The Case for a British Republic* (London: Fourth Estate, 1999)

Friedman, Milton, 'The Social Responsibility of Business Is to Increase Its Profits', *New York Times Magazine*, 13 September 1970

Friedman, Thomas, *Hot, Flat and Crowded: Why the World Needs a Green Revolution – and How We Can Renew Our Global Future* (London: Allen Lane, 2008)

Francis Fukuyama, 'The End of History', *National Interest*, 4 (1989)

Fukuyama, Francis, *Trust, The Social Virtues and the Creation of Prosperity* (New York: Simon & Schuster, 1995)

Furco, A., 'The Role of Service-learning in Enhancing Student Achievement', presentation given at the National Center for Learning and Citizenship board meeting, Santa Barbara, CA (2007)

Furedi, Frank, *Paranoid Parenting: Abandon Your Anxieties and Be a Good Parent* (London: Allen Lane, 2001)

Furedi, Frank, 'Thou Shalt Not Hug', *New Statesman*, 26 June 2008

Furlong, Monica, *The C of E: The State It's In* (London Hodder & Stoughton, 2000)

Gardner, Howard, *Multiple Intelligences: The Theory in Practice* (New York: Basic Books, 1993)

Garland, Bill et al., *Nationwide Community Service* (London: CSV, 2008)

Garner, Joe, 'Trust. . . and the Financial Crisis', speech delivered at the launch of the 2009 Edelman Trust Barometer, 21 July 2009

Gibb, Frances, 'Legal aid cuts: how you could be acquitted and still face huge bill for costs', *The Times*, 17 July 2009

Giddens, Anthony, *The Consequences of Modernity* (Stanford: Stanford University Press, 1991)

Giddens, Anthony, *Modernity and Self-identity: Self and Society in the Late Modern Age* (Cambridge: Polity Press, 1991)

Gintis, Herbert and Khurana, Rakesh, 'Corporate Honesty and Business Education: A behavioural model', in Zak, Paul (ed.), *Moral Markets: The Critical Role of Values in the Economy* (Oxford: Princeton University Press, 2008)

Gladwell, Malcolm, *The Tipping Point: How Little Things Can Make a Big Difference* (London: Little, Brown, 2000)

Gledhill, Ruth, 'God-shaped hole will lead to loss of national sense of identity', *The Times*, 8 May 2008

Glover, Julian, 'Two-thirds believe London bombings are linked to Iraq war', *The Guardian*, 19 July 2005

Godin, Seth, 'Hard-wired to Belong', *RSA Journal*

Golding, William, *Lord of the Flies* (London: Faber and Faber, 1954)

Goodhart, David, 'They're wrong – social mobility is not going downhill', *Sunday Times*, 26 July 2009

Gough, Roger, *With a Little Help from Our Friends: International Lessons for English Local Government* (London: Localis, 2009)

Gray, John, *Black Mass* (London: Penguin, 2003)

Green, Stephen, *Good Value: Reflections on Money, Morality and an Uncertain World* (London: Allen Lane, 2009)

Greenslade, Roy, 'Recruiting working class journalists: what, if anything, can be done?', Greenslade's Blog, 23 July 2009

Griffiths, Sian and Waite, Roger, 'More top English students opt for American universities', *Sunday Times*, 17 February 2008

Grimston, Jack, 'Students at top university revolt over teaching standards', *Sunday Times*, 10 May 2009

Grimston, Jack, 'Play it again Boris', *The Times*, 31 May 2009

Guerrera, Francesco, 'Welch condemns share price focus', *Financial Times*, 12 March 2009

Hamilton-Baillie, Ben, ' Shared Space: Reconciling people, places and traffic', *Built Environment*, 34:2 (2008), pp. 161–81

Handy, Charles, 'What's business for?', in Zak, Paul (ed.), *Moral Markets: The Critical Role of Values in the Economy* (Oxford: Princeton University Press 2008)

Hanser, David, *Architecture of France* (Westport, CT: Greenwood, 2006)

Hardin, Russell, 'From Bodo Ethics to Distributive Justice', *Ethical Theory and Moral Practice*, 2 (1999), pp. 399–413

Hardin, Russell, *Trust* (Cambridge: Polity Press, 2006)

Hardin, Russell, *Trust and Trustworthiness* (New York: Russell Sage Foundation, 2004)

Harford, Tim, 'The Economics of Trust', *Forbes*, 25 September 2006

Hargreaves, Ian, *Journalism: Truth or Dare?* (Oxford: Oxford University Press, 2003)

Harrabin, Roger, Coote, Anna and Allen, Jessica, 'Health in the News: Risk, reporting and media influence', The King's Fund (September 2003)

Harrison, Stephen and Smith, Carole, 'Trust and Moral Motivation: Redundant resources in health and social care?', *Policy & Politics*, 32:3 (2004)

Hauk, Esther and Saez-Marti, Maria, 'On the Cultural Transmission of Corruption', *Journal of Economic Theory* (2002), pp. 311–35

Helliwell, John and Putnam, Robert, 'The Social Context of Well-being', *Philosophical Transactions: Biological Sciences*, 359 (2004), pp. 1435–46

Helliwell, John and Huang, Haifang, 'Well-being and Trust in the Workplace', National Bureau of Economic Research (December 2008)

Hewison, Robert, *The Heritage Industry* (London: Methuen, 1987)

Hitchens, Christopher, *God Is Not Great: The Case against Religion* (London: Atlantic, 2007)

Hobbes, Thomas, *Leviathan* (London: Penguin Classics, [1651] 1982)

Hope, Christopher, 'Post Office closures: the stamp of disapproval', *Sunday Telegraph*, 5 October 2008

Hope, Christopher, 'Record six pubs closing every day due to economic downturn', *Daily Telegraph*, 19 January 2009

Hope, Jenny, 'Drinking just one glass of wine a day can INCREASE risk of cancer by 168%, say the French!', *Daily Mail*, 23 February 2009

Horsburgh, H. J. N., 'The Ethics of Trust', *Philosophical Quarterly*, 10 (1960), pp. 343–54

Hosking, Geoffrey, 'Why we need a history of trust', *Reviews in History* (2002)

House, James S., Landis, Karl R. and Umberson, Debra, 'Social Relationships and Health', *Science*, Reprint Series, vol. 241 (1988)

House, Madeline, Storey, Graham and Tillotson, Kathleen, *The Letters of Charles Dickens 1842–1843* (Oxford: Clarendon Press, 1993)

Hutton, Will, *The State We're In: Why Britain Is in Crisis and How to Overcome It* (London: Jonathan Cape, 1995)

Hyman, Peter, 'Drop GCSEs. We should be teaching our children to think', *The Observer*, 16 August 2009

'Is the law bleeding the NHS to death?', *Sunday Times*, 3 August 2008

James, Oliver, *Affluenza* (London: Vermilion, 2007)

Jay, Antony, *A New Great Reform Act* (West Molesey: 4 Print, 2009)

Jenkins, Simon, *Accountable to None: The Tory Nationalisation of Britain* (London: Penguin, 1996)

Jenkins, Simon, *Thatcher and Sons* (London: Allen Lane, 2006)

Jenkins, Simon, 'We must support the Kensington Road revolution', *Evening Standard*, 21 July 2009

'Jonathan Ross returns to BBC after Sachsgate affair to interview Tom Cruise', *Daily Telegraph*, 22 January 2009

John, Peter, 'The Benefits of Local Citizen Engagement and Dialogue', in Roxburgh, Ian (ed.), *Next Steps for Local Democracy: A Collection of Essays* (London: New Local Government Network, 2008)

Johnston, Philip, 'G20 death: we want a police force, not brute force', *Daily Telegraph*, 8 April 2009

Kellner, Peter, 'Down with people power', *Prospect*, July 2009

Kellner, Peter, 'We should endorse AV', Fabian Society website (2009)

Kelso, Paul, 'Dean Richards given three-year coaching ban after Harlequins bloodgate scandal', *Daily Telegraph*, 18 August 2009

Kemp, Kenny, 'Rebuilding trust', *Sunday Herald*, 14 August 2009

King, Anthony, 'NHS: the nation fears for its future', *Daily Telegraph*, 29 June 2008

Kirby, Douglas, *Emerging Answers: Research Findings on Programs to Reduce Teen Pregnancy* (Washington, DC: National Campaign to Prevent Teen Pregnancy, 2001)

Kirby, Jill, 'From Broken Families to the Broken Society, *Political Quarterly*, 80:2 (2009)

Klitgaard, Robert, 'Subverting Corruption', *Finance and Development*, June 2000

Knight, India, 'Family values return, thanks to the internet', *Sunday Times*, 9 August 2009

Kohn, Marek, *Trust: Self-interest and the Common Good* (Oxford: Oxford University Press, 2008)

Kynaston, David, *The City of London, vol. IV: A Club No More* (London: Chatto & Windus, 2002)

Laville, Sandra, 'Police create most detailed picture of criminal gangs so far', *The Guardian*, 13 July 2009

Layard, Richard, *Happiness: Lessons from a New Science* (London: Allen Lane, 2005)

Layard, Richard, Dunn, Judith and the panel of The Good Childhood Inquiry, *A Good Childhood: Searching for Values in a Competitive Age* (London: Penguin, 2009)

Leach, Ben, 'Two pubs closing every day, new figures show', *Daily Telegraph*, 21 February 2009

Linklater, Magnus, 'What Happened to Playing Fair?', *British Journalism Review*, 19:3 (2008), pp. 62–6

Lloyd, John, *What the Media Are Doing to Our Politics* (London: Constable, 2004)

Loader, Ian and Mulcahy, Aogán, *Policing and the Condition of England: Memory, Politics and Culture* (Oxford: Oxford University Press, 2003)

Lodge, Guy, 'Back in Line?', Institute for Public Policy Research, 21 July 2009

Loveday, Barry, 'Community Policing under New Labour', *Criminal Justice Matters*, 67 (2007), pp .28–9

MacGillivray, Donald, 'When is a fake not a fake? When it's a genuine forgery', *The Guardian*, 2 July 2005

Machiavelli, Niccolò, *The Prince* (Oxford: Oxford University Press, [1513] 2008)

Macintyre, James, 'Public Enemy Number One', *New Statesman*, 16 April 2009

McVeigh, Tracy, Syal, Rajeev and Hinsliff, Gaby, 'G20 protests: how the image of UK police took a beating', *The Guardian*, 19 April 2009

Major, John, speech to the Conservative Group for Europe, 22 April 1993

Mansell, Wade and Meteyard, Belinda, *A Critical Introduction to Law* (Abingdon: Routledge Cavendish, 1995)

Marquand, David, *Britain since 1918: The Strange Career of British Democracy* (London: Weidenfeld & Nicolson, 2008), p. 407.

Marshall, Martin, 'Practice, Politics and Possibilities', *British Journal of General Practice*, 59:565 (2009), pp. 273–82

Meltzer, H. et al., 'Mental Health of Children and Adolescents in Great Britain', Office for National Statistics (2000)

Micklethwait, John, and Wooldridge, Adrian, *God Is Back* (London: Allen Lane, 2009)

Mill, John Stuart, *On Liberty* (London: Longman, 2007)

Miszal, Barbara, *Trust in Modern Societies* (Cambridge: Polity Press, 1996)

Monck, Adrian, *Can You Trust the Media?* (London: Icon, 2008)

Mooney, Chris, *The Republican War on Science* (Basic Books, 2005)

Moorhead, Joanna, 'Would you spy on your child?', *The Guardian*, 17 December 2003

Morgan, William and Streb, Matthew, *How Quality Service-learning Develops Civic Values* (Bloomington: Indiana University Press, 1999)

Mulgan, Geoff, *The Art of Public Strategy: Mobilizing Power and Knowledge for the Common Good* (Oxford: Oxford University Press, 2009)

Mulgan, Geoff, *Good and Bad Power: The Ideals and Betrayals of Government* (London: Penguin, 2006)

Mulgan, Geoff, *Politics in an Antipolitical Age* (Cambridge: Polity Press, 1994)

Murdoch, Iris, *The Sovereignty of Good* (New York: Routledge Classics, 2001)

Murphy, Kevin, 'Cyber Nannies: would you spy on your child?', *The Independent*, 26 May 2006

Murray, Robert and Blessing, Tim, *Greatness in the White House: Rating the Presidents from George Washington through Ronald Reagan* (University Park: Pennsylvania University Press, 1994)

Naish, John, 'Faking it', *Prospect* (2009)

Nelson, Fraser, 'They wish we all could be Californian: the New Tory plan', *Spectator*, 25 February 2009

Nevin, Charles, 'Surveillance over Europe', *Intelligent Life*, Summer 2009

Nordenson, Bree, 'Overload! Journalism's battle for relevance in an age of too much information', *Columbia Journalism Review*, 1 November 2008

Nozick, Robert, *Anarchy, State, and Utopia* (New York: Basic Books, 1974)

Neuberger, Julia, *The Moral State We're In* (London: HarperPerennial, 2005)

Nye, Joseph, Jr and Zelikow, Phillip, *Why People Don't Trust Government* (Cambridge, MA: Harvard University Press, 1997)

Oakeshott, Isabel and Ashton, James, 'Alistair Darling: new law to curb City bonuses', *The Times*, 16 August 2009

Obama, Barack, 'An Honest Government, A Hopeful Future', speech delivered 28 August 2006

Obama, Barack, 'Remarks by the President in State of the Union address', 27 January 2010, available at www.whitehouse.gov

Oakeshott, Isabel, 'Boris Johnson tells Met chief to cut crime – or else', *Sunday Times*, 4 May 2008

Oborne, Peter, *The Triumph of the Political Class* (New York: Simon and Schuster, 2007)

O'Neill, Onora, *A Question of Trust: The BBC Reith Lectures 2002* (Cambridge: Cambridge University Press, 2002)

O'Neill, Rebecca, 'Experiments in Living: The fatherless family', Civitas (September 2002)

O'Neill, Sam, 'Isa Ibrahim: converted to radical Islam online', *The Times*, 18 July 2009

Orwell, George, 'Essay Looking Back on the Spanish Civil War', in *Homage to Catalonia* (Harmondsworth: Penguin, [1938] 1974)

Owen, Jonathan, 'Community? We don't know our neighbours', *The Independent*, 20 January 2008

Packard, Vance, *The Hidden Persuaders* (New York: Ig Publishing, 1957)

Paine, Thomas, *The Rights of Man* (London: Penguin Classics, [1791] 1984)

Palmer, Sue, *Toxic Childhood* (London: Orion, 2006)

'Paradise regained', *The Economist*, 21 December 2000

Patten, Rt Hon. Chris MP, 'Big Battalions and Little Platoons', Seventh Arnold Goodman Lecture (1990)

Paxman, Jeremy, James MacTaggart Memorial Lecture (2007)

Peck, Jules and Phillips, Robert, *Citizen Renaissance* (forthcoming)

Pemberton, Max, 'NHS: have targets become more important than patients?', *Daily Telegraph*, 30 March 2009

Petre, Jonathan, 'Spiritual Britain worships over 170 different faiths', *Daily Telegraph*, 13 December 2004

Plato, *The Republic*, translated with an introduction by Lee, H. D. P. (London: Penguin Classics, 1955)

Porter, Henry, 'The way the police treat us verges on the criminal', *The Observer*, 29 October 2006

'Primary Colours', *The Times*, 23 May 2009

Pringle, Mike, 'The Shipman Inquiry: Implications for the public's trust in doctors', *British Journal of General Practice*, 50:454 (2000), pp. 355–6

Putnam, Robert, *Bowling Alone: The Collapse and Revival of American Community* (New York: Simon & Schuster, 2000)

Puttnam, David, 'Are We Raising the Right Kind of Leaders?', Independent Schools Council Annual Conference, 1 June 2009

Rawls, John, *A Theory of Justice* (Cambridge, MA: Harvard University Press, 1971)

'RBS agree £9.6m pay deal for Stephen Hester', *Daily Telegraph*, 22 June 2009

Reid, Tim, 'Couples say "I do" to lasting love in marriage covenant', *The Times*, 16 February 2005

Reiner, Robert, *The Politics of the Police* (Oxford: Oxford University Press, 2000)

Reiner, Robert, *Law and Order: An Honest Citizen's Guide to Crime and Control* (Cambridge: Polity, 2007)

Rees, Martin, *Our Final Century? Will the Human Race Survive the Twenty-first Century?* (London: Heinemann, 2003)

Rees-Mogg, William, 'This Bill is a panic measure in a tarnished age', *The Times*, 13 July 2009

Reuters, 'UK records first H1N1 death in healthy patient', 10 July 2009

Ronay, Barney, 'Landis drugs ban upheld', *The Guardian*, 30 June 2008

Rousseau, Jean-Jacques, *The Social Contract*, translated by Cranston, Maurice (London: Penguin, [1762] 1968)

Rowe, Michael, *Policing, Race and Racism* (Cullompton: Willan, 2004)

Roxburgh, Iain, 'Overcoming the Obstacles of Devolved Government', in Roxburgh, Iain (ed.), *Next Steps for Local Democracy: Leadership, Accountability and Partnership* (London: New Local Government Network, 2008)

Russell, Jenni, 'We approach others' children at our peril', *Sunday Times*, 16 August 2009

Ruzicka, Jan and Wheeler, Nicholas J., 'The Puzzle of Trusting Relationships in the Nuclear Non-proliferation Treaty', *International Affairs*, 86:1 (2010), pp. 69–85

Sacks, Jonathan, *To Heal A Fractured World. The Ethics of Responsibility* (London: Continuum, 2005)

Sacks, Jonathan, 'Credo: we must guard love in this world of easy pleasures', *The Times*, 25 July 2009

Salinger, J. D., *The Catcher in the Rye* (London: Hamish Hamilton,1951)

Schultz, Matthias, 'Controlled chaos: European cities do away with traffic signs', Spiegel Online, 16 November 2006

Seldon, Anthony, *Blair* (London: Free Press, 2004)

Seldon, Anthony (ed.), *Blair's Britain, 1997–2007* (Cambridge: Cambridge University Press, 2007)

Seldon, Anthony, *Brave New City: Brighton & Hove, Past, Present, Future* (Lewes: Pomegranate Press, 2002)

Seldon, Anthony, *Churchill's Indian Summer: The Conservative Government 1951–1955* (London: Hodder & Stoughton, 1981)

Seldon, Anthony and Ball, Stuart (eds), *The Conservative Century: The Conservative Party since 1900* (Oxford: Oxford University Press, 1994)

Seligman, Martin, *Authentic Happiness: Using the New Positive Psychology to Realise Your Potential for Lasting Fulfilment* (London: Nicholas Brealey Publishing, 2003)

Sen, Amartya, *The Idea of Justice* (London: Allen Lane, 2009)

Sengupta, Kim, 'Soldier's soldier: General Sir Richard Dannatt', *The Independent*, 18 July 2009

Shakespeare, William, *Julius Caesar* (New York: Noble & Noble, [c. 1599] 1938)

Shepherd, Jessica, 'Students less satisfied with their universities, says survey', *The Guardian*, 6 August 2009

Sherman, Lawrence and Strang, Heather, *Restorative Justice: The Evidence* (London: Smith Institute, 2007)

Shipman, Tim and Hickley, Matthew, 'Labour attacks British army chief after he pointedly flies around Afghanistan in US plane', *Daily Mail*, 16 July 2009

Simms, Andrew, 'A salary cap for everyone', *The Guardian*, 6 August 2009

Smith, Adam, *The Wealth of Nations* (New York: Prometheus, [1776] 1991)

Smith, Justin Davis, *The 1997 National Survey of Volunteering* (London: IVR, 1997)

Smith, R., 'Regulation of Doctors and the Bristol Inquiry', *British Medical Journal*, 317 (1998), pp. 1539–40

Smith, Rebecca, 'NHS targets "may have led to 1,200 deaths" in Mid-Staffordshire', *Daily Telegraph*, 18 March 2009

Smith, Richard, 'Research Misconduct: The poisoning of the well', *Journal of the Royal Society of Medicine*, 99 (2006), pp. 232–7

Smithers, Alan, 'Schools', in Seldon, Anthony (ed.), *Blair's Britain, 1997–2007* (Cambridge: Cambridge University Press, 2007), p. 382

'Social trends: the decline of the English divorce', *The Economist*, 16 July 2009.

Solomon, Robert C., and Flores, Fernando, *Building Trust: In Business, Politics, Relationships, and Life* (Oxford: Oxford University Press, 2001)

Sparrow, Andrew, 'Banking bonuses: prospect of return to "business as usual" alarms politicians', *The Guardian*, 3 August 2009

Sparrow, Andrew, 'Poll shows voters want Brown to step up constitutional reform', *The Guardian*, 16 July 2009

Stimson, Henry L., 'The bomb and the opportunity', *Harper's Magazine*, March 1946

Stone, Oliver, *Wall Street* (USA: 20th Century Fox, 1987)

Stratton, Allegra, 'Afghanistan could take 40 years, says new army chief', *The Guardian*, 8 August 2009

Swain, Marianka, 'Pub closures threaten community values', *Country Life*, 2 March 2009

Sylvester, Rachel, 'Inside politics', *Daily Telegraph*, 29 March 2001

Swaine, Jon, Nick Britten and Stephen Adams, 'Swine flu: Government website collapses under demand', *Daily Telegraph*, 24 July 2009

Szinovacz, Maximiliane, 'Living with Grandparents: Variations by cohort, race, and family structure', *International Journal of Sociology and Social Policy*, 16 (1996), pp. 89–123

Sztompka, Piotr, *Trust: A Sociological Theory* (Cambridge: Cambridge University Press, 1999)

Taibbi, Matt, 'The Great American Bubble Machine', *Rolling Stone*, 13 July 2009

Tett, Gillian, 'Untangling the crisis', *Management Today*, April 2009

The ten greatest sporting cheats in history', *The Observer*, 8 July 2001

Thaler, Richard H. and Sunstein, Cass R., *Nudge: Improving Decisions about Health, Wealth and Happiness* (London: Penguin, 2009)

Thompson, James, 'Bupa loses custom for its private medical insurance', *The Independent*, 13 August 2009

Thompson, Mark, 'The trouble with trust', BBC, 15 January 2008

Thomson, Victoria, 'Co-op Bank profits rise as it cashes in on public backlash', *The Scotsman*, 3 April 2009

Tomkins, Richard, 'A religion in recession', *Financial Times Magazine*, 12 July 2008

Toulmin, Tim, 'The PCC did act over phone-tapping', Letters, *The Guardian*, 11 July 2009

Toynbee, Polly and Walker, David, *Unjust Rewards: Exposing Greed and Inequality in Britain Today* (London: Granta, 2008)

Treanor, Jill and Inman, Phillip, 'Banks defend bonus culture as profits jump', *The Guardian*, 3 August 2009

Turley, Anna, *Stronger Together: A New Approach to Tackling Violent Extremism* (London: New Local Government Network, 2009)

Ungoed-Thomas, Jon and Brooks, Helen, 'Revealed: Britain's most lenient judge', *Sunday Times*, 9 August 2009

Unison, 'Unison calls for time on second anniversary of the death of baby Peter', 3 August 2009

Usborne, Simon, 'Cyberchondria: The perils of internet self-diagnosis', *The Independent*, 17 February 2009

Van de Walle, Steven, 'Trust in the Justice System: A comparative view across Europe', *Prison Service Journal*, 183 (2009), pp. 22–6

Vince, Gaia, 'MRSA deaths up 15-fold in a decade', *New Scientist*, 26 February 2004

Wallop, Henry, 'Death of the traditional family', *Daily Telegraph*, 15 April 2009

'Watching the watchdog', *The Guardian*, 10 August 2009

Webster, Philip, 'MPs to begin an 82-day break, after shortest session in decades', *The Times*, 17 July 2009

Weindling, Paul, *Nazi Medicine and the Nuremberg Trials: From Medical War Crimes to Informed Consent* (Basingstoke: Palgrave Macmillan, 2006)

White, Michael, 'Politics is a cruel business', *The Guardian*, 22 July 2009

Whitehead, Tom, 'Police accused of abusing powers as anti-terrorism stop and searches treble', *Daily Telegraph*, 30 April 2009

Widdup, Ellen, 'London school with 100 spy cameras', *Evening Standard*, 21 July 2009

Wiesel, Elie, 'The Perils of Indifference', speech delivered 12 April 1999

Wilkinson, Richard and Pickett, Kate, *The Spirit Level: Why More Equal Societies Almost Always Do Better* (London: Penguin Books, 2009)

Willetts, David, 'More Ball Games', *Childhood Review*, 4 February 2008

Wintour, Patrick, 'Britain's closed shop: damning report on social mobility failings', *The Guardian*, 21 July 2009

Woolcock, Nicola, 'Record A grades prompt plea for new marking plan to split the difference', *The Times*, 21 August 2009

Woolf, Martin, 'Why regulators should intervene in bankers' pay', *Financial Times*, 16 January 2009

Young, Michael and Willmott, Peter, *Family and Kinship in East London* (London: Taylor & Francis, 1954)

Zadek, Simon, Raynard, Peter and Forstater, Maya, 'What Assures? Listening to words of assurance', AccountAbility and PricewaterhouseCoopers (June 2006)

Zak, Paul (ed.), *Moral Markets: The Critical Role of Values in the Economy* (Oxford: Princeton University Press, 2008)

Zevin, Jason, 'The Perils of Popularising Science', *Intelligence Life*, 23 January 2008

Polls, surveys and reports

Appleby and Alvarez, 'British Social Attitudes Survey, 22nd Report: Public Responses to NHS Reform' (2005), quoted in Lord Darzi, 'High Quality Care For All' (June 2008)

Audit Commission, 'When It Comes to the Crunch', 12 August 2009

Bar Standards Board, 'Journalists, bankers, estate agents and politicians the "least trusted professions"', press release, 31 March 2009

Black, Dame Carol, *Working for a Healthier Tomorrow: Review of the Health of Britain's Working Age Population* (London: The Stationery Office, 2008)

British Social Attitudes Survey (1994, 2007, 2009)

Cabinet Office, 'Unleashing Aspiration: The Final Report of the Panel on Fair Access to the Professions' (2009)

Children's Society, 'Good Childhood Inquiry' (2009)

Committee on Standards in Public Life/BMRB Social Research, 'Survey of Public Attitudes towards Conduct in Public Life' (2008)

ComRes, 'The Solicitors Regulation Authority Consumer Research Study 2008' (February 2009)

Conservative Party, 'It's time to inspire Britain's teenagers: National Citizen Service for the 21st century – a six-week programme for every school leaver', 28 May 2009

Corporate Culture, 'Customer Trust Index Summary Findings' (2007)

Darzi, Ara, 'High Quality Care For All: NHS Next Stage Review', final report (June 2008)

Department for Children, Schools and Families, 'Schools, Pupils and their Characteristics: Statistical first release' (January 2009)

Edelman, 'Mid-Year Trust Barometer Report' (2009)

Edelman, 'Trust Barometer Report' (2010)

European Commission, 'Eurobarometer 70' (2008)

Financial Services Authority, 'The Turner Review: A regulatory response to the global banking crisis' (March 2009)

Gallup, 'Trust in Religious Institutions Varies across EU Map', 24 August 2004

'General Election 2005', House of Commons Research Paper 05/33 (2005)

'General Election Results 7 June 2001', House of Commons Research Paper 01/54 (2001)

Gill, Martin and Spriggs, Angela, 'Assessing the Impact of CCTV', Home Office Research, Development and Statistics Directorate (February 2005)

Globescan, 'BBC/Reuters/Media Center Poll: Trust in the Media', 3 May 2006

Hannam, Derry, 'A Pilot Study to Evaluate the Impact of the Student Participation Aspects of the Citizenship Order on Standards of Education in Secondary Schools', report to the DfEE (April 2001)

Hansard Society, 'Audit of Political Engagement 6: The 2009 report, with a focus on political participation and citizenship' (2009)

Hansard, House of Commons Daily Debates, 12 November 2007, col. 491

Hansard Society, 'Restoring Trust in the House of Lords' (July 2009)

Harris Interactive, 'Common Good Survey on Americans' Trust in Their Legal System', 27 June 2005

Hayward, Bruce et al., 'Survey of attitudes towards conduct in public life 2008', Committee on Standards in Public Life, pp. 22–4

Healthcare Commission, 'Investigation into Mid-Staffordshire NHS Foundation Trust' (March 2009)

Herbert, Nick, Keeble, Oscar, Burley, Aidan and Gibbs, Blair, 'Policing for the People: Interim report of the Police Reform Taskforce' (2007)

Hicks, Joe and Allen, Grahame, 'A Century of Change: Trends in UK statistics since 1900', House of Commons Research Paper 99/111, 21 December 1999

House of Commons Communities and Local Government Committee, 'Balance of Power: Central and Local Government', Sixth Report of Session 2008/9, 12 May 2009

House of Commons, 'Speakers Conference (on Parliamentary Representation): Interim Report' (London: The Stationery Office, 2009)

House of Commons, 'The Code of Conduct: The guide to the rules relating to the conduct of Members' (London: The Stationery Office: 2009)

House of Commons Innovation, Universities, Science and Skills Committee, 'Students and Universities', Eleventh Report of Session 2008/9, 20 July 2009

ICM Research, 'BBC Adult Poll' (October 2007)

ICM Research, 'BBC Opinion of the Government Poll' (May 2002)

ICM Research, 'BBC South-East Police Poll' (July 1998)

ICM Research, '*Evening Standard* London Poll' (November 2000)

ICM Research, '*Guardian* Muslim Poll' (July 2005)

ICM Research, '*Guardian* Opinion Poll', 14-16 February 2003

ICM Research, '*Guardian* Opinion Poll' (July 2004)

ICM Research, '*Mirror*/GMTV Labour Five Years Poll' (April 2002)

International Council of Science's Standing Committee on Responsibility and Ethics of Science, 'Ethics and the Responsibility of Science', UNESCO (1999)

Ipsos MORI, 'Annual IBE/Ipsos MORI Survey 2008 of UK Adult Opinion on Business Ethics' (2008)

Ipsos MORI, 'Attitudes to Afghanistan Campaign', 24 July 2009

Ipsos MORI, 'Attitudes towards Policing', 25 February 1999

Ipsos MORI, 'Audit of Political Engagement 3' (December 2005)

Ipsos MORI, 'Can We Have Trust and Diversity?', 19 January 2004

Ipsos MORI, 'End of Year Review' (2008)

Ipsos-MORI, 'Expenses Poll for the BBC', 2 June 2009

Ipsos MORI, 'Ipsos MORI survey shows record demand for independent education' (2008)

Ipsos MORI, 'Most Trusted Profession', 5 February 2008

Ipsos MORI, 'The National College for School Leadership Survey on Britain's Best Leaders', 28 March 2003

Ipsos MORI, 'Only One in Five Say They Trust Journalists to Tell the Truth', 19 June 2009

Ipsos MORI, 'Opinion of Professions: How Well Do They Do Their Jobs?' (2005)

Ipsos MORI, 'Post London Bombings Survey', 5 October 2005

Ipsos MORI, 'Public Attitudes to Climate Change', 23 June 2008

Ipsos MORI, 'Public Perceptions and Patient Experience of the NHS: Winter 2004 Tracking Survey', summary report (2004)

Ipsos MORI, 'Schools Adolescent Lifestyle and Substance Use Survey National Report: Drinking and Drug Use among 13 and 15 Year Olds in Scotland in 2008', 23 July 2009

Ipsos MORI, 'Three in Four Believe that Britain's Governance Needs Improving', 3 June 2009

Ipsos MORI, 'Trust in the Professions: Veracity Index' (2008)

Ipsos MORI, 'Trust in the Professions: Veracity Index' (2009)

Ipsos MORI/BBC, 'Survey on Trust Issues', 22 January 2008

Ipsos MORI/BBC *Horizon*, 'The Origins of Life', 30 January 2006

Ipsos MORI/BVPI, 'General User Survey for East Sussex County Council' (2006)

Ipsos MORI/The Royal Society, 'Concern about Science-related Issues', 6 March 2002

Ipsos MORI/Science Media Centre, 'Public Expects the Impossible from Science', 2 April 2002

Ipsos MORI/The Sun, 'Survey on Britain Today', 23 January 2006

Jansson, Krista, 'British Crime Survey: Measuring crime for 25 years'

The King's Fund, 'NHS Spending, Local Variations in Priorities: An update' (2008)

Local Government Association, 'Online Survey of Councillors' (2009)

Local Government Association Poll (2009)

Local Government Association, Improvement and Development Agency and Regional Improvement and Efficiency Partnerships, 'Leading the Way by Working Together' (July 2009)

Lloyds TSB, 'Over 50s drive down crime rates', press release, July 9 2009

McMaster, Brian, 'Supporting Excellence in the Arts: From Measurement to Judgment', Department for Culture, Media and Sport (January 2008)

Media Standards Trust, 'A More Accountable Press: The need for reform – is self-regulation failing the press and the public?' 9 February 2009

'Membership of UK Political Parties', House of Commons Library Standard Note SG 5125, 13 July 2009, p. 10

Middlesbrough Council, 'Community Consultation Strategy' (2006)

Ministry of Defence, 'Armed Forces Continuous Attitude Survey 2007' (July 2008)

National Advisory Committee on Creative and Cultural Education, 'All Our Futures: Creativity, culture and education' (1999)

National Statistics Online, 'Overview of Families: Cohabiting is fastest growing family type', 4 October 2007

'National Statistics Omnibus Survey', 26 August 2008

NESTA, 'Public Attitudes towards Information about Science and Technology' (October 2005)

New Economics Foundation, 'The Happy Planet Index 2.0', 4 July 2009

Office for National Statistics, 'Population Projections', 23 October 2007

Panel on Fair Access to the Professions, 'Unleashing Aspirations', final report, Cabinet Office Strategy Unit (2009)

Panel on Fair Access to the Professions, 'Unleashing Aspirations', summary and recommendations of full report, Cabinet Office Strategy Unit (2009)

'Power to the People: The report of Power – an independent inquiry into Britain's democracy', Power Inquiry (March 2006)

Reputation Institute, 'The World's Most Reputable Companies: An online study of consumers in 32 countries' (2009)

Social Exclusion Unit, 'Reducing Re-offending by Ex-prisoners' (July 2002)

Social Work Task Force, 'Facing Up to the Task', interim report (July 2009)

Sutton Trust: 'The educational backgrounds of the UK's top solicitors, barristers and judges', briefing note (June 2005)

Sutton Trust, 'University Admissions by School' (2007)

Sutton Trust, 'Applications, Offers and Admissions to Research Led Universities' (2009)

'Tomorrow's Owners: Stewardship of tomorrow's company', Tomorrow's
    Company
Transparency International, 'Corruption Perception Index' (2008)
Transparency International, 'Global Corruption Barometer' (2009)
UK Trade and Investment Defence and Security Organization, 'Securing Success'
    (undated)
UNICEF, 'Child Poverty in Perspective: An overview of child well-being in rich
    countries', UNICEF Innocenti Research Centre (2007)
Van Dijk, Jan, et al, 'The Burden of Crime in the EU – Research Report: A
    comparative analysis of the European Crime and Safety Survey (EU ICS) 2005',
    Gallup Europe (2007)
Walker, Alice, Flatley, John, Kersham, Chris and Moon, Debbie (eds), 'Crime in
    England and Wales 2008/9, vol. 1: Findings from the British Crime Survey and
    police recorded crime', Home Office (July 2009)
Willetts, David, 'More Ball Games: The childhood review' (2008)
YouGov Survey (May 2009) on behalf of Lloyds Pharmacy
YouGov/*Daily Telegraph* Survey, 24–26 October 2006
YouGov/*Daily Telegraph* Survey Results, 27–29 May 2009
YouGov/*Daily Telegraph* Survey Results, 28–30 July 2009
YouGov/*Sunday Times* Survey Results, 16–17 July 2009
'Young People and Crime', Home Office research study 145 (1995)

Websites

Association of British Insurers: www.abi.org.uk
Audit Commission: www.audit-commission.gov.uk
BBC: www.bbc.co.uk
British Security Industry Association: www.bsia.co.uk
Citizen Renaissance: www.citizenrenaissance.com
Community Care: www.communitycare.co.uk
Community Service Volunteers: www.csv.org.uk
Department for Children, Schools and Families: www.dcsf.gov.uk
Department of Health: www.dh.gov.uk
Frank Field: www.frankfield.co.uk
Hansard (House of Commons Daily Debates): www.publications.parliament.uk
Her Majesty's Prison Service: www.hmprisonservice.gov.uk
The Home Office: www.homeoffice.gov.uk
ICM Research: www.icmresearch.co.uk
International Baccalaureate: www.ibo.org
International Olympic Committee: www.olympic.org
Ministry of Defence: www.mod.uk
Ministry of Justice: www.justice.gov.uk
National Association of Primary Care: www.napc.co.uk
National Health Service: www.nhs.uk
National Literacy Trust: www.literacytrust.org.uk
National Trust: www.nationaltrust.org.uk

National Union of Journalists: www.nuj.org.uk
New Economics Foundation: www.neweconomics.org
POLIS: Journalism and Society: www.charliebeckett.org
The Prime Minister's Office: www.number10.gov.uk
Restorative Justice Consortium: www.restorativejustice.org.uk
Street Pianos www.streetpianos.com
United Kingdom Parliament: www.parliament.uk
Transition Town Totnes: totnes.transitionnetwork.org
Trees for Cities: www.treesforcities.org
The Week: www.theweek.com
Wellington College: www.wellingtoncollege.org.uk
The White House: www.whitehouse.gov

NOTES

Introduction: Are we at a turning point for trust?

1 BBC, 'School safety "insult" to Pullman', 16 July 2009

2 *The Times*, 17 July 2009

3 *The Guardian*, 22 July 2009

4 *The Times*, 13 July 2009

5 Interview with Vernon Bogdanor, 29 July 2009

6 Onora O'Neill, *A Question of Trust: The BBC Reith Lectures 2002* (Cambridge: Cambridge University Press, 2002)

7 BBC, 'RBS boss "does the right thing", 18 June 2009

8 John Arlidge, '"I'm doing God's work." Meet Mr Goldman Sachs', *Sunday Times*, 8 November 2009

9 Matt Taibbi, 'The Great American Bubble Machine', *Rolling Stone*, 13 July 2009

10 Vikram Dodd, 'Ali Dizaei, Metropolitan police commander, jailed for four years', *The Guardian*, 8 February 2010

10 BBC, 'Climate scepticism "on the rise"', 7 February 2010

11 Jan Ruzicka and Nicholas J. Wheeler, 'The Puzzle of Trusting Relationships in the Nuclear Non-proliferation Treaty', *International Affairs*, 86:1 (2010), pp. 69–85

12 Edelman, 'Trust Barometer Report' (2010)

13 Ipsos MORI, 'Trust in the Professions: Veracity Index' (2009)

14 O'Neill, *A Question of Trust*

15 Francis Fukuyama, 'The End of History', *National Interest*, 4 (1989)

16 Francis Fukuyama, *Trust: The Social Virtues and the Creation of Prosperity* (New York: Simon & Schuster, 1995)

17 Barbara Misztal, *Trust in Modern Societies: The Search for the Bases of Social Order* (Cambridge: Polity Press, 1996)

18 Piotr Sztompka, *Trust: A Sociological Theory* (Cambridge: Cambridge University Press, 1999)

19 Robert C. Solomon and Fernando Flores, *Building Trust: In Business, Politics, Relationships, and Life* (Oxford: Oxford University Press, 2003)

20 Russell Hardin, *Trust* (Cambridge: Polity Press, 2006)

21 Russell Hardin, *Trust and Trustworthiness* (New York: Russell Sage Foundation, 2004)

22 Anthony Giddens, *The Consequences of Modernity* (Cambridge: Polity Press, 1990)

23 Geoffrey Hosking, 'Why we need a history of trust', *Reviews in History* (2002)

24 Interview with Geoffrey Hosking, 19 February 2010

25 Interview with Frank Field, February 2010

26 Obama, Barack, 'Remarks by the President in State of the Union address', 27 January 2010, available at www.whitehouse.gov

27 Richard H. Thaler and Cass R. Sunstein, *Nudge: Improving Decisions about Health, Wealth and Happiness* (London: Penguin, 2009)

Chapter 1: A new model of trust

1 Fernando Flores and Robert C. Solomon, 'Creating Trust', *Business Ethics Quarterly*, 8 (1998), pp. 205–32

2 Piotr Sztompka, *Trust: A Sociological Theory* (Cambridge: Cambridge University Press, 1999), p. 225

3 Henry L. Stimson, 'The bomb and the opportunity', *Harper's Magazine*, March 1946

4 Seth Godin, 'Hard-wired to Belong', *RSA Journal*, available online.

5 Bruno Bettelheim, *A Good Enough Parent: A Book on Child Rearing* (Toronto: Random House, 1987)

6 Jonathan Sacks, *To Heal A Fractured World: The Ethics of Responsibility* (London: Continuum, 2005), p. 69

7 Robert C. Solomon and Fernando Flores, *Building Trust: In Business, Politics, Relationships, and Life* (Oxford: Oxford University Press, 2003)

8 Russell Hardin, *Trust* (Cambridge: Polity Press, 2006), p. 14

9 Tim Reid, 'Couples say "I do" to lasting love in marriage covenant', *The Times*, 16 February 2005

10 Sandra Laville, 'Police create most detailed picture of criminal gangs so far', *The Guardian*, 13 July 2009

11 Interview with Tony Buzan, 28 July 2009

12 Francis Fukuyama, *Trust: The Social Virtues and the Creation of Prosperity* (New York: Simon & Schuster, 1995)

13 Tim Harford, 'The Economics of Trust', *Forbes*, 25 September 2006

14 Interview with Tony Buzan, 28 July 2009

15 John F. Helliwell and Robert D. Putnam, 'The Social Context of Well-being', *Philosophical Transactions: Biological Sciences*, 350:1449 (2004), pp. 1435–46

16 Richard Layard, *Happiness: Lessons from a New Science* (London: Allen Lane, 2005)

17 Solomon and Flores, *Building Trust*, p. 210

18 Ipsos MORI, 'Only One in Five Say They Trust Journalists to Tell The Truth', 19 June 2009

19 Interview with Burke Trend, 1985

20 Interview with Lord Rees, 6 August 2009

21 Thomas L. Friedman, *Hot, Flat and Crowded: Why the World Needs a Green Revolution – and How We Can Renew Our Global Future* (London: Allen Lane, 2008), p. 301

22 Aristotle, *The Politics*, ed. Trevor J Saunders (London: Penguin Classics, 1981)

23 Confucius, *The Analects of Confucius (Lun Yu)*, tr. Chichung Huang (New York: Oxford University Press), 12.19

24 Cicero, *Pro Sestio*, tr. R. Gardner (Cambridge, MA: Loeb Classical Library, 1958), Chapters 96–100

25 Thomas Hobbes, *Leviathan* (London: Penguin Classics, [1651] 1982), XIII

26 Jean-Jacques Rousseau, *The Social Contract*, tr. Maurice Cranston (London: Penguin, [1762] 1968)

27 Edmund Burke, *Reflections on the Revolution in France* (New York: Oxford University Press, 1999), paragraph 75

28 Alexis de Tocqueville, *Democracy in America*, ed. Richard C. Heffner (New York: Signet Classic, 2001)

29 Thomas Paine, *The Rights of Man* (London: Penguin Classics, [1791] 1984)

30 Iris Murdoch, *The Sovereignty of Good* (New York: Routledge Classics, 2001), p. 47

31 Ibid., p. 40

32 Ibid., pp. 103–4

33 www.nationaltrust.org.uk

34 Jonathan Sacks, 'Credo: we must guard love in this world of easy pleasures', *The Times*, 25 July 2009

35 Rabbi Hillel, Avot 2:4

36 John Donne, *The Complete Poetry and Selected Prose of John Donne*, ed. Charles M. Coffin (London: Modern Library, 1994), Meditation 17

Chapter 2: How is trust lost?

1 Richard Dawkins, *The God Delusion* (London: Bantam Press, 2006)

2 Christopher Hitchens, *God Is Not Great: The Case against Religion* (London: Atlantic, 2007)

3 Geoff Mulgan, *Politics in an Antipolitical Age* (Cambridge: Polity Press, 1994)

4 Marek Kohn, *Trust: Self Interest and the Common Good* (Oxford: Oxford University Press, 2008), p. 64

5 John Rawls, *A Theory of Justice* (Oxford: Oxford University Press, 1999)

6 Onora O'Neill, *A Question of Trust: The BBC Reith Lectures 2002* (Cambridge: Cambridge University Press, 2002), p. 29

7 Maximiliane Szinovacz, 'Living with Grandparents: Variations by Cohort, Race, and Family Structure', *International Journal of Sociology and Social Policy*, 16 (1996), pp. 89–123

8 Nicola Woolcock, 'Key university departments could "implode" without foreign students', *The Times*, 13 August 2009

9 Susannah Hickling, 'Don't exclude the grandparents', *The Times*, 9 June 2009

10 Michael Young and Peter Willmott, *Family and Kinship in East London* (London: Taylor & Francis, 1954)

11 Piotr Sztompka, *Trust: A Sociological Theory* (Cambridge: Cambridge University Press, 1999), p. 98

12 Kathryn Wescott, 'Why are Dutch children so happy?', BBC News, 14 February 2007

13 Russell Hardin, *Trust* (Cambridge: Polity Press, 2006), p. 4

14 Russell Hardin, 'From Bodo Ethics to Distributive Justice', *Ethical Theory and Moral Practice*, 2 (1999), p. 411

15 Ibid., p. 403.

16 BBC, 'Historic Figures: William Beveridge, 1879–1963'

17 Ben Pimlott, 'Giants of poverty yet to be slain', *The Independent*, 1 December 1992

18 Robert Booth, 'Gap between rich and poor narrows, but UK is still one of the world's most unequal countries', *The Guardian*, 22 October 2008

19 Panel on Fair Access to the Professions, 'Unleashing Aspirations', final report, Cabinet Office Strategy Unit (2009)

20 Ibid.

21 David Goodhart, 'They're wrong – social mobility is not going downhill', *Sunday Times*, 26 July 2009

22 Richard Wilkinson and Kate Pickett, *The Spirit Level: Why More Equal Societies Almost Always Do Better* (London: Penguin, 2009), p. 5.

23 Peter Oborne, *The Triumph of the Political Class* (New York: Simon and Schuster, 2007)

24 Simon Jenkins, *Thatcher and Sons* (London: Allen Lane, 2006)

25 James Ashton, Jenny Davey and Kate Walsh, 'The big bonus is back', *Sunday Times*, 28 June 2009

26 Oliver Stone, *Wall Street* (USA: 20th Century Fox, 1987)

27 BBC, 'How Leeson broke the bank', 22 June 1999

28 Mark Tran, 'Arthur Andersen appeals for sympathy', *The Guardian*, 29 January 2002

29 Jenny Booth, 'Blair under pressure over al-Yamamah 'bribes'', *The Times*, 7 June 2007

30 Robert Klitgaard, address, Carter Center Conference on Transparency for Growth in the Americas, 4 May 1999

31 David Kynaston, *The City of London, vol. IV: A Club No More* (London: Chatto & Windus, 2002)

32 Interview with David Kynaston, 21 July 2009

33 Abraham Maslow, 'A Theory of Human Motivation', *Psychological Review*, 50 (1943), pp. 370–85.

34 Oliver James, *Affluenza* (London: Vermilion, 2007),

35 BBC, 'Children "bullied over brands"', 10 August 2008

36 See the New Economics Foundation 'Well-being' programme of work (www.neweconomics. org/gen); see also Jules Peck and Robert Phillips, *Citizen Renaissance*, available online at www.citizenrenaissance.com

37 Interview with Nic Marks, 8 July 2009

38 Jon Ungoed-Thomas and Helen Brooks, 'Revealed: Britain's most lenient judge', *The Times*, 9 August 2009

39 Interview with Tony Travers, 3 August 2009

40 Interview with Polly Toynbee, 5 August 2009

41 Anthony Seldon, *Churchill's Indian Summer: The Conservative Government 1951–1955* (London: Hodder & Stoughton, 1981) OR John Charmley, *Churchill: The End of Glory* (London: Hodder & Stoughton, 1993), p. 401

42 Lars Von Trier, *Antichrist* (Poland: Zentropa Entertainments, 2009)

43 Internet World Stats available at www.internetworldstats.com

44 Interview with Robert Phillips, 16 June 2009

45 David Aaronovitch, *Voodoo Histories: The Role of the Conspiracy Theory in Shaping Modern History* (London: Jonathan Cape, 2009)

46 Interview with Richard Sambrook, 8 July 2009

47 O'Neill, *A Question of Trust*, p. 68.

48 Hardin, *Trust*, p. 101

49 Sam O'Neill, 'Isa Ibrahim: converted to radical Islam online', *The Times*, 18 July 2009

50 Vance Packard, *The Hidden Persuaders* (New York: Ig Publishing, 1957)

51 Gwyn Bevan and Christopher Hood, 'Have Targets Improved Performance in the English NHS' (2006)

52 Antony Jay, *A New Great Reform Act* (West Molesey: 4 Print, 2009), p. 6.

53 Brendan O'Neill, 'Watching you watching me', *New Statesman*, 2 October 2006

54 Henry Porter, 'The way the police treat us verges on the criminal', *The Observer*, 29 October 2006

55 Anthony Giddens, *The Consequences of Modernity* (Cambridge: Polity Press, 1990), p. 80

56 Robert C. Solomon and Fernando Flores, *Building Trust: In Business, Politics, Relationships, and Life* (Oxford: Oxford University Press, 2001), p. 121

Chapter 3: How is trust recovered?

1 Geoffrey Hosking, 'Why we need a history of trust', *Reviews in History* (2002)

2 Anthony Giddens, *The Consequences of Modernity* (Stanford: Stanford University Press, 1991)

3 Hosking, 'Why we need a history of trust'

4 The National Trust, www.nationaltrust.org.uk

5 Hosking, 'Why we need a history of trust'

6 Daniel Finkelstein, 'Car wrecks and Hutus: a guide to good conduct', *The Times*, 16 May 2007

7 Interview with Steve Hilton, 28 July 2009

8 Fraser Nelson, 'They wish we all could be Californian: The New Tory plan', *Spectator*, 25 February 2009

9 Barbara Corcoran, 'The 5 friendliest cities in America', MSNBC, 28 May 2008

10 Jim Collins, *Good to Great* (London: Random House, 2001)

11 Shakespeare, *Julius Caesar*, Act III, Scene 2

12 Martin Seligman, *Authentic Happiness: Using the New Positive Psychology to Realise Your Potential for Lasting Fulfilment* (London: Nicholas Brealey Publishing, 2003)

13 John Elliot and Lauren Quaintance, 'Britain is getting less trusting', *Sunday Times*, 18 May 2003

14 David Goodhart, 'They're wrong – social mobility is not going downhill', *Sunday Times*, 26 July 2009

15 Reputation Institute, 'The World's Most Reputable Companies: An online study of consumers in 32 countries' (2009)

16 Correspondence with Robert Klitgaard, 20 July 2009

17 Robert Klitgaard, 'Subverting Corruption', *Finance and Development*, June 2000

18 David Puttnam, 'Are We Raising the Right Kind of Leaders?', Independent Schools Council Annual Conference, 1 June 2009

19 Esther Hauk and Maria Saez-Marti, 'On the cultural transmission of corruption', *Journal of Economic Theory* (2002), p. 312

20 David Willetts, 'More Ball Games', *Childhood Review*, 4 February 2008, p. 4

21 See for example Robert Murray and Tim Blessing, *Greatness in the White House: Rating the Presidents from George Washington through Ronald Reagan* (University Park: Pennsylvania University Press, 1994)

22 Elie Wiesel, 'The Perils of Indifference', speech delivered 12 April 1999

23 Robin Dunbar, quoted in Malcolm Gladwell, *The Tipping Point: How Little Things Can Make a Big Difference* (London: Little, Brown, 2000), p. 179

Chapter 4: Trust in government, politics and local democracy

1 Barack Obama, 'An Honest Government, A Hopeful Future', 28 August 2006

2 Geoff Mulgan, *The Art of Public Strategy: Mobilizing Power and Knowledge for the Common Good* (Oxford: Oxford University Press 2009), p. 218

3 European Commission, 'Eurobarometer 70', United Kingdom, p. 24

4 Ipsos MORI, 'Three in Four Believe Britain's Governance Needs Improving', 3 June 2009

5 Ibid.

6 House of Commons, 'Speakers Conference (on Parliamentary Representation): Interim Report' (London: The Stationery Office, 2009), p. 5

7 Ipsos MORI, 'Expenses Poll for the BBC', 2 June 2009

8 'Membership of UK Political Parties', House of Commons Library Standard Note SG 5125, 13 July 2009, p. 10

9 Ipsos MORI, 'Three in Four Believe Britain's Governance Needs Improving', 3 June 2009

10 Anthony Seldon, *Blair* (Free Press, 2004), p. 535

11 ICM, '*Evening Standard* London Poll' (November 2000), p. 2

12 ICM, 'Labour Five Years and Royalty Poll' (April 2002), p. 8

13 ICM, 'Opinion of the Government Poll' (May 2002), p. 1

14 ICM, '*Guardian* Opinion Poll' (July 2004), p. 6

15 Interview with David Smith, 15 July 2009

16 Ipsos MORI, 'Expenses Poll for the BBC', 2 June 2009

17 Ipsos MORI, 'Three in Four Believe Britain's Governance Needs Improving', 3 June 2009

18 Ipsos MORI, 'Expenses Poll for the BBC', 2 June 2009

19 Transparency International, 'Global Corruption Barometer' (2009)

20 Transparency International, 'Corruption Perception Index' (2008)

21 Hansard Society, 'Audit of Political Engagement 6: The 2009 report, with a focus on political participation and citizenship' (2009), p. 26.

22 'Power to the People: The report of Power – an independent inquiry into Britain's democracy', Power Inquiry (March 2006)

23 Russell J. Dalton, *Democratic Challenges, Democratic Choices; The Erosion of Political Support in Advanced Industrial Democracies* (Oxford: Oxford University Press, 2004), p. 96.

24 'Best PMs revealed', *BBC History Magazine*, 29 August 2006.

25 Jules Peck and Robert Phillips, *Citizen Renaissance*, available online at www. citizenrenaissance.com.

26 'Power to the People'

27 Ipsos MORI, 'Audit of Political Engagement' (2005)

28 House of Commons Communities and Local Government Committee, 'Balance of Power: Central and Local Government', Sixth Report of Session 2008/9, 12 May 2009, p. 3

29 Simon Jenkins, *Accountable to None: The Tory Nationalisation of Britain* (London: Penguin, 1996), p. 15

30 Ibid., p. 20

31 Ipsos MORI/BVPI, 'General User Survey for East Sussex County Council' (2006)

32 Alexis de Tocqueville, *The Old Regime and the Revolution* (Chicago: University of Chicago Press, 1998), pp. 197–201

33 David Marquand, *Britain since 1918: A Political History* (London: Weidenfeld & Nicholson), p. 187

34 'General Election 2005', House of Commons Research Paper 05/33 (2005); 'General Election Results 7 June 2001', House of Commons Research Paper 01/54 (2001)

35 Interview with Peter Sinclair, 8 July 2009

36 BBC, 'Speaker quits for "sake of unity"', 19 May 2009

37 Andrew Sparrow, 'Poll shows voters want Brown to step up constitutional reform', *The Guardian*, 16 July 2009

38 Mulgan, *The Art of Public Strategy*, p. 227

39 Ipsos MORI, 'Expenses Poll for the BBC', 2 June 2009

40 Parliament website, available at: www.parliament.uk/about/how/elections/constituencies. cfm

41 BBC, 'Miliband backs US-style primaries', 7 August 2009

42 Sam Coates, 'Sarah Wollaston selected to fight Totnes for Tories after open ballot', *The Times*, 5 August 2009

43 'Primary colours', *The Times*, 23 May 2009

44 YouGov/Daily Telegraph Survey Results, 27-29 May 2009, p. 4

45 Hansard Society, 'Political Accountability and Transparency, *Briefing Paper 1: Restoring Trust in the House of Lords'*, July 2009, p. 4

46 YouGov/*Daily Telegraph* Survey Results, 27-29 May 2009, p. 4

47 Ibid.

48 Peter Kellner, 'We Should Endorse AV', Fabian Society, 15 July 2009

49 Dalton, *Democratic Challenges, Democratic Choices*, p. 96

50 Committee on Standards in Public Life/BMRB Social Research, 'Survey of Public Attitudes towards Conduct in Public Life' (2008), p. 30

51 Confucius, *Lun Yu*, 2.3

52 Geoff Mulgan, 'Good and Bad Power: The Ideals and Betrayals of Government' (London: Penguin, 2006), p. 223

53 Cicero, *Pro Sestio*, tr. R. Gardner (Cambridge, MA: Loeb Classical Library, 1958), Chapters 96–100

54 House of Commons, 'The Code of Conduct: The guide to the rules relating to the conduct of Members' (London: The Stationery Office: 2009)

55 Ipsos MORI, 'Expenses Poll for the BBC', 2 June 2009

56 Joseph S. Nye Jr and Philip D. Selikow, *Why People Don't Trust Government* (Cambridge, MA: Harvard University Press, 1997), p. 261

57 Edelman, 'Mid-year Trust Barometer Report' (2009)

58 The White House, Open Government Initiative, available at www.whitehouse.gov/open/innovations

59 'National Statistics Omnibus Survey', 26 August 2008

60 Edelman, 'Mid-year Trust Barometer Report' (2009), p. 4

61 Guy Lodge, 'Back in Line?', Institute for Public Policy Research, 21 July 2009

62 Peter Kellner, 'Down with people power', *Prospect*, July 2009

63 Interview with Tony Travers, 3 August 2009, for whom many thanks for his many insights on local government

64 BBC 'Who cares who wins?', 29 April 2002

65 Local Government Association, Improvement and Development Agency and Regional Improvement and Efficiency Partnerships, 'Leading the Way by Working Together' (July 2009), p. 3

66 Roger Gough, *With a Little Help from Our Friends: International Lessons for English Local Government* (London: Localis, 2009), p. 24

67 Interview with Tony Travers, 3 August 2009

68 Ibid.

69 Isabel Oakeshott, 'Boris Johnson tells Met chief to cut crime – or else', *Sunday* Times, 4 May 2008

70 Interview with Tony Travers, 3 August 2009

71 Iain Roxburgh, 'Overcoming the Obstacles of Devolved Government', in Iain Roxburgh (ed.), *Next Steps for Local Democracy: Leadership, Accountability and Partnership* (London: New Local Government Network, 2008), p. 9

72 Jon Bloomfield, 'Controlling, Cajoling or Co-operating? Central governments' policy approaches towards local government on the issues of performance and cost-effectiveness', *Council of European Municipalities and Regions* (May 2006), pp. 10–11

73 Peter John, *The Benefits of Local Citizen Engagement and Dialogue* (London: New Local Government Network, 2008), p. 39

74 House of Commons Communities and Local Government Committee, 'Balance of Power: Central and Local Government', p. 3

75 Interview with Polly Toynbee, 5 August 2009

76 Bruce E. Cain, Russell J. Dalton and Susan E. Scarrow (eds), *Democracy Transformed? Expanding Political Opportunities in Advanced Industrial Democracies* (Oxford: Oxford University Press, 2003), p. 274

77 Peck and Phillips, *Citizen Renaissance*

Chapter 5: Trust in business, bankers and the economy

1 Adam Smith, *The Wealth of Nations* (New York: Prometheus, [1776] 1991)

2 Herbert Gintis and Rakes Kurana, 'Corporate Honesty and Business Education; A

behavioural model', in Paul Zak (ed.) *The Critical Role of Values in the Economy* (Princeton: Princeton University Press, 2008), pp. 300–327

3 Francis Fukuyama, *Trust: The Social Virtues and the Creation of Prosperity* (New York: Simon & Schuster, 1995), p. 31

4 Kenneth Arrow, 'The Economy of Trust', *Acton Institute; Religion & Liberty*,16:3 (2006), p. 3

5 Edelman, 'Mid-year Trust Barometer Report' (2009), p. 18

6 Corporate Culture, 'Customer Trust Index Summary Findings' (2007)

7 Helliwell, John and Huang, Haifang, 'Well-being and Trust in the Workplace', National Bureau of Economic Research (December 2008), p. 2

8 Edelman, 'Mid-year Trust Barometer Report' (2009)

9 Corporate Culture, 'Customer Trust Index Summary Findings' (2007)

10 Edelman, 'Mid-year Trust Barometer Report' (2009)

11 Ipsos MORI, 'Annual IBE/Ipsos MORI Survey 2008 of UK Adult Opinion on Business Ethics' (2008)

12 Joe Garner, Joe 'Trust. . . and the Financial Crisis', speech delivered at the launch of the 2009 Edelman Trust Barometer, 21 July 2009

13 Interview with Joe Garner, 6 August 2009

14 Interview with Tony Manwaring, 17 July 2009

15 Gillian Tett, 'Untangling the Crisis', *Management Today*, April 2009

16 Interview with Herman Mulder, 30 July 2009

17 Charles Handy, 'What's Business For?', in Paul Zak (ed.) *The Critical Role of Values in the Economy* (Princeton: Princeton University Press, 2008), pp. 328–39

18 BBC, 'RBS boss does "the right thing"', 18 June 2009

19 Interview with Peter Sinclair, 8 July 2009

20 Interview with Polly Toynbee, 5 August 2009

21 Jill Treanor and Phillip Inman, 'Banks defend bonus culture as profits jump', *The Guardian*, 3 August 2009

22 'RBS agree £9.6m pay deal for Stephen Hester', *Daily Telegraph*, 22 June 2009

23 Andrew Sparrow, 'Banking bonuses: prospect of return to "business as usual" alarms politicians', *The Guardian*, 3 August 2009

24 Isabel Oakeshott and James Ashton, 'Alistair Darling: new law to curb City bonuses', *The Times*, 16 August 2009

25 Edelman, 'Mid-year Trust Barometer Report' (2009), p. 3

26 Financial Services Authority, 'The Turner Review: A regulatory response to the global banking crisis' (March 2009)

27. Stephen Davis, Jon Lukomnik and David Pitt-Watson, *Towards an Accountable Capitalism*, IPPR and Friends Provident Foundation (March 2009)

28 Paul Zak (ed.), *Moral Markets: The Critical Role of Values in the Economy* (Princeton: Princeton University Press, 2008), p. xvii

29 BBC, 'Q&A bank bonuses', 9 February 2009

30 BBC, 'Bank reform "needs to be radical"', 1 August 2009

31 Martin Woolf, 'Why regulators should intervene in bankers' pay', *Financial Times*, 16 January 2009

32 Andrew Simms, 'A salary cap for everyone', *The Guardian*, 6 August 2009

33 Edelman, 'Mid-year Trust Barometer Report' (2009), p. 20

34 Robert Peston, 'The new capitalism', BBC, 8 December 2008, p. 6

35 Will Hutton, *The State We're In: Why Britain Is in Crisis and How to Overcome It* (London: Jonathan Cape, 1995), p. 298

36 Peston, 'The new capitalism'

37 Francesco Guererra, 'Welch condemns share price focus', *Financial Times*, 12 March 2009

38 Fukuyama, *Trust*, p. 232

39 Dame Carol Black, *Working for a Healthier Tomorrow; Review of the Health of Britain's Working Age Population* (London: The Stationery Office, 2008), p. 10

40 Business in the Community, 'Emotional Resilience Toolkit', May 2009

41 Edelman, 'Mid-year Trust Barometer Report' (2009)

42 'Tomorrow's Owners: Stewardship of tomorrow's company', Tomorrow's Company

43 Handy, 'What's business for?, pp. 328–39

44 Milton Friedman, 'The Social Responsibility of Business Is to Increase its Profits', *New York Times Magazine*, 13 September 1970

45 Edelman, 'Mid-year Trust Barometer Report' (2009), p. 3

46 Victoria Thomson, 'Co-op Bank profits rise as it cashes in on public backlash', *The Scotsman*, 3 April 2009

47 M Fox, S Forrest, A Ling and M Lynch, *Global Food & beverages: Integrating ESG* (Goldman Sachs, 2007), p. 50

48 Simon Zadek with Peter Raynard and Maya Forstater, *What Assures? Listening to words of assurance* (AccountAbility and PricewaterhouseCoopers, June 2006)

49 Kenny Kemp, 'Rebuilding Trust', *Sunday Herald*, 14 August 2009

50 Interview with Ken Rea, 7 August 2009

51 Edelman, 'Mid-year Trust Barometer Report' (2009), p. 3

52 Ibid., p. 21

53 Jim Collins, *Good to Great: Why Some Companies Make the Leap. . . and Others Don't* (London: Random House, 2001), p. 21

54 Interview with Roger Steare, 22 July 2009

55 W. B. Donham,'The Social Significance of Business', *Harvard Business Review*, 5 (July 1927), pp. 406–19

56 Hauk, Esther and Saez-Marti, Maria, 'On the Cultural Transmission of Corruption', *Journal of Economic Theory* (2002), p. 324

57 Private information

58 Phillip Blond, 'Rise of the red Tories', *Prospect*, 28 February 2009

59 Interview with David Pitt-Watson, 7 August 2009. *The five arms of the civil economy are accountability, responsibility, independent information, relevant and appropriate economic measures,and investigable by civil society*

60 Donovan, Nick, Halpern, David and Sargeant, Richard, 'Life Satisfaction: The state of knowledge and implications for government', Cabinet Office Strategy Unit (2003), p. 17

61 New Economics Foundation, *The Happy Planet Index 2.0* (London: NEF, July 2009), p. 11

62 Interview with Lord Rees, 6 August 2009

63 New Economics Foundation, 'The Happy Planet Index 2.0', 4 July 2009, p. 11

64 Richard Cockett, *Thinking the Unthinkable; Think-tanks and the Economic Counter-revolution 1931–1983* (London: HarperCollins, 1995)

65 Panel on Fair Access to the Professions, 'Unleashing Aspirations', final report, Cabinet Office Strategy Unit (2009)

66 Ibid.

67 Patrick Wintour, 'Britain's closed shop: damning report on social mobility failings', *The Guardian*, 21 July 2009

68 Harry Wallop, 'One in three young people out of work, unemployment statistics show', *Daily Telegraph*, 12 August 2009

Chapter 6: Trust in the police, the law and defence

1 Ipsos MORI/BBC, 'Survey on Trust Issues', 22 January 2008

2 Ipsos MORI/The Sun, 'Survey on Britain Today', 23 January 2006

3 YouGov/*Daily Telegraph* Survey, 24–26 October 2006

4 Terence Blacker, 'The new British way of mourning', *The Independent*, 18 July 2009

5 Ministry of Defence, 'Operations in Iraq: British fatalities', www.mod.uk, accessed 18/08/2009

6 Ministry of Defence, 'Operations in Afghanistan: British fatalities', www.mod.uk, accessed 18/08/2009

7 YouGov/*Daily Telegraph* Survey, 24–26 October 2006

8 Ipsos MORI, 'Attitudes to Afghanistan Campaign', 24 July 2009

9 YouGov/*Sunday Times* Survey Results, 16–17 July 2009

10 YouGov/*Daily Telegraph* Survey Results, 28–30 July 2009

11 Ibid

12 Ian Loader and Aogán Mulcahy, *Policing and the Condition of England: Memory, Politics and Culture* (Oxford: Oxford University Press, 2003), p. 102

13 Correspondence with Robert Reiner, 7 August 2009. See Robert Reiner, *The Politics of the Police* (Oxford: Oxford University Press, 2000)

14 Alice Walker, John Flatley, Chris Kersham, and Debbie Moon, Debbie (eds), 'Crime in England and Wales 2008/9, vol. 1: Findings from the British Crime Survey and police recorded crime', Home Office (July 2009), p. 103

15 'European Social Survey Round 2 Data (2004/2005)', quoted in van de Walle, 'Trust in the Justice System', p. 23

16 Krista Jansson, 'British Crime Survey: Measuring crime for 25 years'

17 British Security Industry Association website, 'Facts and Figures'

18 '2006–2015 Homeland Security & Homeland Defence Global Market Outlook', Homeland Security Research Corporation, cited in UK Trade and Investment Defence and Security Organization, 'Securing Success'

19 Jansson, 'British Crime Survey', p. 27

20 Steven van de Walle, 'Trust in the Justice System: A comparative view across Europe', *Prison Service Journal*, 183 (2009), pp. 22–6

21 Ipsos MORI, 'The National College for School Leadership Survey on Britain's Best Leaders', 28 March 2003

22 Committee on Standards in Public Life/BMRB Social Research, 'Survey of Public Attitudes towards Conduct in Public Life' (2008), p. 22

23 Bar Standards Board, 'Journalists, bankers, estate agents and politicians the "least trusted professions"', press release, 31 March 2009

24 ComRes, 'The Solicitors Regulation Authority Consumer Research Study 2008' (February 2009)

25 Private interview

26 ICM Research, '*Guardian* Muslim Poll', July 2005

27 ICM Research, '*Guardian* Opinion Poll', 14–16 February 2003

28 Gill Allen, 'Andrew Walker: the coroner the MoD couldn't gag', *The Times*, 11 April 2008

29 Christopher Booker, 'Lt-Colonel Rupert Thorneloe and Trooper Joshua Hammond should not have died', *Daily Telegraph*, 4 July 2009

30 Hansard, House of Commons Debates, 12 November 2007, col. 491

31 Kim Sengupta, 'Soldier's soldier: General Sir Richard Dannatt', *The Independent*, 18 July 2009

32 Tim Shipman and Matthew Hickley, 'Labour attacks British army chief after he pointedly flies around Afghanistan in US plane', *Daily Mail*, 16 July 2009

33 Patrick Barkham, 'Stephen Lawrence case Q & A', *The Guardian*, 23rd February 1999

34 Michael Rowe, *Policing, Race and Racism* (Cullompton: Willan, 2004) p. 7

35 ICM Research, 'BBC South-East Police Poll' (July 1998)

36 Ipsos MORI, 'Attitudes towards Policing', 25 February 1999

37 Barry Loveday, 'Community Policing under New Labour', *Criminal Justice Matters*, 67:1 (2007), pp. 28–9

38 BBC, 'Race row police told to "shut up"', 28 August 2008

39 Philip Johnston, 'G20 death: we want a police force, not brute force', *Daily Telegraph*, 8 April 2009

40 Ipsos MORI, 'Post London Bombings Survey', 5 October 2005

41 James Macintyre, 'Public Enemy Number One', *New Statesman*, 16 April 2009

42 Emily Apple, 'Can the police give up confrontation?', *The Guardian*, 23 July 2009

43 Dale Bassett, Andrew Haldenbury, Laurie Thraves, and Elizabeth Truss, 'A New Force', Reform (February 2009)

44 James Macintyre, 'Public Enemy Number One', *New Statesman*, 16 April 2009

45 Tracy McVeigh, Rajeev Syal and Gaby Hinsliff, 'G20 Protests: How the image of UK police took a beating', *The Guardian*, 19 April 2009

46 Ibid.

47 Herbert, Nick, Keeble, Oscar, Burley, Aidan and Gibbs, Blair, 'Policing for the People: Interim report of the Police Reform Taskforce' (2007), p. 30, refers to the policy review 'Crime, Justice and Cohesion', Prime Minister's Strategy Unit (November 2006), p. 13, and comments that the slide in question was removed from the final published document

48 Marian FitzGerald, 'Massaging the crime figures', *The Guardian* 20 July 2009

49 Reiner, Robert, *Politics of the Police* (University of Toronto Press 1992), p xi

50 Private interview

51 Herbert et al., 'Policing for the People', p. 77

52 Joe Hicks and Grahame Allen, 'A Century of Change: Trends in UK Statistics since 1900', House of Commons Research Paper 99/111, 21 December 1999, p. 14

53 Alice Walker, John Flatley, Chris Kersham, and Debbie Moon (eds), 'Crime in England and Wales 2008/9, vol. 1: Findings from the British Crime Survey and police recorded crime', Home Office (July 2009), p. 36

54 Jansson, 'British Crime Survey', p. 9

55 Reiner, Robert, *Law and Order: An Honest Citizen's Guide to Crime and Control* (Cambridge: Polity, 2007), p. 64

56 Jan van Dijk et al., 'The Burden of Crime in the EU – Research Report: A Comparative Analysis of the European Crime and Safety Survey (EU ICS) 2005', Gallup Europe (2007), p. 97

57 Walker et al., 'Crime in England and Wales 2008/9', p. 96

58 Ibid., p. 103

59 Blair, Tony, 'Our Nation's Future: Time for proper debate on law and order', speech delivered 23 June 2006

60 Quoted in Charles Nevin, 'Surveillance over Europe', *Intelligent Life*, Summer 2009

61 Shami Chakrabarti, 'Shami Chakrabarti on human rights', video interview, *The Economist*

62 Tom Whitehead, 'Police accused of abusing powers as anti-terrorism stop and searches treble', *Daily Telegraph*, 30 April 2009

63 Walker et al., 'Crime in England and Wales 2008/9', p. 22

64 Ibid.

65 Marian FitzGerald, Mike Hough, Ian Joseph and Tariq Quereshi, *Policing for London* (Cullompton: Willan, 2002), p. 41

66 Ministry of Justice, 'Prison Population and Accommodation Briefing for 7 Aug 2009'

67 The National Literacy Trust, 'Young Offenders', www.literacytrust.org.uk/socialinclusion/youngpeople/offenders.html

68 BBC, 'Early prison releases top 50,000', 31 March 2009. Early release is defined as up to 18 days before the halfway point of their sentence

69 BBC, 'Why more inmates are reoffenders', 30 January 2007

70 Social Exclusion Unit, 'Reducing Re-offending by Ex-prisoners' (July 2002), p. 3

71 Jon Ungoed-Thomas and Helen Brooks, 'Revealed: Britain's most lenient judge', *Sunday Times*, 9 August 2009

72 Harris Interactive, 'Common Good Survey on Americans' Trust in Their Legal System', 27 June 2005

73 Frances Gibb, 'Legal aid cuts: how you could be acquitted and still face a huge bill for costs', *The Times*, 17 July 2007

74 Judge Sturgess, 1928, cited in Wade Mansell and Belinda Meteyard, *A Critical Introduction to Law* (Abingdon: Routledge Cavendish, 1995)

75 Sutton Trust, 'The educational backgrounds of the UK's top solicitors, barristers and judges', briefing note (June 2005)

76 John Bingham, 'Britain's richest solicitor' guilty of exploiting sick miners for fees', *Daily Telegraph*, 11 December 2008

77 Allegra Stratton, 'Afghanistan could take 40 years, says new army chief', *The Guardian*, 8 August 2009

78 Ministry of Defence, 'Armed Forces Continuous Attitude Survey 2007' (July 2008)

79 Douglas Carswell and Dan Hannan, *The Plan: 12 Months to Renew Britain* (Great Britain: Douglas Carswell, 2008) p. 54

80 Correspondence with Robert Klitgaard, 20 July 2009

81 Barry Loveday, 'Community Policing under New Labour', *Criminal Justice Matters*, 67:1 (2007), pp. 28–9

82 Herbert et al., 'Policing for the People', p. 58

83 Ibid., p. 61

84 Middlesbrough Council, 'Community Consultation Strategy 2006', p. 3

85 Martin Gill and Angela Spriggs, 'Assessing the Impact of CCTV', Home Office Research, Development and Statistics Directorate (February 2005), p. 61

86 John Elliot and Lauren Quaintance, 'Britain is getting less trusting', *Sunday Times*, 18 May 2003

87 Restorative Justice Consortium, www.restorativejustice.org.uk

88 Lawrence W. Sherman and Heather Strang, *Restorative Justice: The Evidence* (London: Smith Institute, 2007), p. 12

Chapter 7: Trust in health, education and social services

1 Julia Abelson, Fiona A. Miller and Mita Giacomini, 'What does it mean to trust a health system? A qualitative study of Canadian health care values', *Health Policy*, 91 (2009), p. 63

2 Association of British Insurers, www.abi.org

3 James Thompson, 'Bupa loses custom for its private medical insurance', *The Independent*, 13 August 2009

4 British Social Attitudes report (2009), quoted in Andrew Cole, 'More Spending on NHS Has Led to Highest Satisfaction Rates in 25 Years, Report Says', *British Medical Journal*, 338:b374 (2009)

5 British Social Attitudes report (2009), quoted in John Carvel, 'Takeoff time for guilt over air travel', *The Guardian*, 28 January 2009

6 Mike Pringle, 'The Shipman Inquiry: Implications for the public's trust in doctors', *British Journal of General Practice*, 50:454 (2000), p. 355

7 Ipsos MORI, 'Trust in the Professions: Veracity Index' (2008)

8 Ipsos MORI, 'Opinion of Professions: How Well Do They Do Their Jobs?' (2005)

9 Ipsos MORI, 'Trust in the Professions: Veracity Index' (2008)

10 Committee on Standards in Public Life/BMRB Social Research, 'Survey of Public Attitudes towards Conduct in Public Life' (2008), p. 22

11 M. W. Calnan and E. Sanford, 'Public Trust in Health Care: The system or the doctor?', *Quality and Safety in Healthcare*, 13:2 (2004), p. 94

12 Ipsos MORI, 'Public Perceptions and Patient Experience of the NHS: Winter 2004 Tracking Survey', summary report (2004), p. 6

13 Ipsos MORI, 'End of Year Review' (2008), p. 16

14 BBC News, 'Infections "the biggest NHS fear"', 30 June 2008

15 Interview with Professor Howard Glennester, 27 July 2009

16 BBC News, 'Infections "the biggest NHS fear"'

17 Ipsos MORI, 'Trust in the Professions: Veracity Index' (2008)

18 Committee on Standards in Public Life/BMRB Social Research, 'Survey of Public Attitudes towards Conduct in Public Life' (2008), p. 22

19 British Social Attitudes survey (2007)

20 Ipsos MORI, 'Ipsos MORI Survey Shows Record Demand for Independent Education' (2008)

21 Department for Children, Schools and Families, 'Schools, Pupils and Their Characteristics: Statistical first release' (January 2009)

22 Gaby Hinsliff, 'How private schools ensure a life of privilege for their pupils', *The Guardian*, 19 July 2009

23 Luren Revans, 'Profession's delight as poll reveals wave of support for social workers', *Community Care*, 3 May 2007

24 Local Government Association poll (2009), www.lga.gov.uk

25 Local Government Association, online survey of councillors (2009), www.lga.gov.uk

26 British Social Attitudes survey (1994)

27 Interview with Professor Howard Glennerster, 28 July 2009

28 Anthony Giddens, *Modernity and Self-identity: Self and Society in the Late Modern Age* (1991), p. 149, quoted in Stephen Harrison and Carole Smith, 'Trust and Moral Motivation: Redundant resources in health and social care?', *Policy & Politics*, 32:3 (2004), p. 372

29 YouGov survey (May 2009) on behalf of Lloyds Pharmacy, www.lloydspharmacy.com

30 Interview with Dr Nick Patton, 9 August 2009

31 Simon Usborne, 'Cyberchondria: The perils of internet self-diagnosis', *The Independent*, 17 February 2009

32 Ibid.

33 Ibid.

34 Interview with Dr Patrick Reade, 11 August 2009

35 David Batty, 'Alder Hey report on use of children's organs', *The Guardian*, 30 January 2001

36 Gaia Vince, 'MRSA deaths up 15-fold in a decade', *New Scientist*, 26 February 2004

37 BBC, 'Infections "the biggest NHS fear"', 30 June 2008

38 Chart based on information from BBC, 'Infections "the biggest NHS fear", 30 June 2008

39 Interviews with Dr Patrick Reade and Dr Nick Patton, 11 August 2009 and 9 August 2009

40 Reuters, 'UK records first H1N1 death in healthy patient', 10 July 2009

41 Jon Swaine, Nick Britten and Stephen Adams, 'Swine flu: government website collapses under demand', *Daily Telegraph*, 24 July 2009

42 Roger Harrabin, Anna Coote and Jessica Allen, 'Health in the News: Risk, reporting and media influence', The King's Fund (September 2003), quoted from BBC Radio 4's *Today* programme website

43 Ibid.

44 Jenny Hope, 'Drinking just one glass of wine a day can INCREASE risk of cancer by 168%, say the French!', *Daily Mail*, 23 February 2009

45 Michael Blastland, 'How to understand risk in 13 clicks', BBC, 11 March 2009

46 Interview with Professor Howard Glennerster, 28 July 2009

47 Interview with Dr Nick Patton, 9 August 2009

48 Department of Health, www.dh.gov.uk

49 'Is the law bleeding the NHS to death?', *Sunday Times*, 3 August 2008

50 BBC, 'Damages "hitting" NHS care', 30 June 2009

51 'Is the law bleeding the NHS to death?'

52 R. Smith, 'Regulation of Doctors and the Bristol Inquiry', *British Medical Journal*, 317 (1998), pp. 1539–40

53 Rebecca Smith, 'NHS targets 'may have led to 1,200 deaths' in Mid-Staffordshire', *Daily Telegraph*, 18 March 2009

54 Ibid.

55 Healthcare Commission, 'Investigation into Mid-Staffordshire NHS Foundation Trust' (March 2009), p. 9

56 Max Pemberton, 'NHS: have targets become more important than patients?', *Daily Telegraph*, 30 March 2009

57 Anthony King, 'NHS: the nation fears for its future', *Daily Telegraph*, 29 June 2008

58 Interview with Professor Howard Glennerster, 28 July 2009

59 The King's Fund, 'NHS Spending, Local Variations in Priorities: An update' (2008), p. 5

60 Interview with Dr Nick Patton, 9 August 2009

61 Department for Children, Schools and Families

62 Polly Curtis and Tracy McVeigh, 'State or private: still the key factor in shaping life for our schoolchildren', *The Observer*, 16 August 2009

63 Sutton Trust, 'University Admissions by School' (2007)

64 Sutton Trust, 'Applications, Offers and Admissions to Research Led Universities' (2009)

65 Cabinet Office, 'Unleashing Aspiration: The Final Report of the Panel on Fair Access to the Professions' (2009)

66 Department for Children, Schools and Families

67 Nicola Woolcock, 'Record A grades prompt plea for new marking plan to split the difference', *The Times*, 21 August 2009

68 International Baccalaureate, www.ibo.org

69 House of Commons Innovation, Universities, Science and Skills Committee, 'Students and Universities', Eleventh Report of Session 2008/9, 20 July 2009, para. 243

70 Jessica Shepherd, 'Students less satisfied with their universities, says survey', *The Guardian*, 6 August 2009

71 Alan Gilbert on Radio 4's *Beyond Westminster*, 15 August 2009

72 Jack Grimston, 'Students at top university revolt over teaching standards', *Sunday Times*, 10 May 2009

73 Sian Griffiths and Roger Waite, 'More top English students opt for American universities', *Sunday Times*, 17 February 2008

74 Derren Hays, 'Community Care survey reveals public ignorance about social work role', Community Care website, 20 September 2004, www.communitycare.co.uk

75 Sally Gillen, 'Reluctance to go on the record frustrates media', Community Care website, 13 August 2009, www.communitycare.co.uk

76 BBC, 'Inquiry into Climbie officials', 12 January 2001

77 BBC, 'Shock as woman returned to home', 22 April 2009

78 'Unison calls for time on second anniversary of the death of baby Peter', Unison press release, 3 August 2009

79 Office of National Statistics, 'Population Projections', 23 October 2007, quoted in Ara Darzi, 'High Quality Care for All: NHS Next Stage Review', final report (June 2008), p. 26

80 Ara Darzi, 'High Quality Care for All: NHS Next Stage Review', final report (June 2008)

81 Interview with Dr Nick Patton, 9 August 2009

82 Ara Darzi, 'High Quality Care for All: NHS Next Stage Review', final report (June 2008)

83 'Fat, unfit NHS staff top the sick league', *The Times*, 19 August 2009

84 Change4Life, www.nhs.uk/Change4Life

85 Abelson et al., 'What does it mean to trust a health system?', p. 64

86 Calnan and Sanford, 'Public Trust in Health Care', p. 96

87 Larry Culliford, 'Teaching Spirituality and Health Care to Third-year Medical Students', *The Clinical Teacher*, 6 (2009), pp. 22–7

88 Appleby and Alvarez, 'British Social Attitudes Survey, 22nd Report: Public Responses to NHS Reform' (2005), quoted in Ara Darzi, 'High Quality Care for All: NHS Next Stage Review', final report (June 2008)

89 NHS Choices, www.nhs.uk

90 Martin Marshall, 'Practice, Politics and Possibilities', *British Journal of General Practice*, 59:565 (2009), pp. 273–82

91 Alan Smithers, 'Schools', in Anthony Seldon (ed.) *Blair's Britain, 1997–2007* (Cambridge: Cambridge University Press, 2007), p. 382

92 Peter Hyman, 'Drop GCSEs. We should be teaching our children to think', *The Observer*, 16 August 2009

93 Interview with Jonathan Smith, 12 August 2009

94 Ellen Widdup, 'London school with 100 spy cameras', *Evening Standard*, 21 July 2009

95 Howard Gardner, *Multiple Intelligences: The Theory in Practice* (New York: Basic Books, 1993)

96 Wellington College, www.wellingtoncollege.org.uk

97 Social Work Task Force, 'Facing Up to the Task', interim report (July 2009), www.dcsf.gov.uk

Chapter 8: Trust in science, religion and ideology

1 Ipsos MORI, 'Trust in the Professions: Veracity Index' (2008)

2 Interview with Martin Rees, 6 August 2009

3 Ipsos MORI/BBC *Horizon*, 'The Origins of Life', 30 January 2006

4 Ipsos MORI, 'Public Attitudes to Climate Change', 23 June 2008

5 The UN Intergovernmental Panel on Climate Change concluded in its Fourth Assessment Report in 2007 that it was 90% certain that human emissions of greenhouse gases rather than natural climatic variations are responsible for warming the planet's surface.

6 Ipsos MORI/The Royal Society, 'Concern about Science-related Issues', 6 March 2002

7 Onora O'Neill, 'A Question of Trust', Reith Lectures 2002, BBC

8 Daniele Fanelli, 'How Many Scientists Fabricate and Falsify Research? A systematic review and meta-analysis of survey data', *PLoS ONE*, 4:5 (May 2009)

9 John Naish, 'Faking it', *Prospect*, 23 July 2009

10 Richard Smith, 'Research misconduct: The poisoning of the well', *Journal of the Royal Society of Medicine*, 99 (May 2006), pp. 232–7

11 Gallup, 'Trust in Religious Institutions Varies across EU Map', 24 August 2004

12 Interview with Richard Harries, 11 August 2009

13 John Micklethwait and Adrian Wooldridge, *God Is Back* (London: Allen Lane, 2009)

14 Monica Furlong, Monica, *The C of E: The State It's In* (London: Hodder & Stoughton, 2000), pp. 216–17

15 Richard Tomkins, 'A religion in recession', *Financial Times Magazine,* 12 July 2008

16 Ruth Gledhill, 'God-shaped hole will lead to loss of national sense of identity', *The Times*, 8 May 2008

17 'Paradise Regained', *The Economist,* 21 December 2000

18 Micklethwait and Wooldridge, *God is Back*

19 Ipsos MORI, 'Trust in the Professions: Veracity Index' (2008)

20 Jonathan Petre, 'Spiritual Britain worships over 170 different faiths', *Daily Telegraph*, 13 December 2004

21 ICM/*The Guardian*, 'Religion Survey', December 2006

22 Andrew Adonis, 'The People's William', *Prospect*, 4 July 2009

23 Jason Zevin, 'The Perils of Popularising Science', *More Intelligent Life*, 23 January 2008

24 Ipsos MORI/Science Media Centre, 'Public Expects the Impossible from Science', 2 April 2002

25 NESTA, 'Public Attitudes towards Information about Science and Technology', October 2005

26 Interview with Ara Darzi, 4 August 2009

27 NESTA, 'Public Attitudes towards Information about Science and Technology', October 2005

28 Elena Curti, 'Does Nolan go too far?' *The Tablet*, 15 August 2009

29 David Batty, 'Catholic Priesthood told to target child abuse', *The Guardian*, 17 September 2001

30 Francis Fukuyama, 'The End of History', *National Interest*, 4 (1989)

31 'Schools "letting down UK science"', BBC, 13 August 2006

32 Interview with Michael Milner.

33 Chris Mooney, *The Republican War on Science* (New York: Basic Books, 2005), p. 267

34 International Council of Science's Standing Committee on Responsibility and Ethics of Science, 'Ethics and the Responsibility of Science', UNESCO (1999)

35 Karen Armstrong, *The Case for God: What Religion Really Means* (London: Bodley Head, 2009)

36 Bidisha, 'An atheist's prayer', *The Guardian*, 17 August 2009

37 John Gray, *Black Mass* (London: Penguin) p. 293

Chapter 9: Trust in communities, families and children

1 Rachel Sylvester, 'Inside Politics', *The Telegraph*, 29 March 2001

2 Ipsos MORI, 'Can We Have Trust and Diversity?', 19 January 2004

3 BBC, 'UK has lost trust in neighbours', 25 May 2004

4 Ipsos MORI, 'Most Trusted Profession', 5 February 2008

5 Myra Butterworth, 'Britons know just nine neighbours by name', *Daily Telegraph,* 25 November 2008

6 Jonathan Owen, 'Community? We don't know our neighbours', *The Independent,* 20 January 2008

7 Seth Godin, 'Hardwired to Belong', *RSA Journal*

8 John Elliott and Lauren Quaintance, 'Britain is getting less trusting', *Sunday Times,* 18 May 2003

9 Ibid.

10 ICM Research, 'BBC Adult Poll', October 2007

11 John Major, speech to the Conservative Group for Europe, 22 April 1993

12 Elliott and Quaintance, 'Britain is getting less trusting'

13 Correspondence with Richard Harries, 19 August 2009

14 Ben Leach, 'Two pubs closing every day, new figures show', *Daily Telegraph,* 21 February 2009

15 BBC, 'UK is losing 52 pubs each week', 22 July 2009

16 Joan Bakewell, 'Resist the cultural vandalism: don't let them close our precious libraries', *The Times,* 20 February 2009

17 Christopher Hope, 'Post Office closures: the stamp of disapproval', *Sunday Telegraph,* 5 October 2008

18 Lloyds TSB Insurance, 'Over 50s Drive Down Crime Rates', press release, 9 July 2009

19 Elliott and Quaintance, 'Britain is getting less trusting'

20 Ibid.'

21 Shaun Bailey, 'What and Who Is it We Don't Trust?', Joseph Rowntree Foundation, 9 October 2008, p. 2

22 BBC, 'UK ghettos claim shocks ministers', 19 September 2005

23 Anna Turley, *Stronger Together: A New Approach to Tackling Violent Extremism* (London: New Local Government Network, August 2009)

24 Audit Commission, 'When It Comes to the Crunch', 12 August 2009, pp. 44, 93

25 Frank Furedi, *Paranoid Parenting: Abandon Your Anxieties and Be a Good Parent* (London: Allen Lane, 2001)

26 The Children's Society, 'Good Childhood Inquiry', 2009

27 Jenni Russell, 'We approach others' children at our peril', *Sunday Times,* 16 August 2009

28 Interview with Suzie Hayman, 10 August 2009

29 Frank Furedi, 'Thou Shalt Not Hug', *New Statesman,* 26 June 2008

30 Russell, 'We approach others' children at our peril'

31 Kevin Murphy, 'Cyber Nannies: would you spy on your child?', *The Independent,* 26 May 2006

32 Joanna Moorhead, 'Would you spy on your child?', *The Guardian,* 17 December 2003

33 'Family breakdown: a key factor', *Daily Telegraph,* 15 November 2006

34 'Social trends: the decline of the English divorce', *The Economist,* 16 July 2009; Jill Kirby, 'From Broken Families to the Broken Society', *Political Quarterly,* 80:2 (April–June 2009)

35 Henry Wallop, 'Death of the traditional family', *Daily Telegraph*, 15 April 2009; Rebecca O'Neill, 'Experiments in Living: The fatherless family', Civitas (September 2002)

36 National Statistics Online, 'Overview of Families: Cohabiting is fastest growing family type', 4 October 2007

37 H. Meltzer et al., 'Mental Health of Children and Adolescents in Great Britain', Office for National Statistics (2000)

38 Elliott and Quaintance, 'Britain is getting less trusting'

39 ICM Research, 'BBC Adult Poll', October 2007

40 Elliott and Quaintance, 'Britain is getting less trusting'

41 India Knight, 'Family values return, thanks to the internet', *Sunday Times*, 9 August 2009

42 Alessandra Buonfino and Geoff Mulgan, *Civility: Lost and Found* (London: Young Foundation, 2009)

43 Matthias Schultz, 'Controlled chaos: European cities do away with traffic signs', Spiegel Online, 16 November 2006

44 Ben Hamilton-Baillie, ' Shared Space: Reconciling people, places and traffic', *Built Environment*, 34:2 (2008), p. 174

45 Simon Jenkins, 'We must support the Kensington Road revolution', *Evening Standard*, 21 July 2009

46 'Play Me, I'm Yours: Sydney 2009', www.streetpianos.com; Jack Grimston, 'Play it again Boris', *The Times*, 31 May 2009

47 T. S. Eliot, *The Waste Land* (1922)

48 Trees for Cities, 'Londoners do want more trees' press release (2009)

49 'Vienna as a model environmental city – Nature in Vienna – 50% green space', Wien International website, www.wieninternational.at. Thank you to Matt Albrighton for suggesting the 20% figure

50 BBC, '"Forty year wait" for allotments', 10 August 2009

51 Thanks to Nina Grunfeld for this information

52 'Some Trust allotment case studies', National Trust website, www.nationaltrust.org.uk

53 Anthony Seldon, *Brave New City: Brighton & Hove, Past, Present, Future* (Lewes: Pomegranate Press, 2002), p. 120

54 Julia Neuberger, *The Moral State We're In* (London: HarperPerennial, 2005), p. xviii

55 'First citizens' jury meets in Bristol', Prime Minister's Office website, 6 September 2007, www.number10.gov.uk

56 Transition Town Totnes, totnes.transitionnetwork.org

57 James S. House, Karl R. Landis and Debra Umberson, 'Social Relationships and Health', *Science*, Reprint Series, vol. 241 (1988)

58 Helen Bowers et al., *Making a Difference through Volunteering* (London: CSV, 2006)

59 Gallup poll for CSV

60 'Young People and Crime', Home Office research study 145 (1995)

61 Douglas Kirby, *Emerging Answers: Research Findings on Programs to Reduce Teen Pregnancy* (Washington, DC: National Campaign to Prevent Teen Pregnancy, 2001)

62 Bill Garland et al., *Nationwide Community Service* (London: CSV, 2008)

63 Rt Hon. Chris Patten MP, 'Big Battalions and Little Platoons', Seventh Arnold Goodman Lecture (1990)

64 Justin Davis Smith, *The 1997 National Survey of Volunteering* (London: IVR, 1997)

65 Derry Hannam, 'A Pilot Study to Evaluate the Impact of the Student Participation Aspects of the Citizenship Order on Standards of Education in Secondary Schools', report to the DfEE (April 2001); R. L. Bradley, 'K-12 Service-learning Impacts: A Review of State-level Studies of Service-learning', in Jim Kielsmeier et al. (eds), *Growing to Greatness 2005: The State of Service-learning Project* (St Paul, MN: National Youth Leadership Council, 2005); William Morgan and Matthew Streb, *How Quality Service-learning Develops Civic Values* (Bloomington: Indiana University Press, 1999)

66 A. Furco, 'The Role of Service-learning in Enhancing Student Achievement', presentation given at the National Center for Learning and Citizenship board meeting, Santa Barbara, CA, (2007); Alberto Dávila and Marie T. Mora, *Civic Engagement and High School Academic Progress: An Analysis Using NELS Data* (Medford, MA: CIRCLE, 2007)

67 CSV Make a Difference Day evaluation report.

68 Sue Palmer, *Toxic Childhood* (London: Orion, 2006), p. 158

69 UNICEF, 'Child Poverty in Perspective: An overview of child well-being in rich countries', UNICEF Innocenti Research Centre (2007)

70 John Ashcroft and Michael Schluter, 'Influencing, Assessing and Developing Relationships', Relationships Foundation Strategy Unit Seminar, 3 March 2009, pp. 6–7

Chapter 10: Trust in the media, culture and sport

1 Ipsos MORI, 'Trust in the Professions: Veracity Index' (2008)

2 Committee on Standards in Public Life/BMRB Social Research, 'Survey of Public Attitudes towards Conduct in Public Life' (2008), pp. 22–4

3 Onora O'Neill, *A Question of Trust: The BBC Reith Lectures 2002* (Cambridge: Cambridge University Press, 2002)

4 Robin Aitken, *Can We Trust the BBC?* (London: Continuum, 2007)

5 Adrian Monck, *Can You Trust the Media?* (London: Icon, 2008)

6 Nick Davies, *Flat Earth News* (London: Chatto & Windus, 2008)

7 Tony Blair, speech given at Reuters, London, 12 June 2007

8 Jeremy Paxman, James MacTaggart Memorial Lecture (2007)

9 Charles Baudelaire, *My Heart Laid Bare*, LIX (1887)

10 Madeline House, Graham Storey and Kathleen Tillotson, *The Letters of Charles Dickens 1842–1843* (Oxford: Clarendon Press, 1993), p. 230

11 Interview with Brian Cathcart, 21 July 2009

12 Ipsos MORI, 'Trust in the Professions: Veracity Index' (2008)

13 Interview with Richard Sambrook, 8 July 2009

14 Steven Barnett, 'On the Road to Self-destruction', *British Journalism Review*, 19:2 (2008), pp. 2–13, using poll data collected by YouGov for the BJR in March 2008

15 Globescan, 'BBC/Reuters/Media Center Poll: Trust in the Media', 3 May 2006

16 Bryan Appleyard, 'A guide to the best 100 blogs', *Sunday Times*, 15 February 2009

17 Bree Nordenson, 'Overload! Journalism's battle for relevance in an age of too much information', *Columbia Journalism Review*, 1 November 2008

18 Official Google Blog, 'We knew the web was big...', 25 July 2008

19 Globescan, 'BBC/Reuters/Media Center Poll: Trust in the Media', 3 May 2006

20 Ipsos MORI/BBC 'Survey on Trust Issues', 22 January 2008

21 Ibid.

22 O'Neill, *A Question of Trust*, p. 56

23 Monck, *Can You Trust the Media?*, p. 2

24 Globescan, 'BBC/Reuters/Media Center Poll: Trust in the Media', 3 May 2006

25 Ipsos MORI, 'Only One in Five Trust Journalists to Tell the Truth', 13 March 2009

26 Personal correspondence with Raymond Kuhn, 30 July 2009

27 Brian Cathcart, 'Journalists: they can't live without us', *New Statesman*, 25 September 2008

28 Charlie Beckett, 'MPs' expenses and the Media: Chequebook journalism pays for political lessons', *Polis*, 10 May 2009

29 Davies, *Flat Earth News*, p. 52

30 Richard Cockett, 'Ball, Chamberlain, and *Truth*', *Historical Journal*, 33 (1990), pp. 131–42, as cited in Anthony Seldon and Stuart Ball (eds), *The Conservative Century: The Conservative Party since 1900* (Oxford: Oxford University Press, 1994), p. 556

31 Information from *The Week*, www.theweek.com

32 George Orwell, 'Essay Looking Back on the Spanish Civil War', in *Homage to Catalonia* (Harmondsworth: Penguin, [1938] 1974) p. 233

33 Interview with Polly Toynbee, 5 August 2009

34 Vian Bakir and David Barlow, 'The End of Trust?', in Vian Bakir and David Barlow (eds), *Communication in the Age of Suspicion: Trust and the Media* (Basingstoke: Palgrave Macmillan, 2007)

35 Monck, *Can You Trust the Media?*, p. 15

36 Jeremy Paxman, James MacTaggart Memorial Lecture (2007)

37 Interview with Polly Toynbee, 5 August 2009

38 Richard Cockett, 'The Party, Publicity and the Media', in Anthony Seldon and Stuart Ball (eds), *Conservative Century: The Conservative Party since 1900* (Oxford: Oxford University Press, 1994) p. 555

39 Ibid., p. 556

40 O'Neill, *A Question of Trust*, p. 96

41 Interview with Brian Cathcart, 21 July 2009

42 Ian Hargreaves, *Journalism: Truth or Dare?* (Oxford: Oxford University Press, 2003), p. 211

43 Brian Cathcart, 'Trust us. We're journalists', *New Statesman*, 5 February 2007

44 O'Neill, *A Question of Trust*, p. 70

45 Interview with Brian Cathcart, 21 July 2009

46 National Union of Journalists Code of Conduct, www.nuj.org.uk

47 Greenslade, Roy, 'Recruiting working class journalists: what, if anything, can be done?', Greenslade's Blog, 23 July 2009

48 Ibid.

49 Edelman, 'Mid-year Trust Barometer Report' (2009)

50 BBC, 'Wikipedia survives research test', 15 December 2005

51 Magnus Linklater, 'What Happened to Playing Fair?', *British Journalism Review*, 19:3 (2008), pp. 62–6

52 Memorandum submitted by Alan Rusbridger to House of Commons Select Committee on Culture, Media and Sport, 11 March 2003, as cited in Media Standards Trust, 'A More Accountable Press: The need for reform – is self-regulation failing the press and the public?' 9 February 2009, p. 13

53 'Watching the watchdog', *The Guardian*, 10 August 2009

54 BBC, 'ITV hit with record £5.68 million fine', 8 May 2008

55 Mark Thompson, 'The trouble with trust', BBC, 15 January 2008

56 Interview with Richard Sambrook, 7 July 2009

57 John Lloyd, *What The Media Are Doing to Our Politics* (London: Constable, 2004)

58 Interview with Brian Cathcart, 21 July 2009

59 Simon Barnes, 'Integrity is at the heart of Arsène Wenger's code', *The Times*, 17 August 2009

60 BBC, 'Richards banned for three years', 17 August 2009

61 International Olympic Committee, www.olympic.org

62 Interview with Ed Smith, 17 August 2009

63 Clarence A. Forbes, 'Crime and Punishment in Greek Athletics', *Classical Journal*, 47:5 (1952), pp. 169–203

64 Interview with Ed Smith, 17 August 2009

65 'The Ten Greatest Sporting Cheats in History', *The Observer*, 8 July 2001

66 Interview with Ed Smith, 17 August 2009

67 Ibid.

68 Interview with Nick Greenslade, 27 July 2009

69 Interview with Nick Greenslade, 17 August 2009

70 Interview with John Inverarity, 27 July 2009

71 Evan Fanning, '"Walking Junkie" Chambers reveals full extent of his drug use', *The Guardian*, 2 March 2009

72 Barney Ronay, 'Landis drugs ban upheld', *The Guardian*, 30 June 2008

73 Rowbottom, Mike, 'Drugs in sport: Graham facing long jail term for lying to inquiry', *The Independent,* 30 May 2008

74 M. Bamberger and D. Yaeger, 'Over the Edge', *Sports Illustrated,* 14 (1997), pp. 62–70

75 Interview with John Inverarity, 27 July 2009

76 Interview with Nick Greenslade, 17 August 2009

77 Donald MacGillivray, 'When is a fake not a fake? When it's a genuine forgery', *The Guardian*, 2 July 2005

78 Michael Clark, *Paradoxes from A–Z* (London: Routledge, 2002) p. 184

79 Robert Hewison, *The Heritage Industry* (London: Methuen, 1987)

80 David A. Hanser, *Architecture of France* (Westport, CT: Greenwood, 2006), p. 40

81 McMaster, Brian, 'Supporting Excellence in the Arts: From Measurement to Judgment', Department for Culture, Media and Sport (January 2008)

82 National Advisory Committee on Creative and Cultural Education, 'All Our Futures: Creativity, culture and education' (1999)

INDEX